OXFORD EARLY CHRISTIAN TEXTS

General Editor

HENRY CHADWICK

━━━━

EUNOMIUS
THE EXTANT WORKS

EUNOMIUS

THE EXTANT WORKS

TEXT AND TRANSLATION BY

RICHARD PAUL VAGGIONE

OXFORD

AT THE CLARENDON PRESS

1987

Oxford University Press, Walton Street, Oxford OX2 6DP

Oxford New York Toronto
Delhi Bombay Calcutta Madras Karachi
Petaling Jaya Singapore Hong Kong Tokyo
Nairobi Dar es Salaam Cape Town
Melbourne Auckland

and associated companies in
Beirut Berlin Ibadan Nicosia

Oxford is a trade mark of Oxford University Press

Published in the United States
by Oxford University Press, New York

British Library Cataloguing in Publication Data
Eunomius
Eunomius: the extant works. —(Oxford early Christian text)
1. Arianism 2. Church history—4th century early church
I. Title II. Vaggione, Paul Richard
273'.4 BT1350
ISBN 0-19-826814-9

Library of Congress Cataloging in Publication Data
Eunomius, Bp. of Cyzicus, ca. 335–ca. 394.
The extant works. (Oxford early Christian texts)
Translated from Greek. Includes bibliography and index.
1. Theology—Collected works—Early church, ca. 20–600.
2. Apologetics—Early church, ca. 30–600.
I. Vaggione, Richard Paul. II. Title. III. Series.
BR65.E6852E5 1987 270.2 86–12656
ISBN 0-19-826814-9

Set by Amaranthus, Warminster, Wilts.
Printed in Great Britain
at the University Printing House, Oxford
by David Stanford
Printer to the University

PREFACE

There are few controversies more alien to the modern mind than the prolonged dispute over the Trinity which occupied the greater part of the fourth century. Not only were the arguments employed of a forbiddingly logical nature, but the polemical depths to which otherwise sober churchmen might be driven in asserting them are unattractive, to say the least. The point at issue, however, was one of relevance to any age: the salvation of humankind and the mystery of the nature of God—a prolonged, careful, deliberate effort to pay God 'the debt which is above all others his due: the acknowledgement that he is what he is.'[1] In an age of theological reappraisal, a clear understanding of the motives, circumstances, and meaning of the original doctrinal development is imperative. In particular, it is important to acquire an accurate and sympathetic understanding of theologians whose positions were eventually rejected. The present edition of the surviving works and fragments of Eunomius of Cyzicus is an attempt to supply this need.

There have been several efforts in this century to produce such an edition. A *Corpus Eunomianum* was projected early in the century by U. von Wilamowitz-Moellendorf, but was never carried out.[2] Werner Jaeger likewise intended to produce an edition in connection with his study of the Eunomian fragments preserved by Gregory of Nyssa, but at the time of his death this had still not appeared.[3] More recently an edition was planned by Bernard C. Barmann but had to be discontinued for personal reasons.[4] Most recently, an edition of the *Liber Apologeticus* has been brought out by the editors of *Sources chrétiennes* in connection with their edition of the *Contra Eunomium* of Basil.[5] In what follows we have attempted

---

[1] Eun., *Apol.* 8.2–3.

[2] So E. Vandenbussche, 'La part de la dialectique dans la théologie d'Eunomius "le technologue" ', *RHE* 40 (1944–5), 47 n. 1.

[3] W. Jaeger, *Gregorii Nysseni Opera* ii (Leiden, 1960), p. vii.

[4] So J. van Parys, 'Grégoire de Nysse. Réfutation de la profession de foi d'Eunome' (Unpublished thesis, Université de Paris, 1968), p. 54.

[5] Basile de Césarée, *Contra Eunome* suivi de Eunome, *Apologie*, edd. B. Sesboüé, SJ, Georges-Matthieu de Durand, OP, Louis Doutreleau, SJ, *Sources chrétiennes* nos. 299, 305 (Paris, 1982), 2 vols. Unfortunately this edition became available too

to present, so far as possible, the whole 'Corpus Eunomianum' —all of the surviving texts and fragments which can reasonably be assigned to Eunomius of Cyzicus—and it is our hope that in so doing we have brought the desired goal somewhat nearer to completion.

Anyone who has attempted a work of this kind cannot but be aware of the large numbers of people who have contributed to it in one way or another. It is with particular regret, therefore, that I am unable to thank individually the many librarians, scholars, and curators who have made their expertise available to me or who have patiently answered repeated requests for information. Some, however, must be singled out for special mention. In the first place I would like to thank the Revd Dr Maurice Wiles for reading over the translations and for making many valuable suggestions (any errors which still remain are entirely my own). I would also like to thank the Revd Dr Henry Chadwick together with the Bampton Electors of the University of Oxford and the Bethune-Baker Trustees of the University of Cambridge for their kindness and generosity, without which this edition would not have been possible. I am particularly grateful to Mr Nigel Wilson of Lincoln College, Oxford, and the Revd Walter M. Hayes of the Pontifical Institute of Medieval Studies for their help in matters of palaeography. Finally, I wish to thank the trustees, scholars, and staff of the Dumbarton Oaks Center for Byzantine Studies, the Catholic University of America, and the Ecumenical Institute for Advanced Theological Studies (Tantur) for allowing me the time and resources to complete this project.

RICHARD PAUL VAGGIONE, OHC

late to be taken account of directly in our own work; I am grateful to Père Doutre-leau for his adoption of our *sigla* and for his comments in vol. ii, p. 198.

CONTENTS

ABBREVIATIONS

There is no consolidated bibliography in this volume, but the reader will find most of the needed material in the various introductions and in the notes. The following abbreviations are used frequently in the notes and apparatus:

A. PATRISTIC AUTHORS AND WORKS

Anast. S., *Monoph.*	Anastasius of Sinai, *Contra Monophysitas Testimonia*
(ps.-)Ath., *Dial.*	(ps.-)Athanasius, *De Sancta Trinitate Dialogi*
Barḥad., *HE*	Barḥadbešabba ʿArbaia, *History of the Holy Fathers*
Basil, *Ep.*	Basil the Great, *Epistulae*
Eun.	*Adversus Eunomium*
Spir.	*Liber de Spiritu Sancto*
Chrys., *Hom. in Mt.*	John Chrysostom, *Homiliae in Matthaeum*
Incomp.	*De Incomprehensibili Dei Natura*
Cyril Alex., *Thes.*	Cyril of Alexandria, *Thesaurus de Sancta et Consubstantiali Trinitate*
Epiph., *Haer.*	Epiphanius, *Adversus Haereses*
Eun., *A, Apol.*	Eunomius, *Liber Apologeticus*
AA, Apol. Apol.	*Apologia Apologiae*
EF, Exp. Fid.	*Expositio Fidei*
F, Fr.	*Fragmenta*
Grg. Naz., *Carm. Vit.*	Gregory of Nazianzus, *Carmen de Vita Sua*
Or.	*Orationes*
Grg. Nyss., *Conf.*	Gregory of Nyssa, *Refutatio Confessionis Eunomii* (= *Eun.*, vulg. ii)
Ep.	*Epistulae*
GN, Eun.	*Contra Eunomium*
Hieron., *Vir. Illus.*	Jerome, *De Viris Illustribus*
Nemesius, *Nat. Hom.*	Nemesius, *De Natura Hominis*
Origen, *Jo.*	Origen, *Commentarii in Joannem*
Philo, *Leg. Alleg.*	Philo Judaeus, *Legum Allegoriae*
Philost., *HE*	Philostorgius, *Historia Ecclesiastica*
Philostratus, *VS*	Philostratus, *De Vita Sophistarum*
Rufinus, *HE*	Rufinus, *Historia Ecclesiastica*
Soc., *HE*	Socrates, *Historia Ecclesiastica*
Soz., *HE*	Sozomen, *Historia Ecclesiastica*

Synesius, *Ep.*	Synesius, *Epistulae*
Thdr. Mops., *Eun.*	Theodore of Mopsuestia, *Contra Eunomium*
Thdt., *Ep.*	Theodoret of Cyrus, *Epistulae*
HE	*Historia Ecclesiastica*
Haer.	*Haereticarum Fabularum Compendium*

B. OTHER ABBREVIATIONS

Adler	*Suidae Lexicon*, ed. A. Adler (Leipzig: B. G. Teubner, 1931), 5 parts.
Albertz	M. Albertz, *Untersuchungen über die Schriften des Eunomius* (Wittenberg: Herrosé und Ziemsen, 1908)
Briquet	C. M. Briquet, *Les Filigranes*, 2nd edn. (Leipzig: Verlag Karl W. Hiersemann, 1923), 4 vols.
BZ	*Byzantinische Zeitschrift*
Cod. Theod.	*Codex Theodosianus*
Cohn and Wendland	*Philonis Alexandrini Opera quae Supersunt*, ed. L. Cohn, P. Wendland (Berlin: G. Reimer, 1896–1930), 7 vols.
Courtonne	Saint Basile, *Lettres*, ed. Yves Courtonne (Paris: Société d'édition 'les belles lettres', 1957), 3 vols.
EO	*Echos d'orient*
Excerpta Valesiana	Ammiani Marcellini, *Rerum Gestarum Libri*, excerpta Valesiana
GCS	*Die griechischen christlichen Schriftsteller der ersten drei Jahrhunderte*
Gothofredus	Iacobi Gothofredi, *Codex Theodosianus cum Perpetuis Commentariis* (Lyon: Huguetan and Revaud, 1665)
Hahn	A. Hahn, *Bibliothek der Symbole und Glaubensregeln der alten Kirche*, dritte Auflage (Breslau: Verlag E. Morgenstern, 1897)
Henry	Photius, *Bibliothèque*, ed. René Henry (Paris: Société d'édition 'les belles lettres', 1959), 7 vols.
J	W. Jaeger, *Gregorii Nysseni Opera* (Leiden: E. J. Brill, 1921 ff.) (All references to the *Contra Eunomium* are to the 2nd edn., 1960)
JTS	*Journal of Theological Studies*
Mason	*The Five Theological Orations of Gregory of Nazianzus*, ed. A. J. Mason (Cambridge University Press, 1899)
Mommsen	*Theodosiani Libri XVI*, ed. Th. Mommsen, Paul M. Meyer (Berlin: Weidmann, 1905), 2 vols.
Nauck	*Tragicorum Graecorum Fragmenta*, ed. Augustus Nauck, rev. Bruno Snell (Hildesheim: Georg Olms Verlagsbuchhandlung, 1964)

Opitz	*Athanasius' Werke*, ed. H.-G. Opitz (Berlin and Leipzig: Walter de Gruyter, 1935 ff.), vols. 2 and 3
Pearson	*The Fragments of Sophocles*, ed. A. C. Pearson (Cambridge University Press, 1917), 3 vols.
PG	*Patrologiae Cursus Completus*, accurante J.-P. Migne, *Series Graeca*
PL	*Patrologiae Cursus Completus*, accurante J.-P. Migne, *Series Latina*
PO	*Patrologiae Orientalis*, ed. R. Graffin, F. Nau
P-W	*Real-Encyclopädie der classischen Altertumswissenschaft*, ed. A. Pauly, G. Wissowa, *et al.* (1893 ff.)
RACh	*Reallexikon für Antike und Christentum* (Stuttgart, 1950–)
Rettberg	C. H. G. Rettberg, *Marcelliana. Accedit Eunomii ΕΚΘΕΣΙΣ ΠΙΣΤΕΩΣ Emendatior* (Göttingen: Vandenhoek and Ruprecht, 1794)
REG	*Revue des études grecques*
RHE	*Revue d'histoire ecclésiastique*
SC	*Sources chrétiennes*
TU	*Texte und Untersuchungen*
Waltz	*Anthologie grecque*, ed. P. Waltz (Paris: Sociéte d'édition 'les belles lettres', 1928), 3 vols.

GENERAL INTRODUCTION

The author of the works contained in this volume has been largely neglected by modern scholars, but it is clear from the writings of his contemporaries that they afforded him an eminence which the meagreness of his surviving fragments does little to suggest. Almost every major theological figure of Eunomius' own age undertook to refute him. To mention only those who are said to have composed full-scale treatises against him, we find that Apollinarius,[1] Basil the Great,[2] Didymus the Blind,[3] Diodore of Tarsus,[4] Gregory of Nyssa,[5] Theodore of Mopsuestia,[6] Theodoret of Cyrus,[7] and Sophronius[8] are all said to have written treatises 'Contra Eunomium'. Today only the works of Basil and Gregory are extant in full, but the sheer number and eminence of Eunomius' opponents demonstrates his importance in their eyes and suggests that our own neglect has been misplaced.

Eunomius represents the second generation of Arian thinkers, that is, the generation which attempted to carry on the theological work of Arius and Eusebius of Nicomedia after the break-up in the 340s of the original anti-Nicene coalition.[9] Together with his teacher, Aetius, Eunomius represents this tradition in its most

---

[1] So Philost., *HE* viii.12 (*GCS* 21.114.1–5), Hieron., *Vir. illus.* 120 (*PL* 23.711A).

[2] Basil, *Eun.* i–iii (*PG* 29.497–669, also *SC* 299, 305).

[3] So Hieron., *Vir. illus.* 109 (*PL* 23.705A), 120 (*PL* 23.711A). Perhaps to be identified with Books iv–v of (ps.-)Basil, *Eun.*? See the literature cited in M. Geerard, ed., *Clavis Patrum Graecorum* ii (Brepols-Turnhout, 1974), p. 142, no. 2837.

[4] So Barḥad., *HE* 17 (*PO* 23.315.13) and Ebed-jesus, *Carmen* 18 in J. S. Assemani, *Bibliotheca Orientalis Clementino-Vaticana* iii (Romae: Typis Sacrae Congregationis de Propaganda Fide, 1725), pars i, p. 29, line 6.

[5] Grg. Nyss., *Eun.* I–III (*J* i and ii).

[6] Cf. R. P. Vaggione, 'Some Neglected Fragments of Theodore of Mopsuestia's *Contra Eunomium*', *JTS* 31 (1980), 403–70.

[7] Cf. Thdt., *Haer.* v.2 (*PG* 83.449C), *Ep.* 113 (*SC* 111.64.11–12), 116 (*SC* 111.70.26), 146 (*SC* 111.176.18–19).

[8] Photius, *Cod.* 5 (Henry i.8.8–15), 138 (Henry ii.107.31).

[9] For a general discussion, cf. Thomas A. Kopecek, *A History of Neo-Arianism* i–ii (The Philadelphia Patristic Foundation, 1979); for a more specialized treatment, cf. Elena Cavalcanti, *Studi Eunomiani*, Orientalia Christiana Analecta no. 202 (1976).

extreme form. In his view, any assertion of a similarity of essence between Father and Son must lead to an assertion of their identity in essence and hence to a denial of the reality of the persons. The only way to avoid this and to guarantee the substantial reality of the persons is to assert that the essence of the Son is *not similar* (*anomoios*) to the essence of the Father. Because of this assertion, the followers of Aetius and Eunomius have generally been known as 'anomoeans'.

Eunomius himself was a Cappadocian of relatively humble origins. To recapitulate briefly the earlier portions of his life, he was born sometime toward the end of the decade 320-30 in the small village of Oltiseris on the Galatian border.[10] Originally trained as a shorthand writer, he went to Constantinople in search of a literary education after the death of his parents.[11] From there he went on to Antioch and Alexandria, where he became the disciple of Aetius, and, together with him, became part of the entourage of Eudoxius, bishop successively of Antioch (358-60) and Constantinople (360-70). Ordained deacon by Eudoxius, he took a full part in the controversies of the age, and at the time the first works found in this volume were written had already begun to acquire an identity separate from that of his master. The events which followed, and which led to the composition of Eunomius' surviving works, are discussed in the introductions to each. When Eunomius finally died in exile (*c.*394) after some thirty-five years of literary activity, the impact of his person and writings could be described by an admirer as follows:

It was there [at Dakora in Cappadocia] that Philostorgius, then twenty years old and staying in Constantinople, saw him. He praises Eunomius extravagantly and describes his understanding and character as 'incomparable'. He also speaks flatteringly of the great distinction of his facial appearance and of his limbs. He even likens the words of his mouth to pearls—though a little further on he admits (if unwillingly) that his voice had a lisp. Nor was he ashamed of the lisp; he extols it as extremely elegant.[12] Likewise, the white blemishes which disfigured and spotted his

---

[10] So *GN* I (*J* i.33.17, 57.21-58.1, ii.309.15); Sozomen's assertion in *HE* vii.17 (*GCS* 324.21-325.1) that Eunomius' πατρίς was Dakora near Caesarea seems to be based on a false deduction from the fact that in later life he had an estate there.

[11] Cf. Thdr. Mops., *Eun.*, Fr. iv, *Gk.* 8-28, *Syr.* 37-63 (Vaggione, op. cit., 421-2, 424-5) and *GN* I (*J* i.39.21-3, cf. 56.20-4).

[12] The 'lisp' need not have been a speech defect. The use of the Cappadocian

face he strives to make into a bodily ornament. He praises all his works extravagantly but says that his letters surpass the others by far.[13]

These letters, like much else written by Eunomius, are lost, but the testimony of his contemporaries, both positive and negative, confirms the power of his impact on others.

The loss of so many of Eunomius' works is not due simply to the vicissitudes of time. In a decree dated 4 March 398, the Emperor Arcadius, responding to renewed heretical activity in the years following the death of Theodosius the Great,[14] and perhaps acting at the instigation of the then newly-elected archbishop of Constantinople, John Chrysostom,[15] ordered all Eunomian works to be burnt.[16] Contemporary authors mention the carrying out of this decree.[17] Between the efforts of Arcadius' ministers and the work of the intervening centuries little now remains of what must once have been a sizeable literary inheritance.

The three works which have in fact come down to us in whole or in part were all occasioned by a single controversy lasting over a period of twenty years (360–83). The first salvo in this controversy was fired by Eunomius himself in his earliest surviving work, the *Liber Apologeticus*. A reply to this was published by Basil the Great in his treatise, the *Adversus Eunomium*, and was answered in its turn by Eunomius in his *Apologia Apologiae*. To this Gregory of Nyssa produced yet another answer in his own *Contra Eunomium*, refuting at the same time a further work by Eunomius entitled the *Expositio Fidei*. These, together with fragments which include a scholion on the *Syntagmation* of Aetius and part of a work entitled *De Filio*, constitute the entire known surviving corpus of Eunomius'

language was still widespread in the fourth century, particularly among persons like Eunomius from a rural background (cf. Basil, *Spir.* xxix.74.50-2 [*SC* 17bis.514]); even Cappadocians with a rhetorical training could have a pronounced accent (cf. Philostratus, *VS* ii.13.594). It may be that the 'lisp' which Philostorgius found so elegant was simply the remnants of a Cappadocian accent.

13 Philost., *HE* x.6 (*GCS* 128.10-20).

14 See Synesius, *Ep.* 5 (*PG* 66.1341c); cf. *Gothofredus*, vi, pp. 152-3.

15 Consecrated 26 February 398; compare Theodosius' attitude as reported by Sozomen, *HE* vii.12 (*GCS* 316.9-15) with that of Chrysostom in, e.g., his *Hom. in Mt.* 46.1.2 (*PG* 58.477 ad medium), first suggested by C. Baronius, *Annales Ecclesiastici* (Lucae: typis Leonardi Venturini, 1740), vi.281, anno 398, section lxxviii.

16 *Cod. Theod.* xvi.5.34 (Mommsen i, pars post., p. 866).

17 Philost., *HE* xi.5 (*GCS* 135.26-7), Nicephorus Callistus, *HE* xiii.1 (*PG* 146.925c).

literary output, a theological corpus almost entirely dogmatic in character.

The one-sided nature of what has come down to us is emphasized by what is known of Eunomius' two remaining lost works. The historian Socrates Scholasticus mentions a work by Eunomius in seven volumes usually designated the *Commentary on Romans*, though Socrates does not actually say that it was a commentary.[18] Likewise, as we saw above, Philostorgius tells us that the *Letters* of Eunomius surpassed all his other works. Photius had read some forty of them, though he claims that in writing them Eunomius displayed his ignorance of the laws of epistolary style.[19] Apart from a single fragment of the *Commentary on Romans*, not a single line which can be ascribed to either of these works survives. That they were not isolated phenomena is suggested by the other known products of the Eunomian school,[20] and by surviving indications of Eunomius' own wider interests.[21] We can gauge the extent of our loss if we think how different our appreciation of the Cappadocians would be if time had preserved to us only their dogmatic treatises and we had lost all of their exegetical, ascetical, and mystical works.

The reason for this one-sidedness soon becomes apparent. Whatever the actual range of Eunomius' interests, his writings as preserved inevitably reflect the interests of his adversaries. Quite apart from the deliberate efforts at destruction mentioned above, there was simply no incentive for Orthodox scribes to copy heretical

[18] Soc., *HE* iv.7 (*PG* 67.473A).

[19] Photius, *Cod.* 138 (Henry ii.107.17–108.21).

[20] Notably the *Ecclesiastical History* of Philostorgius (together with two epigrams in the *Palatine Anthology* ix.193–4 [Waltz vii.77]) and a lost work by Eunomius' disciple Theophronius entitled Περὶ τῆς γυμνασίας τοῦ νοῦ (Soc., *HE* v.24 [*PG* 67.648C], Soz., *HE* vii.17 [*GCS* 325.1–5]). To this may be added the extremely interesting commentary on Job published by Dieter Hagedorn in his *Der Hiob-kommentar des Arianers Julian* (Berlin: Walter de Gruyter, 1973), a work which is correctly identified by Hagedorn as very closely related to the *Apology* of Eunomius (ibid., p. lv). There is also considerable evidence of Eunomian editing of such works as the *Clementine Homilies* (*GCS*, 2nd edn., pp. vii–ix) and the *Apostolic Constitutions*, together with the longer recension of the *Ignatian Epistles* (cf. Hagedorn, op. cit., pp. xxxvii–lii). Finally we may mention two Easter homilies preserved among the *spuria* of John Chrysostom (*SC* 67) which, while certainly anomoean, may or may not be Eunomian.

[21] Cf., e.g., Eunomius' speculation on the population of the world as recorded by Nemesius of Emesa, *Nat. Hom.* (*PG* 40.575A–B).

literature unless they had some specific purpose in doing so. This is illustrated by the way in which our two surviving complete works, the *Liber Apologeticus* and the *Expositio Fidei*, have come down to us. Both have been preserved because at some point they were bound up with a copy of their respective refutations by Basil and Gregory. One scribe went so far as to warn his readers in a marginal comment that his sole purpose in copying it was ἵνα δεικνύται ἡ γραφή and to tell them to beware of the book's heretical teachings.[22] In a similar way, the one other work of Eunomius which has come down to us, the *Apologia Apologiae*, has been preserved only in the quotations of it made by Gregory of Nyssa in his refutation. Though, as we shall see, there is little reason to suspect deliberate falsification (as opposed to tendentious misrepresentation!), the reader of Eunomius' works must always be aware that even when he is able to read a given work in full, he is still to some extent seeing him through his adversaries' eyes.

Despite the fact that this causes considerable difficulties in interpretation, there can be no doubt that even in this attenuated form Eunomius' works represent an interesting and valuable body of material. In trying to make them available to a wider modern audience, it is our hope that some of the richness which, for good or ill, so clearly fascinated their ancient hearers will have come through.

----

[22] Eun., *Apol.* 1, apparatus, codex G.

EUNOMII LIBER APOLOGETICUS
THE APOLOGY

INTRODUCTION

I. TITLE

We have already remarked that almost all of the surviving works of Eunomius derive from a single controversy. The first of these is the so-called *Liber Apologeticus*. In using this, its traditional name, however, we do not mean to prejudge the question as to whether this was its original title. The name given to it in the manuscripts[1] and in the title of Basil's *Adversus Eunomium*[2] is Ἀπολογητικός, but some modern scholars have contended that its original title was Ἀπολογία.[3] This contention is based on references in Basil the Great and Philostorgius (discussed below), and on the fact that Eunomius' second apology, a defence of this one, was entitled Ὑπὲρ τῆς ἀπολογίας ἀπολογία.[4] A statement of Gregory of Nyssa, moreover, seems to clinch the case, for he tells us flatly that ἐκείνῳ μὲν γὰρ ἦν τῷ λόγῳ Ἀπολογία τὸ ὄνομα.[5] In spite of this, a close examination of the evidence shows that the case is not so simple.

For one thing, there is good reason to believe that Gregory of Nyssa did not himself possess a copy of the *Liber Apologeticus* and that all his information about it derives either from Basil or from the second apology of Eunomius which he was refuting.[6] This means that we cannot look to Gregory for any independent information as to what the original title of this work may have been, and that the statement quoted above is simply a gloss intended to explain the title of Eunomius' later work. In order to obtain any new information we must turn to the *Adversus Eunomium* of Basil.

[1] See the apparatus criticus ad loc. The longer title found in G (perhaps added by a different hand) is also found in B and in these manuscripts' numerous progeny.

[2] Basil, *Eun.* i (*PG* 29.497-8), though the remark of the editors that 'Tot sunt fere tituli varii, quot codices' is abundantly borne out by the list provided in the new edition of Basil (*SC* 299, p. 139). All references to Basil in what follows are to column numbers in *PG* 29, also used in the new edition.

[3] As asserted in Albertz, p. 5, and Fr. Diekamp, 'Literargeschichtlichen zu der Eunomianischen Kontroverse', *BZ* 18 (1909), 1.

[4] So *GN* i (*J* i.29.26; 42.24-43.1), ii (*J* i.392.7-10).

[5] Ibid., i (*J* i.43.4-5, cf. 45.5-6).

[6] See the discussion of Gregory's quotations below, pp. 25-6.

We have already noted that in the title of Basil's work, Eunomius' treatise is referred to as the Ἀπολογητικός. In the course of the work itself, however, Basil frequently uses the word ἀπολογία, though he nowhere states that this was the title of the treatise.[7] Most of these uses are connected with Basil's claim that Eunomius had no right to use 'apology' as a literary category (see discussion below), and are usually accompanied by some uncomplimentary phrase expressive of this critique: ἐν ἀπολογίας εἴδει,[8] ἐν ἀπολογίας πλάσματι,[9] τῷ τῆς ἀπολογίας προκαλύμματι,[10] ἡ περὶ τὴν ἀπολογίαν σκηνή,[11] and τὸ τῆς ἀπολογίας . . . δρᾶμα.[12] The remaining references all reflect the same pattern and are part of Basil's attempt to deny Eunomius any right to use this particular literary form.[13] Moreover, with a single exception all these occurrences are to be found in the same chapter of Basil's work (i.2). This suggests the source of the word ἀπολογία, for it is in this chapter that Basil discusses the opening paragraph of Eunomius' treatise, a paragraph in which Eunomius describes his purpose as being πρὸς ἀπολογίαν.[14] Here, then, we have an explanation of Basil's use of this word which does not give us any reason to suppose that the title he found in his copy of Eunomius' treatise was any different from that found in our own. Basil cannot provide us with a definitive solution to our problem.

The same statement also applies to the mention of this work found in the *Ecclesiastical History* of Philostorgius. The two sources which give us our knowledge of this passage both use ἀπολογία merely to describe the literary character of the work and shed no new light on its title.[15] In the end we are left with a single piece of evidence, the title of the second apology, Ὑπὲρ τῆς ἀπολογίας ἀπολογία, but since Eunomius was under no obligation to use the same word in both cases, this too is inconclusive. It seems, then, that while the possibility that Ἀπολογία was the original title cannot be excluded, there is no reason to overturn the unanimous witness of the manuscript tradition.[16]

---

[7] The one possible exception is Basil, *Eun.* i.2 (501B) where Basil specifically mentions a 'title': . . . ἐξ αὐτῆς τῆς ἐπιγραφῆς τὴν ἀρχὴν ποιησάμενος. This confirms that the work had a title but does not tell us what it was.

[8] Basil, *Eun.* i.2 (501B).   [9] Ibid. (501C).   [10] Ibid. (504A).

[11] Ibid. (504B).   [12] Ibid. (504B).   [13] Ibid., i.2 (505A, B), ii.1 (573B).

[14] Eun., *Apol.* 1.13-14.   [15] Philost., *HE* viii.12 (*GCS* 114.2, 17).

[16] There is an unfortunate lacuna in the manuscripts of Photius just at the point where he is about to tell us what the title is, *Cod.* 137 (Henry ii.105.41-2).

II. DATE AND OCCASION

If the title of Eunomius' work cannot be determined conclusively, its general significance remains unimpaired, for the very word 'apology' raises the question of the occasion which warranted such a presentation. By definition an 'apology' presupposes a legal context if not a trial proper, and in their criticisms of his work both Basil[17] and Gregory[18] claimed that Eunomius chose this manner of presentation only to gain sympathy as an injured party, alleging that his so-called 'apology' had never in fact been presented in public. Nevertheless, and despite obvious evidence that the work had been revised for publication,[19] Eunomius contended vehemently in his second apology that the earlier work had been presented at a public trial.[20] Since it is difficult to see what he might have gained from lying about so professedly public an event, and it is clear that Gregory and Basil are disingenuous to say the least,[21] it seems that we must take his contention seriously; but if so, we must ask when such an apology can have been presented.

In seeking an answer to this question, we are fortunate in that Basil's reply to Eunomius, the *Adversus Eunomium*, provides us with a *terminus ante quem*. This work can be dated generally by its references to Constantius' persecution of the Orthodox and by its mention of events surrounding the years 359-60;[22] this suggests that Basil took advantage of Julian's edict of toleration, and the confusion following his death in 363, to bring out his own work. A more precise date is provided by a letter of Basil which can be dated to the end of 364 or the beginning of 365 telling us that he had sent a copy of this work to Leontius the Sophist.[23] In all likelihood, then, Basil produced this work during his years of monastic solitude at Annesoi, most probably during the period of his retirement from Caesarea in deference to Bishop Eusebius (362-5).[24] This surmise

---

[17] Basil, *Eun.* i.2 (501B-505B).   [18] *GN* I (*J* i.42.16-62.22).

[19] Cf. *Apol.* 1.15 ('by setting out for you in writing an expression') and 2.1-2 ('those who may come across this work in the future').

[20] Eun., *Apol. Apol.* i, below pp. 100-1.

[21] See the remarks by L. R. Wickham, 'The Date of Eunomius' *Apology*: A Reconsideration', *JTS* 20 (1969), 238-9.

[22] Basil, *Eun.* i.2 (504C-505B).   [23] Basil, *Ep.* 20.25-32 (Courtonne i.51).

[24] NB Basil's comment in *Ep.* 13 (Courtonne i.42) on each season's characteristic product: in springtime, flowers; in summer, wheat; in autumn, fruit; in winter, books!

could be raised to near certainty if we could accept the authenticity
of Basil's correspondence with Apollinaris, for this correspondence
contains verbal reminiscences of the *Adversus Eunomium* and must
(if authentic) be dated to about this period.[25] Eunomius' treatise,
then, must have appeared sometime during the period preceding
Basil's retirement, so that we must look for the event which
occasioned it at some point prior to the year 362.

In considering the possibilities, two events stand out as having a
prima facie likelihood; both are to be found in the *Ecclesiastical
History* of Philostorgius. The first is the defence of his position
made by Eunomius before Eudoxius and the assembled clergy of
Constantinople when accused of heterodoxy by members of his own
Church at Cyzicus.[26] The second is an appearance before the
Emperor Constantius at Antioch in response to an accusation by
Acacius of Caesarea. Since the latter failed to appear, the matter
was still in abeyance when Constantius died in November of 361.[27]
The reason for thinking of these events as possible occasions for
Eunomius' apology is Philostorgius' choice of words in describing
them: of the one he says, ἐντεῦθεν εἰς ἀπολογίαν ὁ Εὐνόμιος τῷ
Κωνσταντινουπόλεως κλήρῳ καταστάς . . .[28] and of the other, καὶ
παραγεγονότα εἰς ἀπολογίαν κελεύει καταστῆναι . . .[29] In the latter
case at any rate, Eunomius' accuser never put in an appearance, so
it seems unlikely that there was an opportunity for him to present
a defence. This makes the former of the two possibilities seem more
likely since, as has been rightly pointed out,[30] several of the points
at issue on that occasion are in fact discussed in the extant
apology.

In spite of this, however, there are other and more powerful
reasons for maintaining that neither of these events could have been
the occasion for our apology. We may note first of all, as Basil had

[25] Basil, *Ep.* 361-4 (Courtonne iii.220-6); cf. G. L. Prestige, *St. Basil the Great
and Apollinaris of Laodicea* (London: SPCK, 1956), pp. 10, 19 ff., 24 ff.

[26] Philost., *HE* vi.1 (*GCS* 70.2-71.2); also mentioned with considerable dif-
ferences by Soz., *HE* vi.26 (*GCS* 273.7-15) and Thdt., *HE* ii.29 (*GCS* 166.13-167.6).
This is the occasion accepted by Diekamp (op. cit., 5-6) and, following him, by E.
Vandenbussche, 'La part de la dialectique dans la théologie d'Eunomius "le techno-
logue"', *RHE* 40 (1944/5), 61 f. n. 1; also by E. Cavalcanti, *Studi Eunomiani*,
Orientalia Christiana Analecta 202 (1976), p. 24.

[27] Philost., *HE* vi.4 (*GCS* 71.23-73.6).

[28] Ibid., vi.1 (*GCS* 70.12-13).   [29] Ibid., vi.4 (*GCS* 71.28-9).

[30] By Diekamp, op. cit., 5-6 (see below p. 9).

already done,[31] that the parties to whom this apology is addressed are not clearly delineated, a lack which would be difficult to understand if this address had been presented before the clergy of Constantinople in response to charges arising from Eunomius' own diocese.[32] A stronger reason, however, is provided by something that Eunomius himself says in his second apology:

εἰ γὰρ τὸ ἆθλον . . . νίκης ἐστὶ γνώρισμα καὶ τέλος, μηνύει δὲ τὴν δίκην ἡ νίκη, συνεισάγει δὲ πάντως ἑαυτῇ τὴν κατηγορίαν ἡ δίκη, ὁ τὸ ἆθλον διδοὺς ἀναγκαίαν εἶναι φήσει καὶ τὴν ἀπολογίαν.[33]

If a reward . . . is the token and crown of victory, and a victory indicates a trial, and a trial inevitably implies an accusation, the one who grants the reward must admit that of necessity there was a defence.

In this passage Eunomius was trying to use Basil's own words against him, since in his reply to the first apology Basil had admitted that Eunomius received the bishopric of Cyzicus as the 'reward' of his impiety.[34] While it is true that Eunomius nowhere states in so many words that this was the case, it would rather ruin the point of his argument if it was not. This means that Eunomius must have delivered his apology *before* he received the bishopric of Cyzicus, in which event he cannot have done so on either of the occasions mentioned by Philostorgius since by then he already was a bishop.[35]

It seems, then, that we must turn to two earlier possibilities, both mentioned by Basil, the councils of Ariminium/Seleucia (September 359) and Constantinople (January 360).[36] In assessing these possibilities we are somewhat hampered by the fact that Gregory has not preserved the section of Eunomius' reply to Basil, from which the above fragment comes, in its original order.[37] None the less, a careful comparison of the surviving fragments with the comments made by Basil shows that Eunomius indeed discussed both events.[38] In the case of the former he replied to Basil's accusation that at Seleucia he had been convicted by default (Ἀλλὰ

---

[31] Basil, *Eun.* i.2 (504c).   [32] See Wickham, op. cit., 238.
[33] Eun., *Apol. Apol.* i (*J* i.60.12-16).   [34] Basil, *Eun.* i.2 (505A/B).
[35] That is, assuming with most commentators that Soc., *HE* iv.7 (*PG* 67.472c), followed by Soz., *HE* vi.8 (*GCS* 248.4-11), cf. vii.6 (*GCS* 307.15-18), is wrong in placing this under Valens.
[36] Basil, *Eun.* i.2 (504c-504A); Basil, of course, denies that a defence was presented at either.
[37] *GN* i (*J* i.29.21-2).   [38] See below pp. 100-1.

σιωπήσαντες ἑάλωσαν)[39] by saying that while this was indeed the case (σιωπῶντες ἑάλωμεν),[40] faced with a packed jury he could have done nothing else.[41] In the case of the second, although Eunomius did not actually mention the Council by name,[42] it is clear from a comment of Gregory that he had turned his attention to the events at Constantinople as well.[43] Though it is no longer possible to restore the original order, it seems that there too Eunomius was responding directly to the accusations of Basil. To Basil's demand to know the locale of this trial and the identity of the accusers,[44] he replied that it was a council of great importance, and that its members came from every region.[45] To Basil's charge that in any case no defence was needed there,[46] he answered that indeed there was a mortal combat at which Basil himself had been present,[47] and that contrary to his own inclinations he had been forced by intermediaries to make his defence.[48] Furthermore, he went on to say that while he himself had presented his arguments at the appropriate time, Basil had been too late,[49] apparently meaning by this that he had presented his own arguments before the council itself while Basil had declined to appear, only putting forward a reply at a much later date.[50] It is difficult to find any known event to which this might apply other than the Council of Constantinople. Moreover, despite Basil and Gregory's patently 'economic' approach to the narration of these events, it can be shown that this understanding of the events is consistent with their statements.[51] It seems, then, that Eunomius made the claim that he had given his apology at the Council of Constantinople in January of 360 and that he had received the bishopric of Cyzicus as the reward of a successful defence. The probable date of this work's

[39] Basil, *Eun.* i.2 (504c).   [40] Eun., *Apol. Apol.* i (*J* i.44.5; 51.17-18).
[41] Ibid. (*J* i.44.4-7; 51.17-21; cf. 44.15-18; 47.8-11).
[42] Ibid. (*J* i.49.9-13; 50.3).   [43] *GN* I (*J* i.50.18-23).
[44] Basil, *Eun.* i.2 (504c).   [45] Eun., *Apol.Apol.* i (*J* i.49.9-22; 50.3-10).
[46] Basil, *Eun.* i.2 (505A).   [47] Eun., *Apol. Apol.* i (*J* i.49.16-22).
[48] Ibid. (*J* i.51.23-8).

[49] Ibid.; cf. Gregory's acidic résumé of the significance of this argument, *GN* I (*J* i.51.6-12).

[50] This seems to be the import of his abuse at *Apol. Apol* i (*J* i.63.2-10), cf. Wickham, op. cit., 236. Gregory, moreover, seems to confirm Basil's silence at *GN* I (*J* i.50.18-23). For a discusion of Basil's role at this council, see S. Giet, 'Saint Basile et le concile de Constantinople de 360', *JTS* 6 (1955), 94-9.

[51] Cf. Wickham, op. cit., 238-9.

publication, then, would be sometime late in 360 or 361, with
Basil's reply appearing during the years immediately following.

III. STRUCTURE AND CONTENTS

The general concerns of this Council are clearly reflected in the
Liber Apologeticus, as they are, indeed, in other works appearing
about this time. Although, as we noted earlier, Eunomius' defence
of his position before the clergy of Constantinople was not the
occasion of our own Apology, the arguments recorded by Philostorgius as having been used there provide an excellent summary of
its general approach:

καὶ γὰρ ἀνόμοιον τῷ πατρὶ τὸν υἱὸν οὐ μόνον οὐδαμῶς ἐν οἷς ἐδημηγόρησε
δογματίζειν ἐφωράθη, ἀλλά γε καὶ ὅμοιον κατὰ τὰς γραφὰς ἀνακηρύττειν
ἐπαρρησιάζετο. τὸ μέντοι ὅμοιον κατὰ τὴν οὐσίαν οὐ προσίετο, ἴσον εἰς βλασφημίαν λέγων εἶναι ὅμοιον κατ᾽ οὐσίαν λέγειν τῷ πατρὶ τὸν υἱὸν καὶ μὴ
ὁμοιότατον φρονεῖν κατὰ τοὺς μονογενεῖ θεῷ πρὸς τὸν ἀπαθῶς γεγεννηκότα
πατέρα προσήκοντας λόγους.[52]

For not only had he never been found to teach in his public preaching that
the Son is 'dissimilar' to the Father, he had boldly proclaimed that he is
'similar to him in accordance with the Scriptures'. He did not, moreover,
accept (the formula) 'similar in essence' but asserted that it is just as
blasphemous to say the Son is 'similar to the Father in essence' as it is *not*
to account him 'most similar' to him in accordance with the passages which
speak of the Only-begotten God in relation to the Father who impassibly
begot him.

In using the phrase ὅμοιος κατὰ τὰς γραφάς ('similar in accordance
with the Scriptures'), Eunomius was adopting a formula which had
been used not only by the Council of Constantinople,[53] but also by
those of Sirmium IV,[54] Thracian Nike,[55] and Ariminium[56] (all in
359) in response to the homoeousian formula ὅμοιος κατ᾽ οὐσίαν
('similar in essence') adopted at Ancyra in 358.[57] In the *Liber
Apologeticus* Eunomius several times condemns the formula ὅμοιος
κατ᾽ οὐσίαν,[58] and one of his principal concerns is to show that the
assertion of a *similarity* of essence inevitably implies an *identity* of

[52] Philost., *HE* vi.1 (*GCS* 70.15-22).   [53] Hahn, no. 167, p. 208.
[54] Hahn, no. 163, p. 204.   [55] Hahn, no. 164, p. 206.
[56] Hahn, no. 166, p. 208.   [57] Hahn, no. 162, pp. 201-2.
[58] Eun., *Apol.* 11.6-9, 18.12-13, 20.9-10, 24.26.

essence as well.[59] While he nowhere uses the actual phrase ὅμοιος κατὰ τὰς γραφάς, he alludes to it in asserting that we must accept the likeness of the Son to the Father 'in accordance with his own words'.[60] One of the major purposes of the *Liber Apologeticus*, then, is to show that Eunomius' own teaching is conformable in this respect to the teaching of the Council. In pursuing his arguments in greater detail, however, we shall have to turn to the question of the structure of the work.

At first sight, this structure seems perfectly obvious and straightforward. At the very beginning of his work Eunomius presents the basis on which he intends to proceed, a short Trinitarian Creed in three sections which had come down to him from the Fathers.[61] Although it is apparent that the ultimate basis of this creed is 1 Cor. 8: 6, Basil tells us that it was indeed used by some of the Fathers and that it had been presented to Alexander of Alexandria (Bishop, AD 312–28) by Arius in token of his faith.[62] As the creed stands, we are told that some undisputed secondary matters have been omitted, but we are not told what they were.[63] The most likely guess is that a paragraph on the resurrection of the dead such as that which closes the *Expositio Fidei*[64] has been passed over,[65] but in any case it is evident that in this creed Eunomius found 'that essential faith which is common to all who are concerned either to seem or to be Christians'[66] on which he proposed to base his defence.

However this may be, in the immediate introduction to his main argument Eunomius provides us with an explicit statement of how he intends to make use of it:

πειρασόμεθα ὡς ἂν οἷοί τε ὦμεν εἰς τοὐμφανὲς ἀγαγεῖν ἣν αὐτοὶ περὶ τούτων τυγχάνομεν ἔχοντες δόξαν, ἤτοι προτιθέντες τὴν λέξιν, εἶθ' ὕστερον ἐκκαλύπτοντες τὴν ἔννοιαν, ἢ καὶ προκειμέναις ταῖς ἐννοίαις τὰς φωνὰς ἐφαρμόζοντες...[67]

We shall try, therefore, so far as we can, to make the opinion we hold with regard to these arguments explicit—either we shall first set out the text of

---

[59] e.g. Eun., *Apol.* 11.4-9.   [60] Eun., *Apol.* 22.4-5, cf. 12.6-7.
[61] Eun., *Apol.* 4.6-7; the creed itself is at *Apol.* 5.1-7 = Hahn, no. 190, pp. 260-1.
[62] Basil, *Eun.* i.4 (509B).   [63] Eun., *Apol.* 6.3-4.
[64] Eun., *Exp. Fid.* 5.1-12.
[65] A suggestion first made by J. A. Fabricius, *Bibliotheca Graeca* viii (Hamburg: Christian Liebezeit, 1717), p. 267.
[66] Eun., *Apol.* 6.1-2.   [67] Ibid., 6.17-20.

the profession and then disclose its meaning, or, after setting out the meaning, we shall then apply it to the verbal expressions of the text.

On the basis of this programme it is possible to construct what is, on the surface at least, a very satisfactory outline of the main features of the *Liber Apologeticus*:

Yet, while this analysis clearly does reflect the external structure of the Apology, in other ways it is less adequate as a full expression of Eunomius' meaning. This is suggested by a statement made by Eunomius himself on the methods by which theological enquiry is to be pursued:

δυεῖν γὰρ ἡμῖν τετμημένων ὁδῶν πρὸς τὴν τῶν ζητουμένων εὕρεσιν, μιᾶς μὲν καθ' ἣν τὰς οὐσίας αὐτὰς ἐπισκοπούμενοι, καθαρῷ τῷ περὶ αὐτῶν λόγῳ τὴν ἑκάστου ποιούμεθα κρίσιν, θατέρας δὲ τῆς διὰ τῶν ἐνεργειῶν ἐξετάσεως, ἣν ἐκ τῶν δημιουργημάτων καὶ τῶν ἀποτελεσμάτων διακρίνομεν, οὐδετέραν τῶν εἰρημένων εὑρεῖν ἐμφαινομένην τὴν τῆς οὐσίας ὁμοιότητα δυνατόν.[68]

There are two roads marked out to us for the discovery of what we seek —one is that by which we examine the actual essences and with clear and unadulterated reasoning about them make a judgement on each; the other is an enquiry by means of the actions, whereby we distinguish the essence on the basis of its products and completed works—and neither of the ways mentioned is able to bring out any apparent similarity of essence.

In some ways this might almost be taken as a summary of the contents of the treatise. In any case, it makes clear that there are two methods of doing theology, the one a priori where, by an analysis of the essences as revealed by their names (e.g. ἀγέννητος, γέννημα), we come to an understanding of the things signified, the other a posteriori where, by an analysis of the effects, we are able to discern the essence which caused them. On the basis of this

[68] Ibid., 20.5–10.

methodological distinction, it is possible to detect a more subtle structure underlying the surface features of the work, one which gives us a more satisfactory understanding of Eunomius' meaning:

Even in this rough outline we can see that the composition of Eunomius' Apology is more integrally linked to his basic approach to theology than the more mechanical analysis presented earlier would lead us to believe.[69] Beneath the apparently simple structure of his treatise we are led by a two-fold way to the acceptance of his contention that neither way 'is able to bring out any apparent similarity of essence'.

IV. AUTHENTICITY

The authenticity of the work found in our manuscripts as the *Liber Apologeticus* of Eunomius is guaranteed by the quotations of it preserved by Basil of Caesarea. Questions have arisen, however, over those chapters which Basil does *not* quote.[70] Although he cites almost every chapter of the work in the course of his refutation, he passes over chapters 14, 21-4, and 26-8, some eight in all. Of these, only chapters 26-8 pose a real problem. There is no reason whatsoever to doubt the authenticity of chapter 14, which fits perfectly into its context, and scarcely less that of chapters 21-4, which

---

[69] For a more detailed analysis based on similar principles, cf. Th. Dams, 'La controverse Eunoméenne' (unpublished dissertation [place lacking], 1951), pp. 12-14 (a copy is available in the Bodleian Library, Oxford); cf. also L. R. Wickham, 'The Syntagmation of Aetius the Anomoean', *JTS* 19 (1968), 537-40 (hereafter referred to as Wickham, 'Syntagmation').   [70] e.g. Albertz, pp. 6-7 ff.

cannot without violence be separated from the main body of the work.[71] Since neither of these sections adds a great deal that is new to the argument, the most probable reason for their omission is the demonstrable tendency of these authors to quote less fully as they proceed with their work. Certainly it is impossible to think of any reason why a forger would have added them!

Chapters 26-8, however, pose a different problem. We can set aside chapter 28 for the moment because it clearly requires special treatment, and deal only with chapters 26-7. The authenticity of these chapters has been doubted because, despite the tight organization of the treatise as a whole, they seem to have only a very general relationship with what precedes.[72] Although there is nothing in them which is incompatible with the rest of the treatise, their creed-like character, together with the obviously transitional nature of the paragraph which introduces them,[73] suggests a distinct change of literary gears. A certain amount of thought, however, suggests a less sinister explanation. Many of those who opposed Eunomius were suspicious not only of his theology, but also of his theological method, a suspicion which they expressed by calling him the 'logic-chopper', ὁ τεχνολόγος.[74] In view of the systematic and highly technical nature of most of the work, it is not difficult to understand that in concluding his defence Eunomius might have wanted to present a more popular and immediately comprehensible version of his opinions, one untainted by the presence of the much-maligned τέχνη. There are, however, more concrete reasons for believing these chapters to be integrally related to the rest of the work. If we consider the latter part of chapter 27 (clearly the original ending of the work) in relation to Eunomius' introductory remarks in chapters 2 and 3, we find that the parallelism is almost exact: in both there is the same appeal to an audience actually present and to a wider range of future readers;[75] there is the same exhortation to avoid anything which might distort

---

[71] Cf. Albertz, pp. 7-8. [72] Ibid., pp. 10-11.

[73] Eun., *Apol.* 25.27-26.3.

[74] Cf., e.g., *GN* II (*J* i.402.28); the burden of the accusation was, as Eunomius himself recognized (*Apol.* 21.6-8), that he 'perverted the truth (of Scripture) by his clever inventions and use of argument.' The powerful interest in logic is borne out by all the works contained in this volume, but in Eunomius' own view, of course, he was merely providing the confirmation (πίστωσις) of what was to any unbiased eye the real meaning of Scripture, cf. *Apol.* 6.10-12, 21.8 ff., etc.

[75] Eun., *Apol.* 27.17-19~2.1-2.

the judgement and to ignore the appeals of influential men;[76] there is the same dichotomy between present joys and pains and the sure reward promised to the faithful in the future.[77] Parallels so exact must, in the absence of contrary evidence, be taken as showing that the passages in question come not only from the same author,[78] but from the same work.

Before passing on to a discussion of chapter 28, let us deal with two passages said to provide this evidence. The first of these is the introductory paragraph of Eunomius' concluding remarks:

Τούτων δὴ πάντων εὐκρινῶς μὲν καὶ πλατύτερον ἐν ἑτέροις ἡμῖν ἀποδεδειγμένων, ἐν βραχεῖ δὲ νῦν πρὸς ὑμᾶς ὡμολογημένων, εὐχόμεθα τούς τε παρόντας ὑμᾶς . . .[79]

Since we demonstrated all these things with clarity and at greater length ἐν ἑτέροις and have now professed them again by way of summary, we beseech not only you who are present . . .

We have left the phrase ἐν ἑτέροις untranslated for the moment because it is precisely the point at issue. These words have usually been understood as referring to earlier and presumably larger works of Eunomius.[80] If this could be shown to be the case, it would be unlikely that these chapters belong with the rest of the work, for the *Liber Apologeticus* was almost certainly Eunomius' first published effort. This is deduced not only from Eunomius' own statements,[81] but also from the assertion of Basil that he had previously hidden his opinions and had only now (presumably for the first time) brought them out in his ἄθεον κήρυγμα.[82] A comparison of the passage quoted above, however, with Eunomius' earlier statements in the introduction to chapter 26 shows that the usual understanding of ἐν ἑτέροις is mistaken. In that passage,[83] after clearly alluding to an immediately preceding longer dis-

---

[76] Eun., *Apol.* 27.19-23~2.2-11. [77] Eun., *Apol.* 27.23-42~3.1-9.
[78] As suggested by Albertz, p. 8. [79] Eun., *Apol.* 27.16-18.
[80] Thus W. Whiston's translation in *Primitive Christianity Reviv'd* i (London, 1711), p. 28, 'We have elsewhere with greater care, and more largely demonstrated these things . . .', plainly gives this impression, and Fabricius, op. cit., p. 301 n., makes the explicit statement, 'Notandus hic locus quo ad uberiora sua scripta jam ante illud tempus edita Eunomius provocat.' Albertz, pp. 8-9 also clearly bases his arguments on such a translation, as does B. C. Barmann, 'The Cappadocian Triumph over Arianism' (unpublished Ph.D. thesis, Stanford University, 1966), pp. 54-5. [81] Eun., *Apol.* 1.7-10.
[82] Basil, *Eun.* i.2 (501B-C). [83] Eun., *Apol.* 26.1-3.

cussion, the author goes on to say that, in order not to weary his hearers by the length of his discourse, he proposes to present the force of his arguments in a few words (ἐν βραχεῖ). In the present passage, the author begins his appeal to his hearers by saying that he had previously presented his arguments 'at greater length' ἐν ἑτέροις, and that he had just now made his profession in a few words (ἐν βραχεῖ). Unless, then, we are prepared to divide these chapters yet again and separate the passage which opens them from that which closes them, we shall have to conclude that the reference in both is to the same thing, the earlier part of the work. The correct translation of this passage, then, must be as follows:

Since we demonstrated all these things with clarity and at greater length *in the other parts of our discourse* and have now professed them again by way of summary, we beseech not only you who are present . . .

We can deal with the remaining passage more briefly. In the closing part of Basil's *Adversus Eunomium* there is a statement identified by the editor as coming from Eunomius which bears no apparent resemblance to any known portion of the work.[84] This has been taken to indicate that a section has dropped out and been replaced by the matter now found in chapters 26-7.[85] The most natural understanding of this passage in context, however, would be as a rebuke directed at Eunomius and as a caution not to use his previous arguments, now proved fruitless. In this case, there ought to be a passage earlier in the work of which this alleged quotation is a paraphrase. A perusal of Eunomius' chapter on the Holy Spirit, that refuted by Basil in the preceding passage, shows that this is in fact the case. That chapter contains a passage which corresponds almost exactly to that mentioned by Basil,[86] the sole difference being that Basil has considerably abbreviated the argument and has supplied a suppressed premise. In view of the positive evidence cited above, then, and the fact that these chapters do occupy a logical place within the work itself, they must be regarded as

[84] Basil, *Eun.* iii.6 (665D-668A); the passages so identified are, of course, purely editorial, though following in part the usage of the manuscripts.

[85] As by Albertz, pp. 11-12; he also cites in the same place another fragment of Eunomius as not corresponding to any extant portion of the apology. This is Basil, *Eun.* i.23 (564A), but this passage is clearly a paraphrase of *Apol.* 11.1-12, the portion of the work there being refuted; cf. also Basil, *Eun.* ii.8 (588B), where the argument of *Apol.* 12.6-10 is summarized.

[86] Eun., *Apol.* 25.19-25.

forming an integral part of the *Liber Apologeticus*, and indeed as marking the proper conclusion of the work.

With this in mind, we may now turn to the one remaining section of the treatise, chapter 28. That this chapter forms an independent unit can scarcely be denied, and it has clearly been appended to the work by a later hand. Whether the hand in question was that of Eunomius or of a disciple cannot now be determined. In any case, it clearly reflects Eunomian doctrine and teaching, and in the absence of any independent title in the manuscripts we have given it the name *Confessio Eunomiana*. As it stands it possesses a marked creed-like character and may be divided into two paragraphs or sections. The first, 28.1-17, deals with the various ranks of the chain of being, beginning with the Unbegotten and then proceeding to each of the beings derived from him in their proper order: the Son, the Holy Spirit, all other created beings. In each case it is shown that there can be no similarity of essence between the members of the intelligible hierarchy. The second and shorter section, 28.17-26, tries to show the same thing on the basis of Holy Scripture. It seems unlikely that either section ever circulated independently of the other. While the manuscripts themselves give us no indication of the original purpose of this short work, it is a very attractive hypothesis that it is one of those 'Introductory Works' (λόγον εἰσαγωγικόν) said by Gregory of Nazianzus to have been used in Eunomian missionary work among the less educated.[87] If so, it may have become attached to our treatise simply because at some point it followed the *Liber Apologeticus* in a collection of Eunomian works and was copied consecutively by a scribe without his noticing that in doing so he had passed from one work to another.[88] In any event, if it cannot certainly be ascribed to Eunomius himself, this short work can still provide us with a valuable witness to the teaching of the Church he founded.

V. THE MANUSCRIPTS[89]

a. *Manuscripts CIG*

Taken together, these three manuscripts form the main independent witnesses to our text. Before discussing the relationships

[87] Grg. Naz., *Or.* 29.1 (Mason 74.6-11).

[88] As happened in MS F of the *Expositio Fidei*; see the apparatus at *Exp. Fid.* 4.16 and the discussion on p. 137.

[89] I am most grateful to Mr Nigel Wilson of Lincoln College, Oxford for

between them, however, we will attempt briefly to identify and describe each manuscript.

C   *Codex Parisinus (olim Colbertinus) graecus 965, fos. 1ʳ–17ᵛ, saeculi xi.*[90]

This manuscript, by far the oldest known to us, consists of the first 17 folios (out of 215) of a volume also containing the *Adversus Eunomium* and *De Spiritu Sancto* of Basil. It is written on parchment in a single column of 24 lines, each folio measuring 22 × 17 cm. The hand is a clear and legible minuscule making use of few abbreviations or contractions. On fos. 1ʳ, 2ʳ, 3ʳ, 4ʳ, 4ᵛ, 5ʳ, 5ᵛ, 6ʳ, 6ᵛ, 7ᵛ, 16ʳ (?), 17ᵛ a later hand has added a series of abusive comments usually consisting of the single word ἀνάθεμα, but in a few cases more extensive; none of these comments shed any additional light on the text. Presumably the same scribe who was responsible for these comments is also responsible for crossing out the closing lines of chapter 28 (21-6) which appear on fo. 17ᵛ together with the opening chapter of Basil's *Adversus Eunomium*. In contrast with most other manuscripts of the *Liber Apologeticus*, the portions of the treatise refuted by Basil are not designated in the margin, though Basil's quotations of Eunomius in the *Adversus Eunomium* are so distinguished. On fos. 1ʳ–5ᵛ, 6ᵛ, and 7ᵛ a hand of the late fifteenth or early sixteenth century has added a series of extensive comments in Latin. In the seventeenth century, this volume formed part of the library of Jean-Baptiste Colbert (1619–83), and its number in his collection (no. 4529) is written at the top of fo. 1ʳ. Colbert had the volume rebound in red moroccan leather with his arms on the front and his monogram (*JBC*) repeated several times on the back. In 1732 this manuscript entered the Bibliothèque Royale (now the Bibliothèque Nationale) together with the rest of Colbert's collection and has remained there ever since. Unfortunately, there is no information as to its prior history.

examining all of these manuscripts (as well as those of the *Expositio Fidei*) with an eye to verifying their dates and provenance. Except where specifically indicated to the contrary, the suggested dates of composition and possible identities of some of the scribes are his.

[90] I am indebted to the kindness of M. Charles Astruc, Conservateur au Département des Manuscrits, Bibliothèque Nationale, for much of the detailed information about this manuscript (personal letter, 3 March 1979).

I   *Codex Athous monasterii Iviron 354 [376] (Lampros 4474),*
     fos. 1ʳ-16ʳ, verisimile saeculi xiv.

As in the case of C, the *Liber Apologeticus* occupies the first place
in this codex, immediately followed by the *Adversus Eunomium*
and *De Spiritu Sancto* of Basil.[91] The manuscript is written on
paper in a single column of 25 lines, each folio measuring 13.5 ×
20.5 cm. It is written in a clear, though not wholly regular
minuscule employing few abbreviations or contractions. Although
the work of several second-hand correctors can be discerned in the
text of the *Adversus Eunomium*,[92] no such corrections are visible in
the *Liber Apologeticus*. Apart from one exception on fo. 12ᵛ, there
are no marginal notes or comments, although the portions of the
treatise refuted by Basil in the *Adversus Eunomium* are distinguished by a stroke placed against the line in the margin. In
contrast to the same manuscript's treatment of the *Adversus
Eunomium*, no use is made of red ink in initial letters or titles. We
have been unable to obtain any information as to this manuscript's
earlier history.

G   *Codex Gudianus graecus 85, fos. 1ʳ-9ʳ, saeculi xiv medii vel*
     exeuntis.[93]

Codex G is virtually unique in containing the *Liber Apologeticus*
alone, unaccompanied by any other work. It is written on paper in
a single column of 35 lines, each folio measuring 21 × 14.5 cm.
There is a very faint and otherwise unknown watermark in the form
of a bell with a line on either side visible across the fold between fos.
3ʳ and 6ʳ.[94] The written portion of the manuscript is preceded and
followed by two uninscribed folios which are in fact joined together
(those at the beginning of the book are unfoliated, those at the end

[91] The latter is surely what is intended by the entry in S. Lampros, *Catalogue of
the Greek Manuscripts on Mount Athos* ii (Cambridge University Press, 1900),
p. 95.

[92] W. Hayes, 'Greek Recentiores, (Ps.-)Basil, *Adversus Eunomium*, IV-V', in
J. R. O'Donnell (ed.), *Essays in Honour of Anton Charles Pegis* (Toronto: Pontifical
Institute of Medieval Studies, 1974), pp. 350-1.

[93] I am indebted to Dr Helmar Härtel and Dr Wolfgang Milde of the Herzog
August Bibliothek Wolfenbüttel for much information about this manuscript,
particularly to Dr Härtel for the tracing of the watermark (personal letters 26 Oct.
1977, 4 Nov. 1977, and 29 May 1978).

[94] It is most similar to watermark no. 3945 listed in Briquet i, pp. 247 ff., and
deriving from Bologna, 1321.

form fos. 10 and 11). The paper used for these folios is entirely different from that of the inscribed portion and bears a different watermark; the blank folios are wholly unconnected with those bearing the written text and were presumably added when the book was rebound for the Wolfenbüttel Library.[95] In the course of this rebinding the pages were trimmed and some parts of the folio numbers were cut off. Since there is no indication of any earlier system of numbers, that now found in the manuscript is presumabiy original and was there when the manuscript was rebound. This raises another question. If the manuscript as we have it is complete, an explanation must be found as to why Orthodox scribes should have secured the independent transmission of an heretical text.[96] The most reasonable explanation is that it was intended to illustrate the arguments employed by Basil in his *Adversus Eunomium*, an explanation rendered the more likely by the fact that the passages quoted in that work are distinguished by a mark in the margin. This suggests that our manuscript was once part of a larger whole. If, as we have suggested, the present foliation is original, there is a strong possibility, even probability, that our manuscript is a detached portion of a larger one similar to those already considered. Thus, as in the case of C and I, G would once have been followed by the *Adversus Eunomium* and (perhaps) *De Spiritu Sancto* of Basil from which it has now become detached. If so, however, there is no surviving manuscript of the *Adversus Eunomium* with which it can now be identified.[97] The manuscript is written in a highly compressed though clear minuscule making consistent use of abbreviations and contractions. The scribe himself is apparently responsible for a variant appearing in the margin of fo. 7ᵛ which has passed down into the tradition of this manuscript's numerous progeny.[98] In addition to this, three hands can be discerned in the marginal notations. The first is responsible for

---

[95] For the binding see F. Koehler, *Die Gudischen Handschriften* (Wolfenbüttel: Verlag Julius Zwissler, 1913), p. 51.

[96] Their reluctance to do so is shown by the marginal comment on fo. 1ʳ of this very manuscript (cf. *Apol.* 1.1, apparatus).

[97] I am indebted for this information to the kindness of the Revd Walter J. Hayes, SJ, who has examined the manuscripts for me (personal letter, 15 Feb. 1978).

[98] See the apparatus at *Apol.* 25.6. G has περιβολήν in the text with the correct μεταβολήν in the margin; B, followed by A and F, has written μεταβολήν in the text but kept περι- between the lines as a variant; VMOS (all copies of B) have written both sequentially, περὶ μεταβολήν.

a relatively lengthy caveat to the reader on fo. 1ʳ (for the text, see apparatus). Another hand has added the phrase ἔκθεσις πίστεως to the margin of fo. 2ʳ directly opposite *Apol.* 7.1, and is apparently responsible for the bracket appearing at this point in the text as well as on fo. 1ᵛ opposite *Apol.* 5.1. This same hand has also added the comment τραγέλαφος in the margin of fo. 2ᵛ opposite *Apol.* 8.4. Finally, another much later hand (Holsatius?) has added the probably correct conjecture ἐπισφ(αλές) to the margin of fo. 1ʳ in place of the ἀσφαλές of the manuscripts.[99] Since the seventeenth century this manuscript has been part of the collection of Marquardus Gudius (1635-89), now in the Herzog August Bibliothek Wolfenbüttel. Although there is no direct information as to the previous whereabouts of this manuscript, the Italian origin of many of the copies made from it suggests Italy as the most likely possibility.[100]

There are numerous indications that these three manuscripts derive ultimately from an exemplar at some remove from the autograph, one, moreover, already joined to a copy of Basil's refutation.[101] To take only the external evidence, we may note that the contents of two of the codices (CI) are identical and that the same may very probably have been true of the third. Moreover, all three have a marginal notation in connection with Eunomius' discussion of the Holy Spirit in *Apol.* 25.1: C and G have the surely original ση(μείωσ)αι while I has περὶ τοῦ ἁγίου πνεύματος. Again, all three manuscripts agree in a number of obvious errors: the omission of πίστις in *Apol.* 6.1; the reading καὶ λεγόντων καὶ γενομένων at *Apol.* 8.6, shown to be an erroneous banalization by Eunomius' own quotation of the passage, etc. Yet if these readings and shared characteristics show the ultimate common origin of these manuscripts, many others show the extent by which they differ. To begin with, we may note that I and G must derive from a common ancestor, though not an immediate one. They agree in

[99] See the apparatus at *Apol.* 1.19.

[100] In view of the copies made by Friedrich Lindenbrog (LW) it appears that this manuscript was acquired during his trip to Italy in 1606-7, though it cannot be excluded that he may have made the copies in Italy (in that case it was presumably bought by Gudius during his trip, 1659-63). See my article, 'An Appeal to Antiquity', cited in section c below.

[101] The Revd George Dennis, SJ, who has examined the manuscripts, informs me that in his view there is evidence of two separate transcriptions from uncial to minuscule (personal communication, March 1978).

error against C eight times and share a common omission,[102] while
I agrees with C against G only three times,[103] and G and C against
I only four.[104] The picture which this presents is that of two groups
of manuscripts originally descended from a common exemplar
which have become sufficiently distinct in the course of time to
occupy quite separate branches of their common family tree.

This raises the problem of the means by which this text has been
transmitted. We have already remarked several times that the main
reason for its preservation appears to have been a desire to illustrate
the arguments used by Basil in his *Adversus Eunomium* — indeed,
two of the manuscripts are still bound up with this work and the
same may have been true of the third. The problem is the relation
of this work to the text tradition of Basil. This tradition has been
studied intensively by Walter M. Hayes as regards Books iv and v of
Basil's work (originally separate),[105] and both C and I belong to the
same family of manuscripts in Hayes's stemma, that designated
beta. Unfortunately it is not clear how the stemma of the authentic
books (i–iii) is related to the stemma presented by Hayes.[106] Despite
this, we may still draw attention to a number of interesting points.
The first is that of the fourteen complete manuscripts belonging to
Hayes's family *beta*, only two contain the work of Eunomius — a
strong indication of the reluctance of scribes to copy this work. The
second is the possible origin of the tradition represented by
manuscripts I and G. I (designated *t* by Hayes) is closely related to
two others, the ninth-century D (Codex Athous monasterii

---

[102] Eun., *Apol.* 1.14, 6.10, 10.13-14, 11.16, 13.9, 15.11, 25.13, 24; omission,
Apol. 11.9.

[103] Eun., *Apol.* 7.11, 16.10, 25.17.

[104] Eun., *Apol.* 13.8, 13 (CB), 26.1 (if I is correct at this point), 27.22. Père
Doutreleau informs me that in his view Codex I ought to be connected with C rather
than with G. This conclusion, however, appears to be based on the assumption that
G almost always represents the correct reading and hence that where C and I agree
they are reflecting a common ancestor different from G; in my view this agreement is
to be explained in most cases because C and I jointly reflect the original reading,
e.g. *Apol.* 13.12, where C and I read the certainly correct ἀσεβέστατον as opposed to
G's εὐσεβέστατον.

[105] W. M. Hayes, *The Greek Manuscript Tradition of (Ps.)Basil's Adversus
Eunomium Books IV-V* (Leiden, 1972); see also the article cited above, n. 92.

[106] The Revd M. J. Hayes, SJ (personal letter, 19 Mar. 1975) informed me that
Bernard C. Barmann had concluded that the two traditions were probably identical;
Père Doutreleau has since informed me (personal communication) that they are in
fact different, as is now confirmed by the *SC* edition of Basil.

Vatopedi 68) and the fourteenth-century *g* (Codex Athous monasterii Vatopedi 58), though it is a copy of neither.[107] Since I is itself an Athonite manuscript, it is not unreasonable to suppose that all three ultimately derive from an original formerly on Athos and that manuscript G is from a similar source. This supposition is considerably strengthened by the discovery that in the mid-fourteenth century there was a considerable revival of interest in Eunomius in connection with the Palamite controversy. Since it can be demonstrated that participants in the controversy had actually read Eunomius' apology, and codices G and I date from just this time, it seems likely that we owe the preservation of this work in part to the passions stirred up by the Palamite controversy.[108]

b. *Manuscripts BVMOSAF*

All of the manuscripts in this group are directly or indirectly copies of G through their common exemplar, codex B. Since they do not bear directly on the text, we have not included them in the apparatus, with the exception of B itself. Since this manuscript's independence of G cannot be ruled out absolutely (Père Doutreleau informs me that this is in fact his own view), we have decided to include its readings in the apparatus. For a description and discussion of the remaining manuscripts (VMOSAF) the reader is referred to my article, 'The Other Half of a Controversy: The Rediscovery of one of Basil's Opponents in Renaissance Italy', in *Proceedings of the Patristics, Medieval, and Renaissance Conference* [Villanova, PA] 6 (1981), pp. 101-16.[109]

B   *Codex Monacensis (sive Bavaricus) graecus 512, fos. 1^r-18^v, saeculi xv.*[110]

Codex B, the oldest member of this group, contains along with its first entry, the *Liber Apologeticus* of Eunomius, three other short

---

[107] See Hayes, op. cit. n. 92, pp. 350-1, 355-7, stemma p. 360.

[108] For a discussion and references, see the article cited in section b immediately below; there is reason to believe that codex G entered Italy in connection with the Council of Florence (1438-55).

[109] Together with the rest of Cardinal Grimani's library, codex B was given to the library of San Antonio di Castello in Venice; all of the copies of this codex (VMOSAF) can be connected directly or indirectly with this library and more specifically with participants in the Council of Trent (1545-63).

[110] I am indebted to Dr Karl Dachs and Dr Erwin Arnold of the Bayerische Staatsbibliothek München for information on the details of this manuscript.

works, two of which have been passed on to some of its numerous descendants.[111] It is written on parchment in a single column of 22 lines, each folio measuring 21.6 × 14.3 cm. The hand is a neat and clear minuscule making moderate use of contractions and abbreviations and may perhaps be that of Ioannes Thettalos Scutariotes (*fl. c.*1460).[112] On the blank page opposite fo. 1^r the contents of the manuscript have been written first in Greek, then in Latin, and a number of Latin notes are to be found in the margin of fo. 3^v. The passages of the work refuted by Basil are marked in the margin. The binding is Italian, most probably Florentine. A now erased, but still (with difficulty) legible entry on the verso side of the front endpiece informs us that this manuscript formerly belonged to the famous collection of Cardinal Domenico Grimani (1460-1523), son of Doge Antonio Grimani of Venice (1436-1523). It is not known when or under what circumstances it entered the Bayerische Staatsbibliothek in Munich, where it now resides.[113]

V   *Codex Vossianus graecus Q 13, fos. 22^r-38^v, saeculi xvi.*

M   *Codex Monacensis (sive Bavaricus) graecus 58, fos. 294^r-308^r, saeculi xvi.*

O   *Codex Vaticanus Ottobonianus graecus 112, fos. 18^r-28^r, saeculi xvi (24 October/November 1542).*

S   *Codex Vesontionus Sequanorum graecus 408 (Suppl. Gr. D 13), fos. 141^r-151^r, saeculi xvi.*

A   *Codex Ambrosianus graecus C 255 inf., fos. 91^r-100^r, saeculi xvi.*

---

[111] The *Hermiae irrisio gentilium* and the *Dialogus SS. Basilii et Gregorii*; several of the other manuscripts also have treatises in common (for a discussion, see my article cited above).

[112] As suggested by Mr Nigel Wilson; cf. M. Vogel and V. Gardthausen, *Die griechischen Schreiber des Mittelalters und Renaissance* (= *Centralblatt für Bibliothekswesen*, Beiheft 33 [Leipzig, 1909]), pp. 197-8; Scutariotes' dated manuscripts run from 1442 to 1494.

[113] Père Doutreleau informs me that in his view B is an independent witness to the exemplar of G. Although this cannot be excluded absolutely, the 14th-century date of G as established by Nigel Wilson's analysis of the palaeography and the watermark (see above) suggests, as the most economical theory, that B is derived from G, since everything in it can be explained on this basis; moreover, in view of the rarity of the text and the Italian origin of B one would presumably have to suppose another lost copy of Eunomius (and Basil?) in Italy, which, though not impossible, is difficult. Either view makes little difference to our understanding of the text.

F   *Codex Matritensis graecus O. 9, tractatus 10, saeculi xvi.*

c. *Manuscripts PWLH*

All of the remaining manuscripts are relatively late copies of one or another of those already discussed. For a description and discussion of these manuscripts see my article, 'An Appeal to Antiquity: The Seventeenth and Eighteenth Century Manuscripts of the Heretic Eunomius', in *Arianism: Historical and Theological Reassessments*, ed. Robert C. Gregg (The Philadelphia Patristic Foundation, 1985), pp. 335-60.[114]

P   *Codex Parisinus suppl. graecus 294, fos. 2ʳ-19ᵛ, saeculi xvii ineuntis.*

W   *Codex Gudianus graecus 100, pp. 1-147, saeculi xvii.*

L   *Codex Lindenbrogius graecus, Hamburg Cod. Theol. 1518 in 4°, saeculi xvii.*

H   *Codex Gudianus graecus 89, pp. 1-147, saeculi xvii.*

d. *Manuscripts TEYQRJN*

All the manuscripts in this group are directly or indirectly copies of V, formerly in the possession of Canon Isaac Vossius of Windsor (1618-89). For a description and discussion, see the article cited in section c.[115]

T   *Codex Tenisonius graecus, Lambeth 802 (a), fos. 1ʳ-22ᵛ, saeculi xvii.*

E   *Codex Cantabrigiensis Collegii Emmanuelis 249, pp. 1-31, saeculi xvii.*

Y   *Codex Tenisonius graecus, Lambeth 802 (b), pp. 9-82, saeculi xvii.*

Q   *Codex Oxoniensis Collegii Reginensis 187, fos. 1ʳ-15ᵛ, saeculi xvii.*

---

[114] P (described as 'ex bibliotheca Friderici Lindenbrogii J. C.') appears to have belonged to Émery Bigot (1626-89), as did N. W and L belonged to Friederich Lindenbrog (1573-1648); H is mainly in the hand of Marquardus Gudius (1635-89).

[115] All of these manuscripts except N (copied c.1657 for Émery Bigot) can be associated with one or another of the participants in the late 17th- and early 18th-century controversies over Socinianism and Arianism in England. For a detailed discussion, see my article cited above.

R   *Codex Bodleianus graecus Cherry 25 (9799), pp. 37-88, saeculi xvii exeuntis* (c.*1700*).

J   *Codex Cantabrigiensis Collegii Sanctissimae et Individuae Trinitatis O.2.3. (1107), fos. 7ʳ-15ʳ, saeculi xviii ineuntis* (*verisimile* c.*1710*).

N   *Codex Parisinus suppl. graecus 270, fos. 272ʳ-279ᵛ, saeculi xvii.*

e. *Quotations by Basil and Gregory*

The quotations of the *Liber Apologeticus* made by Basil in the course of his refutation are potentially of great importance, and enable us at several points to get behind the manuscript tradition to what clearly must have been the original text. At the same time caution must be exercised in using them. Not only is it apparent that Basil was frequently paraphrastic and often not concerned with verbal accuracy, but there is evidence of some mutual influence between the texts of the *Liber Apologeticus* and the *Adversus Eunomium*. For instance, at *Apol.* 2.1 IGB read the probably correct αἰτοῦμεν while C reads αἰτοῦμαι.[116] While it is not impossible that αἰτοῦμαι was Eunomius' original reading, or that the variant represents a very early division of the text, the possibility of mutual influence cannot be excluded.[117]

The quotations of the *Liber Apologeticus* made by Gregory of Nyssa present quite different problems, primarily because there is every reason to suspect that he did not actually have a copy of it. All his information, therefore, would have come from Basil or from the second apology of Eunomius. Certainly most of his direct quotations of the *Liber Apologeticus* are also to be found in Basil and several show distinct verbal resemblances. For instance, in quoting *Apol.* 7.10-11 Gregory uses not the ἀκολουθεῖ of the manuscripts and of Basil's direct quotation, but the (παρ)ἕπεσθαι of his subsequent detailed discussion.[118] Again, it is clear that Gregory's quotation of *Apol.* 8.14-18 is (despite a lacuna in his manuscripts) not based on Eunomius' original but on the more

---

[116] My thanks to the Revd M. J. Hayes, SJ, for checking the manuscripts of Basil at this point (personal letter, 15 Feb. 1978).

[117] A likely point at which this might have taken place is when the marginal notes were added indicating passages refuted by Basil.

[118] *GN* I (*J* i.214.21-2) quoting Basil, *Eun.* i.5 (517C, 520A).

streamlined version of Basil.[119] Yet again, in quoting *Apol.*
19.12-14 we find that although the quotation itself is a paraphrase
and differs from both Eunomius and Basil,[120] in Gregory's subsequent comments he reproduces one of Basil's remarks almost
exactly, thus showing that he had the latter's work in front of him
when composing this passage.[121] While it is clear that some of
Gregory's quotations do not derive from Basil, the general weight of
evidence suggests that he did not himself possess a copy of the *Liber
Apologeticus*. Most of his quotations, therefore, are of use as
witnesses to the text of Basil; where they are of independent worth,
it is as witnesses to Eunomius' own quotations of his earlier work in
the second apology. In those cases Gregory indeed enables us to get
behind the manuscript tradition to the work of Eunomius himself.

VI. EDITIONS AND TRANSLATIONS

c   Guilielmi Cave, *Scriptorum Ecclesiasticorum Historia Lite-
raria* i (Londini: Typis T. H. & Impensis Richardi Chiswell
ad insigne Rosae Coronatae in Coemiterio D. Pauli, 1688),
pp. 170-6.[122]

This partial edition prepared by the Revd William Cave, Canon of
Windsor (1637-1713), is the first appearance of any portion of
Eunomius' apology in print. It includes only chapters 1.1-6.4 and
27.16-28.26 and is accompanied by the Latin translation of Cave's
assistant, Henry Wharton (1664-95). Chapter 28 is correctly
printed under a separate heading: *Eunomii Confessio Fidei,
Apologiae suae calci subjecta.* The edition is based on Codex T ('ex
Codice Tenisoniano', p. 170) though Codex Y, a defective copy in
Wharton's hand with a Latin translation, was apparently the
printer's copy—it lacks just those portions of the work published by
Cave and is now bound up in the same volume with T.

[119] *GN* II (*J* i.245.1-5) quoting Basil, *Eun.* i.11 (537A).

[120] *GN* III.x (*J* ii.296.7-9), cf. Basil, *Eun.* ii.25 (629C).

[121] *GN* III.x (*J* ii.296.9-25), cf. Basil, *Eun.* ii.28 (632B-D).

[122] A second, pirated edition appeared at Geneva a few years later (1705),
describing itself as 'nunc auctior facta'; Eunomius' work appears on pp. 138-41.
A new authorized edition was issued in 1740 at Oxford with the corrections prepared
by the author before his death. Eunomius is found in vol. i, pp. 219-23. Finally,
Cave's text was reprinted yet again in Jacobus Basagne's *Thesaurus Monumentorum
Ecclesiasticorum et Historicorum*, nova editio (Antwerp, 1725), pp. 181-4.

William Whiston, M.A., *Primitive Christianity Reviv'd* i-iv
(London: Printed for the Author; And are to be Sold by the
Booksellers of London and Westminster. 1711), i, pp. 1-30;
iv, appendix pp. 50-3.

This English translation by William Whiston (1667-1752) marks
the first appearance in any form of the complete *Liber Apologeticus*. The translation of the apology proper includes only
chapters 1-27, but chapter 28 ('*Eunomius's* large Creed', i, p. 30)
is found in an appendix at the end of all. The translation is clearly
based on a manuscript derived from V and is very probably a
rendering of J.[123] Though the translation is frequently perceptive,
Whiston was more concerned to present a clear exposition of his
own 'Eusebian' position than to render the thought of Eunomius
exactly.

v[f]   Io. Alberti Fabricii, *Bibliothecae Graecae* viii (Hamburgi:
        Sumtu [*sic*] Christiani Liebezeit, 1717), pp. 262-305.

        Julianus Garnier (ed.), *Sancti Patris Nostri Basilii Caesareae
        Cappadociae Archiepiscopi Opera Omnia quae exstant . . .*
        i (Parisiis: typis & sumptibus Joannis Baptistae Coignard,
        Regis architypographi ac Bibliopolae ordinarii, 1721),
        pp. 618-30.[124]

The edition of Johann Albert Fabricius of Hamburg (1644-1729)
marks the *editio princeps* of the complete Greek text and, with
some modifications, has remained the commonly received or
'vulgate' text to this day. Included along with the Greek text is a
modified form of the Latin translation of 'Holsatius', apparently
Jacobus Fabricius of Schleswig-Holstein (i.e. 'Holsatius', 1589-
1645). The text is said to be based on three manuscripts, the
'codices Gudii, Lindenbrogii, Tenissonii'. The last is clearly the
manuscript (Y) used by Cave in his printed edition. The other two
are somewhat more obscure. The 'codex Lindenbrogii' is
apparently L, but the readings of the 'codex Gudii' do not cor-
respond exactly with those of any of the copies of G owned by
Gudius. The most probable explanation is that Fabricius made

---

[123] Formerly in the possession of Roger Gale (1672-1744); for a detailed discussion, see the article cited in section c above.

[124] A second, Latin edition of Garnier's work appeared at Venice in 1750; the text
of Eunomius appearing in vol. i, pp. 325-33 is a straight reprint of the translation
as it appears in Garnier.

a transcript for his own use and introduced some new errors in doing so, in which case his 'codex Gudii' is our own codex W. When the well-known Maurist, Dom Julianus Garnier (1670–1725), came to produce his famous edition of Basil, he reprinted Fabricius' text with only minor alterations, though he did not include any of Fabricius' notes or critical apparatus. He did, however, keep Fabricius' paragraph divisions, and these have been transmitted to subsequent editions. As Fabricius based these primarily on the location of Basil's quotations, the meaning of the text is sometimes obscured. In our own edition we have kept Fabricius' paragraph divisions in order to facilitate reference, but where the sense requires it we have printed the text consecutively.

v^g *Sancti Patris Nostri Basilii Caesareae Cappadociae Archiepiscopi Opera Omnia quae Exstant* . . . editio Parisina altera, emendata et aucta . . . opera et studio Juliani Garnier, i (Parisiis: apud Gaume Fratres, Bibliopolas, 1839), pars ii, pp. 887–907.[125]

This third, revised edition of Garnier also contains a revised edition of the *Liber Apologeticus*. In addition to a revised preface, readings from Codex C have been included in the text or added to the notes. Thus, although the text is still basically that of Fabricius, both it and the translation have been improved at several points. It has certainly been the best previously available printed text.

v^m J.-P. Migne (ed.), *S. P. N. Basilii Caesareae Cappadociae Archiepiscopi Opera Omnia quae Exstant* . . . ii (= *PG* 30) (Parisiis: Apud Garnier Fratres, editores et J.-P. Migne Successores, 1888), cols. 835C–868C.

The edition of Migne is by far the most readily available text of Eunomius, and while like the others considered it is based on Fabricius, it is also in part composite. The Greek text printed is, with some minor differences, that of the third edition of Basil mentioned above (v^g). The translation and notes, however, are those of Fabricius with minor alterations and additions; there is nothing to indicate that the same is not also true of the text. Migne's purpose in so combining and altering texts is unclear, for the notes of v^g would have clarified his text at several points.

---

[125] This text was later republished in J. D. Goldhorn (ed.), *Sancti Basilii . . . et Sancti Gregorii . . . opera dogmatica selecta* (Leipzig, 1854), pp. 578–615.

VII. A NOTE ON γεν(ν)ητός AND ἀγέν(ν)ητος

It has been frequently noted that the manuscripts of many Greek authors display a tendency to confuse the words ἀγένητος and ἀγέννητος and their derivatives.[126] This is no less true of those of Eunomius. The tendency of Fabricius and later editors has been to regularize this usage. A consideration of Eunomius' use of these words shows that there is no hard and fast distinction between them —indeed, at *Apol.* 13.7-14 the whole argument depends on their being used interchangeably. We have therefore made no effort to regularize Eunomius' usage in this respect but have tried to follow the manuscript tradition as closely as possible. The same principle has also been applied to the other works which appear in this volume.

---

[126] Cf., e.g., G. L. Prestige, *God in Patristic Thought* (London: SPCK, 1952), pp. 42 ff.

CONSPECTUS SIGLORUM

C   Codex Parisinus (olim Colbertinus) graecus 965, fos. 1^r-17^v, saeculi xi.

I   Codex Athous monasterii Iviron 354 [376] (Lampros 4474), fos. 1^r-16^r, verisimile saeculi xiv.

G   Codex Gudianus graecus 85, fos. 1^r-9^r, saeculi xiv medii vel exeuntis.

B   Codex Monacensis (sive Bavaricus) graecus 512, fos. 1^r-18^v, saeculi xv.

V   Codex Vossianus graecus Q 13, fos. 22^r-38^v, saeculi xvi.

M   Codex Monacensis (sive Bavaricus) graecus 58, fos. 294^r-308^r, saeculi xvi.

O   Codex Vaticanus Ottobonianus graecus 112, fos. 18^r-28^r, saeculi xvi (24 October/November 1542).

S   Codex Vesontionus Sequanorum graecus 408 (Suppl. Gr. D 13), fos. 141^r-151^r, saeculi xvi.

A   Codex Ambrosianus graecus C 255 inf., fos. 91^r-100^r, saeculi xvi.

F   Codex Matritensis graecus O. 9, tractatus 10, saeculi xvi.

P   Codex Parisinus suppl. graecus 294, fos. 2^r-19^v, saeculi xvii ineuntis.

W   Codex Gudianus graecus 100, pp. 1-147, saeculi xvii.

L   Codex Lindenbrogius graecus, Hamburg Cod. Theol. 1518 in 4°, saeculi xvii.

H   Codex Gudianus graecus 89, pp. 1-147, saeculi xvii.

T   Codex Tenisonius graecus, Lambeth 802 (a), fos. 1^r-22^v, saeculi xvii.

E   Codex Cantabrigiensis Collegii Emmanuelis 249, pp. 1-31, saeculi xvii.

Y   Codex Tenisonius graecus, Lambeth 802 (b), pp. 9-82, saeculi xvii.

Q   Codex Oxoniensis Collegii Reginensis 187, fos. 1^r-15^v, saeculi xvii.

R   Codex Bodleianus graecus Cherry 25 (9799), pp. 37-88, saeculi xvii exeuntis (c. 1700).

J   Codex Cantabrigiensis Collegii Sanctissimae et Individuae

Trinitatis O.2.3 (1107), fos. 7^r-15^r, saeculi xviii ineuntis (verisimile c.1710).

N   Codex Parisinus suppl. graecus 270, fos. 272^r-279^v, saeculi xvii.

b   Excerpta quae in Basilii *Adversus Eunomium* libris inveniuntur.

v^g Textus vulgatus iuxta editionem Parisinam alteram Dom Juliani Garnier (1839).

v^m Textus vulgatus iuxta editionem J.-P. Migne (1888).

g   Excerpta quae in Gregorii Nysseni *Contra Eunomium* libris inveniuntur.

STEMMA

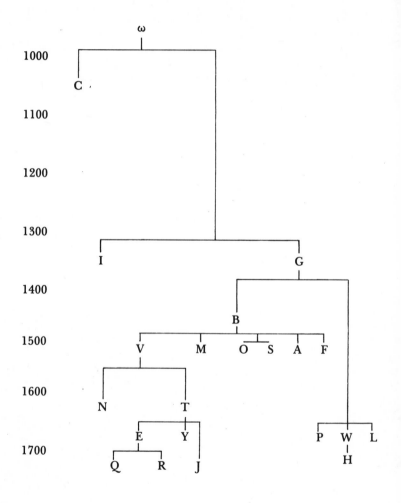

ΕΥΝΟΜΙΟΥ ΑΠΟΛΟΓΗΤΙΚΟΣ
THE APOLOGY OF EUNOMIUS

ΕΥΝΟΜΙΟΥ ΑΠΟΛΟΓΗΤΙΚΟΣ

1. ^aΤὸ μὲν συκοφαντεῖν καὶ διαβάλλειν τινὰς ἐξ ἀκολάστου γλώττης
καὶ γνώμης ἀγνώμονος μοχθηρῶν καὶ φιλαπεχθημόνων ἔργον εἰδότες, τὸ
δὲ τοὺς ἐκ διαβολῆς εἶναι δόξαντας πονηροὺς πάσῃ προθυμίᾳ πειρᾶσθαι τὸ
ψεῦδος τοῖς ἐλέγχοις ἀποτρέπειν ἀνδρῶν σωφρόνων καὶ μετὰ τῆς ἰδίας
5 εὐβουλίας τὴν τῶν πολλῶν ἀσφάλειαν περὶ πολλοῦ ποιουμένων,^a ηὐχόμεθα
μὲν λόγῳ τὴν γνῶσιν ἀμφοῖν ἔχοντες, μήτε τῆς προτέρας ποτὲ γενέσθαι
μοίρας καὶ τῆς ὑστέρας τὴν πεῖραν διαφυγεῖν. ἐπειδὴ δὲ μὴ κατὰ γνώμην
ἐκβῆναι συνέβη τὸ τέλος, ποικίλως καὶ πολυτρόπως διά τε λόγων καὶ
πράξεων παρὰ πολλοῖς κατασκευασθείσης ἡμῶν ψευδοῦς δυσφημίας (ἀλγει-
10 νῆς μὲν ἡμῖν, βλαβερᾶς δὲ τοῖς πιστεύουσιν) ὑπό τινων πονηρῶν καὶ
μηδὲν ὀκνούντων λέγειν ἢ πράττειν ἀνθρώπων, καὶ τῶν ἀκεραιοτέρων ταῖς
τῶν διαφόρων κατηγορίαις τὴν ἀλήθειαν μετρούντων, οὐ κρίσει τὰς καθ'
ἡμῶν διαβολὰς προσιεμένων, ἡμῖν τε αὐτοῖς λυσιτελεῖν ᾠήθημεν πρὸς
ἀπολογίαν καὶ τοῖς ἀβασανίστως τὰ λεγόμενα δεχομένοις πρὸς ἀσφάλειαν,
15 ἔγγραφον εἰς ὑμᾶς ἐκθέσθαι τῆς ἑαυτῶν δόξης τὴν ὁμολογίαν, εἴ πως διὰ
ταύτης τήν τε προλαβοῦσαν ἀποτριψαίμεθα βλασφημίαν καὶ πρὸς τὸ λοιπὸν
τοὺς μὲν πονηροὺς ἀτολμοτέρους, τοὺς δὲ λίαν εὐχερεῖς ἀσφαλεστέρους
παρασκευάσαιμεν, τοῖς μέν, τὸ ψευδῆ λέγειν ἐπιδεές, τοῖς δέ, τὸ πισ-
τεύειν ἐπισφαλὲς ὑποδείξαντες, συναποδεικνυμένης τῇ παρ' ἡμῶν ἀληθείᾳ
20 τῆς κατ' ἀμφοῖν κολάσεως· ἡ γὰρ πρὸς τὸ ψεῦδος κοινωνία κοινὴν ἀμφο-
τέροις κατεργάζεται τὴν τιμωρίαν.

---

1. ^{a-a} Basil, *Eun.* i.2 (504A); the column numbers throughout are those found in
PG 29.

Εὐνομίου Ἀπολογητικός CI: Εὐνομίου τοῦ δυσσεβοῦς ἀπολογητικὸς πρὸς ὃν ἔγραψε
τοὺς ἀντιρρητικοὺς ὁ μέγας Βασίλειος GB: sed fortasse ἀπολογία est legendum, v.
supra pp. 3 ff.   Post titulum add. G monitum sequentem: ση(μείωσ)αι: οὗτος
ὁ λόγος, οὐ δι' ἄλλο τι γέγραπται, ἢ ἵνα δεικνύται ἡ γραφή· ἃ γὰρ λέγει περὶ θεοῦ ὡς
ἀγέννητος· καὶ γέν'ν'ητος ὁ υἱός, καὶ ἕτερα ὅσα ληρεῖ, ἀσεβέστατά εἰσι· καὶ ἔξω τῆς εὐσεβοῦς
ἡμῶν πίστεως· πρόσχες γοῦν ὁ ἀναγινώσκων, ἵνα μὴ παρατραπῇς τῆς εὐθείας ὁδοῦ:-
1. 1 μὲν codd.: μὲν οὖν *b*   2 μοχθηρῶν codd. *b*: πονηρῶν *b* var.   9 πολλοῖς
CGB: πολλῆς I   10 πιστεύουσιν CIG: πιστεύουσι B   14 τὰ λεγόμενα
δεχομένοις C: λεγομένοις IGB   16 ἀποτριψαίμεθα C: ἀποτρεφαίμεθα IGB
19 ἐπισφαλές sic recte coniecit G marg. necnon et Holsatius et Whiston: ἀσφαλές
codd.

THE APOLOGY OF EUNOMIUS

1. If slandering or defaming people with unbridled tongue or hostile intent is a mark of knaves and wranglers, the zealous effort of those who have slanderously been called evil to refute the falsehood through argument is a sign of prudence, the work of people who by their personal discretion set great store on the common welfare. We used to hope, indeed, that we could keep our knowledge of both these things merely verbal: since we had no part in the former, we hoped to escape the trial of the latter as well. Events, however, did not turn out as we intended. With a crafty and varied cunning, both by words and deeds, a lying allegation had been trumped up against us in the minds of many, an allegation as painful to ourselves as it was harmful to those who believed it.[1] Originally concocted by the kind of good-for-nothings who won't scruple to say or do anything, it was then taken up by the sort of simpletons who measure truth by partisan accusations and who unthinkingly accepted the slanders brought against us. We have decided, therefore, to profit ourselves by way of apology and, by way of caution, to help those who have thoughtlessly accepted these charges by setting out an expression of our opinions in writing. Perhaps by this means we can eliminate the aforesaid slander and, for the rest, make the wicked less daring and the reckless more cautious, showing the former the uselessness of spreading lies and the latter the danger of believing them. By thus showing the truth of our position we shall demonstrate what correction is due them both, for fellowship in a common lie will work in both a common retribution.

---

[1] The allegation was that Eunomius believed the Son to be unlike the Father in *all* senses, not only in some, i.e. not 'in accordance with the Scriptures' as taught by the Council.

2. [a]Αἰτοῦμεν δὲ πρὸ πάντων ὑμᾶς τούς τε νῦν ἀκουσομένους καὶ τοὺς εἰς ὕστερον ἐντευξομένους,[b] [c]μὴ τῷ πλήθει διακρίνειν ἐθέλειν τῆς ἀληθείας τὸ ψεῦδος, τῇ πλείονι μοίρᾳ τὸ κρεῖττον συνάπτοντας,[c] [d]μήτε μὴν ἀξιώμασιν ἤ τινων ἀλαζονείᾳ προσέχοντας ἀμαυροῦσθαι τὴν διάνοιαν, ἢ τῇ
5 τάξει τῶν προλαβόντων τὸ πλεῖον νέμοντας ἀποφράττειν τὰς ἀκοὰς τοῖς ὑστέροις,[ad] τὴν δὲ τοῦ σωτῆρος ἡμῶν Ἰησοῦ Χριστοῦ διδασκαλίαν παντὸς μὲν ἀνθρώπων ἀριθμοῦ, πάσης δὲ φιλοτιμίας ἢ φιλονεικίας, συνηθείας τε αὖ καὶ συγγενείας, καὶ συλλήβδην εἰπεῖν, πάντων ὅσα τοῖς τῆς ψυχῆς κριτηρίοις ἐπισκοτεῖν εἴωθεν προτιμήσαντας, τῇ πρὸς τὴν ἀλήθειαν εὐνοίᾳ
10 κρίνειν τὰ λεγόμενα· μεγίστη γὰρ μοῖρα πρὸς τὴν τῆς ἀληθείας διάγνωσιν ἡ πρὸς αὐτὴν οἰκείωσις.

3. [a]Πρὸς δὴ τούτοις μηδ᾽ ἡμῖν χαλεπαίνειν εἰ τύφου μὲν ἀμελήσαντες καὶ φόβου, τῆς δὲ παραυτίκα χάριτος καὶ ἀσφαλείας τὴν ὑπὲρ τῶν μελλόντων ἄδειαν προτιμήσαντες καὶ πάσης ἐπιγείου κακοπαθείας θανάτου τε προσκαίρου φοβερωτέραν τὴν κατὰ τῶν ἀσεβῶν ὡρισμένην ἀπειλὴν εἶναι κρίναντες, παντὸς
5 ἐπικαλύμματος γυμνὴν ἐκτιθέμεθα τὴν ἀλήθειαν.[a] Οὔτε γάρ, κατὰ τὸν ἀπόστολον εἰπεῖν, ἄξια τὰ παθήματα τοῦ νῦν καιροῦ πρὸς τὴν μέλλουσαν ἀποκαλύπτεσθαι δόξαν,[b] οὐδ᾽ ὁ σύμπας κόσμος πρὸς ἀπόλαυσιν καὶ δεσποτείαν ἰσόρροπον ἀντάλλαγμα τῆς ἰδίας ἑκάστου ψυχῆς,[c] πολὺ καθ᾽ ἑκάτερον ἀπόλαυσίν τε καὶ κόλασιν ὑπερβαλλόντων τὰ παρόντα τῶν προσδοκωμένων.

4. Ἀλλ᾽ ἵνα γε μὴ τούτοις ἐπὶ πλεῖον ἐνδιατρίβοντες πέρα τοῦ μέτρου μηκύνωμεν τὸν λόγον, ἐπ᾽ αὐτὴν ἤδη τρεφώμεθα τῆς πίστεως τὴν ὁμολογίαν ἐξ ἧς εὐμαρὴς καὶ ῥᾳδία γένοιτ᾽ ἂν τοῖς βουλομένοις τῆς ἡμετέρας γνώμης κατανόησις. ἀναγκαῖον δὲ ἴσως τοὺς περὶ τούτων λόγους
5 ποιουμένους καὶ δόξης οἰκείας εὐθύνας ὑπέχοντας μὴ ταῖς τῶν πολλῶν ἀμελῶς ἑαυτοὺς ἐκδιδόναι γνώμαις, [a]τὴν δὲ κρατοῦσαν ἄνωθεν ἐκ τῶν

---

2. [a-a]Basil, *Eun.* i.3 (505B-508A)   [b]*GN* ; (*J* i.45.8-10)   [c-c]*GN* I (*J* i.45.18-20; 48.17-18)   [d-d]Cf. *GN* I (*J* i.55.16-20)   3. [a-a]Basil, *Eun.* i.3 (508C)   [b]Rom. 8: 18   [c]Cf. Matt. 16: 26   4. [a-a]Basil, *Eun.* i.4 (509C-D)

---

2. 1 αἰτοῦμεν IGB*b* var.: αἰτοῦμαι C*b*   3 συνάπτοντας codd.*bg* ad 45.19 f.: συνάψοντας *b* var.: προσάπτοντας *g* ad 48.18   4 ἤ τινων ἀλαζονείᾳ προσέχοντας om. *b*   5 πλεῖον codd.: πλέον *b*   8 ὅσα IG: ὥσα C   τοῖς om. G sed corr.   τῆς GB: om. CI   9 εἴωθεν CG: εἴωθε I   3. 1 ἡμῖν IG: ἡ μὲν C   8 πολὺ CIG: πολ᾽ B   4. 3 ἐξ ἧς CI: ἐξῆς GB   3-4 τῆς . . . κατανόησις CGB: ἡ τῆς . . . κατανόησις I   5 μὴ IGB: καὶ C   6 ἐκ codd.: παρὰ *b*

2. Above all we implore those who are about to hear us now, as well as any who may come across this work in the future: don't try to distinguish truth from falsehood by mere numbers, confusing the better with the more numerous part; don't darken your minds by paying attention to some people's ranks or arrogance; don't give so much attention to earlier speakers that you shut your ears to those who come after. Rather, honour the teaching of our Saviour Jesus Christ above any mere number of persons, above every consideration of dignity or love of rivalry, indeed, above every relation or kinship — or to put it briefly, above all the things which so often darken the soul's power of judgement. Make your decision with a partiality for the truth, for the greatest part of the discernment of truth is to adopt her as one's own.

3. Moreover, we ask you not to judge us harshly if, caring nothing for either arrogance or fear ourselves, and preferring the assurance of things to come to any present favour or security, we reckon the threats levelled against the ungodly more fearful than any earthly suffering or temporal death, and so lay out unveiled the naked truth. 'For', as the Apostle says, 'the sufferings of this present time are not worth comparing with the glory that is to be revealed',[b] nor is the whole world with all its pleasures and dominion a fit exchange for anyone's soul,[c] by so much do things which are to come, both joys and punishments, outstrip those which are present.

4. But not to waste further time on all this and unduly prolong the discourse, let us turn to that very profession of faith by which those who wish to do so may acquire an easy and convenient knowledge of our opinion. For it does not behove those who are to discourse of such matters and to present an account of their doctrine to give in to the majority opinion without thought; rather, after first setting out as a kind of rule or norm that pious and

πατέρων εὐσεβῆ παράδοσιν ὥσπερ τινὰ γνώμονα καὶ κανόνα προεκθεμένους, ἀκριβεῖ τούτῳ συγχωρεῖν χρῆσθαι κριτηρίῳ πρὸς τὴν τῶν λεγομένων ἐπίκρισιν.[a]

5. [a]Πιστεύομεν εἰς ἕνα θεόν, πατέρα παντοκράτορα,
ἐξ οὗ τὰ πάντα,
καὶ εἰς ἕνα μονογενῆ υἱὸν θεοῦ, θεὸν λόγον, τὸν
κύριον ἡμῶν Ἰησοῦν Χριστόν, δι' οὗ τὰ πάντα,[b]
5   καὶ εἰς ἓν πνεῦμα ἅγιον, τὸν παράκλητον,[a] ἐν ᾧ
πάσης χάριτος διανομὴ κατὰ τὴν συμμετρίαν πρὸς τὸ συμφέρον ἑκάστῳ δίδοται τῶν ἁγίων.[c]

6. [a]Ἡ μὲν οὖν ἁπλουστέρα καὶ κοινὴ πάντων πίστις ὅσοις τὸ δο-
κεῖν ἢ τὸ εἶναι χριστιανοῖς ἐπιμελές (ὡς ἐν ἐπιδρομῇ κεφαλαιωδέστερον
εἰπεῖν) αὕτη,[a] λειπομένων ἔτι τῶν δευτέρων ὧν διὰ τὸ τέως ἀναμφισβήτητον
παρέλκειν ἡγούμεθα τὴν μνήμην. ἡμεῖς δ' εἰ μὲν ἑωρῶμεν ἐπάναγκες
5 εἶναι τοῖς ἅπαξ τὰς φωνὰς παραδεξαμένοις ἀπαράτρεπτον συνδιασῴζειν
τοῖς ὀνόμασι τὴν ἀληθῆ διάνοιαν, ἢ τοὺς ἡμᾶς ἀσεβείας γραφὴν[b] γραφα-
M 841 μένους μετὰ τὴν ὁμο|λογίαν ταύτην ἐλευθέρους ἀφιέντας τῶν ἐγκλημάτων,
καθαρευούσης αὐτῶν τῆς διανοίας πάσης καθ' ἡμῶν πονηρᾶς ὑπονοίας,
τοῦτον ὅρον καὶ πέρας τῶν ἰδίων ἂν ἐποιησάμεθα λόγων, ἀσφαλῆ τὴν ἡσυ-
10 χίαν ἡμῖν ἐγγυωμένης τῆς ὁμολογίας· ἐπειδὴ δὲ μή, εἴτε διὰ κακόνοιαν
ἤ τινα γνώμης μοχθηρίαν ἑτέραν, παρατρέπειν καὶ διαφθείρειν τὴν ἔννοιαν ἐπιχειροῦσιν αὐτάρκης πρὸς πίστωσιν τῆς ἀληθείας (οὐ γὰρ ἂν Σαβέλ-
λιος ὁ Λίβυς καὶ Μάρκελλος ὁ Γαλάτης καὶ Φωτεινὸς καὶ εἴ τις ἄλλος
τῶν τὴν αὐτὴν τούτοις μανίαν μανέντων συλλόγων ἱερατικῶν καὶ κοινωνίας
15 μυστηρίων καὶ περιβόλων ἐκκλησιαστικῶν εἴργοντο), μηθ' ἡμῖν ἱκανὴ
πρὸς διάλυσιν τῶν ἐπενεχθέντων ἐγκλημάτων, ἀλλὰ δεῖ τινων ἀκριβεστέρων

5. [a-a]Basil, Eun. i.4 (512A)   [b]Cf. 1 Cor. 8: 6   [c]Cf. 1 Cor. 12: 7 and
8: 6 var.   6. [a-a]Basil, Eun. i.4 (512A, 513A)   [b]Cf. Eun., Apol. Apol. i
(J i.46.11-12)

7 προεκθεμένους C: προεκτιθεμένους IGB: προεκθέμενοι b   8 συγχωρεῖν codd.:
om. b   χρῆσθαι codd.: χρησώμεθα b   5. 3 υἱὸν θεοῦ codd.: υἱὸν τοῦ θεοῦ b
θεὸν λόγον IGB: θεοῦ λόγον C   5 ἓν πνεῦμα ἅγιον codd.b: τὸ πνεῦμα τὸ ἅγιον
b var.   τὸν IGB: τὸ Cb   6. 1 ἁπλουστέρα codd.b ad 513A: ἁπλουστέρα
πίστις b ad 512A   πίστις b ad 513A: om. codd. et b ad 512A   2 κεφαλαιωδέστερον CIb: κεφαλαιωδέτερον GB   4 δ' IGB: δὲ Cb   10 μὴ εἴτε C: μήτε
IGB   13 Μάρκελλος IGB: Μάρκελος C   καὶ εἴ τις C: ἤ τις IGB

governing tradition which has come down from the fathers, they should agree to use that as the exact standard by which to judge what is said:[2]

> **5.** We believe in one God, the Father almighty, from whom are all things;
> And in one only-begotten Son of God, God the Word, our Lord Jesus Christ, through whom are all things;[b]
> And in one holy Spirit, the Counsellor, in whom is given to each of the saints an apportionment of every grace according to measure for the common good.[c]

6. Apart from certain secondary matters which, being still undisputed, we have decided not to bring up, this is that essential faith which (speaking generally and by way of summary) is common to all who are concerned either to seem or to be Christians. Now if we could see that those who had once accepted the sounds [which make up this profession] must of necessity keep their real meaning undistorted along with the words, or that once we had presented it those bringing the indictment of impiety against us would let us go free of these charges, their minds then cleansed of every evil suspicion about us, we would have made it the measure and term of our arguments, for the profession itself would have guaranteed our undisturbed tranquillity. But in fact, when people have deliberately set out to twist and distort its significance, whether through ill-will or some other perverse inclination, it is neither itself an adequate confirmation of the truth, nor does it suffice us for the refutation of these alleged charges. Otherwise, neither Sabellius the Libyan, Marcellus the Galatian, Photinus,[3] or anybody else who may join them in their mad rage would ever have been excluded from the priestly assemblies, fellowship of the sacraments, or ecclesiastical precincts. On the contrary, this profession requires

---

[2] According to Basil, *Eun.* i.4 (509B) this creed (Hahn no. 190) was in fact used by some of the Fathers 'in the simplicity of their hearts', and had been presented by Arius to Alexander of Alexandria in token of his faith.

[3] These three figures are frequently joined together as symbolic of modalism, though they were not all contemporaries. Sabellius was originally condemned by Pope Callistus I (217-22). Marcellus of Ancyra, however, was accepted by some councils (Rome, *c.*340; Sardica, 343) and condemned by others (Jerusalem, 336; Antioch, 339, 345; Sirmium, 351, Ancyra, 359, etc.); his disciple, Photinus of Sirmium, shared in his condemnation (Antioch, 345; Sirmium, 351).

λόγων πρὸς τὴν τῆς διανοίας ἐξάπλωσιν, πειρασόμεθα ὡς ἂν οἷοί τε ὦμεν εἰς
τοὐμφανὲς ἀγαγεῖν ἣν αὐτοὶ περὶ τούτων τυγχάνομεν ἔχοντες δόξαν, ἤτοι
προτιθέντες τὴν λέξιν, εἶθ' ὕστερον ἐκκαλύπτοντες τὴν ἔννοιαν, ἢ καὶ
20 προχειμέναις ταῖς ἐννοίαις τὰς φωνὰς ἐφαρμόζοντες, οὐ λυμαινομένης τῇ
ἀληθείᾳ τῆς κατὰ τὴν τάξιν ταύτην ἐναλλαγῆς, ἀρκούντων δηλαδὴ τῶν
αὐτῶν ἡμῖν πρός τε τὴν ἡμετέραν αὐτῶν ἀπολογίαν καὶ τὸν τῶν ἡμᾶς γρα-
ψαμένων ἔλεγχον.

7. ᵃ Εἴς τοίνυν κατά τε φυσικὴν ἔννοιαν καὶ κατὰ τὴν τῶν πατέρων
διδασκαλίαν ἡμῖν ὡμολόγηται θεός, μήτε παρ' ἑαυτοῦ μήτε παρ' ἑτέρου
γενόμενος, ἑκάτερον γὰρ αὐτῶν ἐπίσης ἀδύνατον. ἐπειδή γε δεῖ κατὰ
ἀλήθειαν τό τε ποιοῦν τοῦ γενομένου προϋπάρχειν καὶ τὸ ποιούμενον
5 τοῦ ποιοῦντος εἶναι δεύτερον, μήτε δ' αὐτὸ ἑαυτοῦ πρότερον ἢ ὕστερον
εἶναι δύνασθαι, μήτε ἕτερόν τι πρὸ τοῦ θεοῦ. ἢ γὰρ ἂν ἐκεῖνο πρὸ τοῦ
δευτέρου τὸ τῆς θεότητος ἔσχεν ἀξίωμα,ᵃ τὸ γάρ τοι δυνατὸν εἶναι λέγειν
ὑφ' ἑτέρου τι γίνεσθαι (ἀληθὲς ὄν) ἐπὶ γενητῶν ἂν ἔχοι χώραν, κἀπὶ τῶν
ὑπὸ θεοῦ γενομένων τάττοιτο δικαίως. ᵇοὐκοῦν εἰ μήτε αὐτὸς ἑαυτοῦ
10 μήθ' ἕτερόν τι αὐτοῦ προϋπάρχειν δέδεικται, πρὸ δὲ πάντων αὐτός, ᶜἀκο-
λουθεῖ τούτῳ τὸ ἀγέννητον,ᶜ ᵈμᾶλλον δὲ αὐτός ἐστιν οὐσία ἀγέννητος.ᵇᵈ
περιττὸν μὲν ἴσως καὶ παρέλκον δόξει τισὶ τὰ πολλοῖς ὁμολογούμενα κατα-
σκευάζειν ὡς ἀμφίβολα. οὐ μὴν ἀλλά γε διὰ τοὺς σοφίαν οἰομένους τὴν
πρὸς τὰ φανερὰ μάχην ἢ πρὸς μέμψιν καὶ συκοφαντίαν παρεσκευασμένους
15 δεῖ τινος ἀκριβεστέρας παρατηρήσεως ἡμῖν.

8. ᵃ Ἀγέννητον δὲ λέγοντες, οὐκ ὀνόματι μόνον κατ' ἐπίνοιαν ἀνθρωπίνην σεμνύνειν οἰόμεθα δεῖν, ἀποτιννύναι δὲ κατ' ἀλήθειαν τὸ πάντων

---

7. ᵃ⁻ᵃBasil, *Eun.* i.5 (513D-516A)   ᵇ⁻ᵇBasil, *Eun.* i.5 (517B)   ᶜ⁻ᶜGN I
(*J* i.214.21-2; 215.13-14)   ᵈ⁻ᵈBasil, *Eun.* i.5 (517C, 520A), GN i (*J*
i.215.16-17)   8. ᵃ⁻ᵃBasil, *Eun.* i.5 (520C), 8 (528A); cf. *GN* II (*J* i.238.26-9)

19 προτιθέντες CG corr.: προστιθέντες IB   7. 4 τε codd.: om. *b*   γενομένου codd.: γινομένου *b*   5 δ' codd.: δὲ *b*   9 δικαίως CIG: δικαίων B sed
corr.   οὐκοῦν codd.: Ἄρ' οὖν *b*   εἰ μήτε CI*b*: εἰμί τε GB   10 μήθ'
codd.: μήτε *b*   10-11 ἀκολουθεῖ codd.*b*: (παρ)έπεσθαι *g* et *b* ad 517C-520A
11 ἀγέννητον GB*bg*: ἀγένητον CI   αὐτός codd.*b* var.: αὐτό *bg*   ἀγέννητος
CGB*bg*: ἀγένητος I   8. 2 σεμνύνειν IGB*b*: σεμνυνόμενοι C   ἀποτιννύναι δὲ
κατ' ἀλήθειαν codd.: ἐκτιννύναι δὲ αὐτῷ *b*

additional arguments to bring out its underlying meaning. We shall try, therefore, so far as we can, to make the opinion we hold with regard to these arguments explicit: either we shall first set out the text of the profession and then disclose its meaning, or, after setting out the meaning, we shall then relate it to the verbal expressions of the text. No distortion of the truth will result from this interchange of order, for these approaches are clearly both sufficient, not only for our own defence, but also for the refutation of our accusers.

7. It is in accordance, therefore, both with innate knowledge and the teaching of the fathers that we have made our confession that God is one, and that he was brought into being neither by his own action nor by that of any other, for each of these is equally impossible. In fact, just as the maker must be in existence before the thing he brings into being, and the thing made must be later than its maker, by the same token a thing cannot exist before or after itself, nor anything else at all before God. If it did, it would surely be the first which had the dignity of Godhead rather than the second; for after all, anything which can be said to come into existence by the action of another (granted that this is in fact the case) has itself to be placed among created beings, and must properly be ranked among things which have come into existence by the action of God. So then, if it has now been demonstrated that God neither existed before himself nor did anything else exist before him, but that he is before all things, then what follows from this is the Unbegotten, or rather, that he is unbegotten essence. To some people it will seem useless and superfluous to develop an argument for things that are commonly acknowledged as though they were subject to doubt. They are not. But because there are some who think it wisdom to contest the obvious, or who have their objections and slanders ready, we will need some more precise investigation.

8. When we say 'Unbegotten', then, we do not imagine that we ought to honour God only in name, in conformity with human invention; rather, in conformity with reality, we ought to repay

ἀναγκαιότατον ὄφλημα τῷ θεῷ, τὴν τοῦ εἶναι ὅ ἐστιν ὁμολογίαν.[b] [c]τὰ
γάρ τοι κατ' ἐπίνοιαν λεγόμενα ἐν ὀνόμασι μόνοις καὶ προφορᾷ τὸ εἶναι
M 844 ἔχοντα ταῖς φωναῖς | συνδιαλύεσθαι πέφυκεν,[a] ὁ δὲ θεός, καὶ σιωπώντων
καὶ φθεγγομένων καὶ γεγενημένων καὶ πρὸ τοῦ γενέσθαι τὰ ὄντα, ἥν τε
καὶ ἔστιν ἀγέννητος.[c] [d]ἀλλὰ μὴν οὐδὲ κατὰ στέρησιν· εἴ γε τῶν κατὰ
φύσιν αἱ στερήσεις εἰσὶ στερήσεις, καὶ τῶν ἕξεων δεύτεραι.[d] οὔτε δὲ
κατὰ φύσιν ἥν τις τῷ θεῷ γένεσις, οὔτε προτέραν ἔχων ταύτην εἶτα στερη-
10 θεὶς γέγονεν ἀγέννητος. ἐπεὶ καὶ λίαν ἐστὶν ἀσεβὲς ὡς λυμαντικὸν τῆς
ἀληθοῦς περὶ θεοῦ ἐννοίας καὶ τῆς τελειότητος αὐτοῦ (μᾶλλον δὲ τῆς τῶν
ἐφευρόντων διανοίας) τὸ λέγειν ὅλως ἐστερῆσθαί τινος τὸν θεόν, δηλονότι
τῶν φύσει προσόντων, οὐ γὰρ ἄν τις εἴποι σωφρονῶν ἐστερῆσθαι τινά τινος
τῶν μὴ πρότερον ὑπαρχόντων. [e]εἰ δὲ μήτε κατ' ἐπίνοιαν μήτε κατὰ στέρη-
15 σιν, ὡς ὁ ῥηθεὶς ἔδειξε λόγος, μήτε ἐν μέρει τὸ ἀγέννητον (ἀμερὴς γάρ),
μήτε ἐν αὐτῷ ὡς ἕτερον (ἁπλοῦς γὰρ καὶ ἀσύνθετος), μήτε παρ' αὐτὸν
ἕτερον (εἷς γὰρ καὶ μόνος αὐτός ἐστιν ἀγέννητος), αὐτὸ ἂν εἴη οὐσία
ἀγέννητος.[e]

9. [a]Ἀγέννητος δὲ ὢν κατὰ τὴν προλαβοῦσαν ἀπόδειξιν, οὐκ ἄν ποτε
πρόσοιτο γένεσιν ὥστε τῆς ἰδίας μεταδοῦναι τῷ γεννωμένῳ φύσεως, ἐκφύ-
γοι τ' ἂν πᾶσαν σύγκρισιν καὶ κοινωνίαν τὴν πρὸς τὸ γεννητόν.[a] εἰ γάρ
τις κοινοποιεῖν πρὸς ἕτερον ἢ μεταδιδόναι τινὶ τῆς οὐσίας ταύτης ἐθελή-
5 σειεν, ἤτοι κατὰ διάστασιν καὶ μερισμὸν ἢ κατὰ σύγκρισιν τοῦτο κατα-
σκευάσειεν ἄν· ὁπότερον δ' ἂν λέγηται τούτων, πολλαῖς ἀτοπίαις (βλασφη-
μίαις δὲ μᾶλλον) ὁ λόγος ἐνσχεθήσεται. εἴτε γὰρ διαιροῖτο καὶ μερίζοιτο,

---

[b]Cf. Exod. 3: 14, Rom. 1: 20-3   [c-c]Eun., *Apol. Apol.* ii (*J* i.271.17-22,
272.13-16)   [d-d]Basil, *Eun.* i.9 (532A); according to Basil this observation is
derived from Aristotle's *Categories,* cf. *Cat.* 12a26-34   [e-e]Basil, *Eun.* i.11
(537A); *GN* II (*J* i.238.15-16, 245.1-5, cf. 238.11-12)   9. [a-a]Basil, *Eun.* i.16
(548c), 17 (552A)

---

4 μόνοις codd.: μόνον *b*   τὸ om. C sed corr.   6 καὶ φθεγγομένων καὶ
γεγενημένων (γεγονότων ad 271.21) Eun., *Apol. Apol.* teste *g*: καὶ λεγόντων καὶ
γενομένων male codd.   γενέσθαι codd.*g* ad 272.15f.: γεγονέναι *g* ad 271.21
14 εἰ δὲ μήτε codd.: Οὐκοῦν εἰ μήτε *bg*   15 ὡς ὁ ῥηθεὶς ἔδειξε λόγος codd.: om.
bg   τὸ ἀγέννητον codd.: om. *bg*   16 καὶ ἀσύνθετος codd.: om. *b*
17 αὐτός ἐστιν codd.: om. *bg*   9. 2 γένεσιν codd.: γέννησιν *b*   γεννωμένῳ
CIG*b*: γενομένῳ B   3 τ' codd.: τε *b*   4-5 ἐθελήσειεν IGB: ἐθελήσιεν C
5 διάστασιν IGB: διάστησιν C sed corr. alia manu   7 ἐνσχεθήσεται C: ἐνεχθήσεται
IGB

him the debt which above all others is most due God: the acknowledgement that he is what he is.[b] Expressions based on invention
have their existence in name and utterance only, and by their
nature are dissolved along with the sounds [which make them up];
but God, whether these sounds are silent, sounding, or have even
come into existence, and before anything was created, both was
and is unbegotten. He is not such, however, by way of privation; for
if privatives are privatives with respect to the inherent properties of
something, then they are secondary to their positives.[d] But birth has
never been an inherent property of God! He was not first begotten
and then deprived of that quality so as to become *un*begotten!
Indeed, if to say that God has been deprived of anything at all is
impious in the extreme as being destructive of the true notion of
God and of his perfection (or rather, destructive of the minds of
those who invent such things)', then it must surely be impious to say
this with respect to things which belong to his nature, for no one of
sound mind would say that a thing had been deprived of something
which it did not previously possess. So then, if, as shown by the
preceding argument, 'the Unbegotten' is based neither on invention
nor on privation, and is not applied to a part of him only (for he is
without parts), and does not exist within him as something separate
(for he is simple and uncompounded), and is not something
different alongside him (for he is one and only he is unbegotten),
then 'the Unbegotten' must be unbegotten *essence*.

9. But if God is unbegotten in the sense shown by the foregoing
demonstration, he could never undergo a generation which
involved the sharing of his own distinctive nature with the offspring
of that generation, and could never admit of any comparison or
association with the thing begotten. Still, if anyone did want to
make this essence a common property with some other or give
something else a share in it, he would have to argue either on the
basis of separation and division or on the basis of comparison; yet
whichever of these he chooses, the argument will be entangled in
manifold absurdities (or rather, blasphemies). If he proceeds on the

οὐκ ἔτ' ἀγέννητος εἴη (ὃ μὴ πρότερον ἦν, τοῦτο ἐκ τῆς διαιρέσεως γιγνό-
μενος), ἀλλὰ μὴν οὔτ' ἄφθαρτος (τοῦ μερισμοῦ τὸ τῆς ἀφθαρσίας ἀξίωμα
10 λυμαινομένου), εἴτε τὴν πρὸς ἕτερον δέχοιτο σύγκρισιν, τῆς συγκρίσεως
οὐκ ἐξ ἀκοινωνήτων γιγνομένης, [b]κοινοποιηθήσεται τὸ τῆς οὐσίας ἀξίωμα,
εἰ δὲ τοῦτο καὶ τοὔνομα, ὥστ' ἐξ ἀνάγκης δεῖν τοὺς τούτῳ τῷ λόγῳ βιαζο-
μένους ἢ τὴν προσηγορίαν ἀκοινώνητον φυλάττειν βουλομένους ἀκοινώνητον
M 845 ταύτῃ συνδια | σώζειν καὶ τὴν οὐσίαν, ἢ ταύτης μεταδοῦναί τινι πειρωμένους
15 μεταδιδόναι καὶ τῆς προσηγορίας ὥσπερ καὶ τῆς οὐσίας.[b] χωλεύοι γὰρ ἂν
αὐτοῖς ἡ φιλοτιμία λειπομένην παρέχουσα θατέρῳ μέρει τὴν χάριν, μετὰ τοῦ
μηδ' ἄξιον ἐργάζεσθαι λόγου τὴν διαφορὰν (ἀκριβολογουμένους περὶ τὴν
προσηγορίαν), εἴ γε ὀνόματι μόνῳ ὁ μὲν ὑπερέχοι, ὁ δὲ ἐλαττοῖτο. εἰ
δὲ τῆς αὐτῆς μεταδοῦναι φωνῆς ὁ τῆς ἀκολουθίας ἀναγκάζει λόγος, μεταδι-
20 δότωσαν φιλοτιμότερον καὶ τῆς ἰσότητος, οὐκ εὑρισκομένου τινὸς ἐν
ὅτῳ θήσονται τὴν ὑπεροχήν.

10. [a]Οὐ γὰρ δὴ τοῦτ' ἂν εἴποιεν, ὡς κοινὴ μὲν ἀμφοῖν ἡ οὐσία,
τάξει δὲ καὶ τοῖς ἐκ χρόνου πρεσβείοις ὁ μέν ἐστι πρῶτος, ὁ δὲ δεύτερος, ἐπειδή γε δεῖ προσεῖναι πάντως τοῖς ὑπερέχουσι τὸ τῆς ὑπεροχῆς
αἴτιον. οὐ συνέζευκται δὲ τῇ οὐσίᾳ τοῦ θεοῦ οὐ χρόνος, οὐκ αἰών, οὐ
5 τάξις. ἥ τε γὰρ τάξις δευτέρα τοῦ τάττοντος, οὐδὲν δὲ τῶν τοῦ θεοῦ
ὑφ' ἑτέρου τέτακται. ὅ τε χρόνος ἀστέρων ποιά τίς ἐστι κίνησις,[b] ἀστέ-
ρες δὲ οὐ τῆς ἀγεννήτου μόνον οὐσίας καὶ νοητῶν ἁπάντων, ἀλλὰ καὶ τῶν
πρώτων σωμάτων γεγόνασιν ὕστεροι.[c] περὶ γὰρ αἰώνων τί δεῖ καὶ λέγειν,
σαφῶς τῆς γραφῆς διαγορευούσης πρὸ τῶν αἰώνων ὑπάρχειν τὸν θεόν,[ad] καὶ
10 τῶν κοινῶν λογισμῶν ἐπιμαρτυρούντων; οὐ γὰρ μόνον ἀσεβές, ἀλλὰ καὶ
κομιδῇ καταγέλαστον, τοὺς ἓν μόνον παραδεξαμένους ἀγέννητον ἢ προϋπάρ-

---

[b-b]Cf. Basil, *Eun.* ii.24 (628C)   10. [a-a]Basil, *Eun.* i.19 (553C-D)   [b]Cf.
Plato, *Timaeus* 37C-39E   [c]Gen. 1: 14 ff.   [d]Ps. 54(55): 20

19 μεταδοῦναι IGB: μεταδιδόναι C   20 φιλοτιμότερον CI: φιλοτιμώτερον GB
10. 1 τοῦτ' C: τοῦτο IGBb   εἴποιεν codd.: εἴποιμεν b   2-3 δεύτερος codd.b:
ὕστερος b var.   3 προσεῖναι b: προεῖναι codd.   πάντως codd.: om. b
τοῖς codd.: ἐν τοῖς b   4 οὐ χρόνος CIb: ὁ χρόνος GB   7 μόνον IGb: μόνου C
8 ὕστεροι codd.b: δεύτεροι b var.   γὰρ codd.: δὲ b   9 σαφῶς τῆς γραφῆς
codd.: τῆς Γραφῆς σαφῶς b

basis of separation and division, then God cannot be unbegotten already (what he was not before is precisely what he becomes as a result of the separation),[4] but then again, God cannot be incorruptible either (division is destructive of the whole principle of incorruption); on the other hand, if he undertakes the comparison of this essence with something else, then, since a comparison cannot be made between things with nothing in common, the fundamental principle of the essence will be made common. But if that happens, the name will be made common as well, so that those who persist in this line of reasoning will of necessity be obliged either to keep the designation uncommon if they want to keep the essence uncommon too, or, if they want to share that out with something, they must share out the designation just as they do the essence. Indeed, if it is really only in name that the one is pre-eminent and the other less, the very prodigality which bestows the missing grace on the other part will prove a hindrance to them, while the verbal distinction will not work out properly either (assuming they are using the designation in the strict sense). But if the reasoning on which this argument is based forces them to share out the actual vocable, let them the more prodigally share out the equality as well, for we have found nothing on the basis of which they can establish a pre-eminence.

10. They certainly cannot say this, that while the essence is common to both, it is in order, and in a superiority based on time that the one is first and the other second, for after all, the cause of pre-eminence must surely be an inherent property of the things which are pre-eminent. But neither time nor age nor order have ever been joined to the essence of God. Order is secondary to the one who orders, but nothing which pertains to God has ever been ordered by another. Time is a certain motion of the stars,[b] but the stars came into being not only later than the essence of the Unbegotten and all intelligible beings, but even later than the first corporeal objects.[c] As for the ages, what can be said? The Scriptures themselves clearly state, 'God exists before the ages',[d] and the

---

[4] This series of arguments is difficult to render in English because in it Eunomius is making use of a tradition in which ontology is 'the projected shadow of logic' (Proclus, *The Elements of Theology*, ed. E. R. Dodds (Oxford University Press, 1933), p. xxv). Thus in the present instance the same words represent both logical operations and ontological realities: if *we* are said to know the divine essence by the logical operation of distinguishing or separating it from something else, then the essence itself is considered to have been distinguished or separated.

χειν τι τούτου φάσκειν ἢ συνυπάρχειν ἕτερον. εἴτε γὰρ προϋπάρχοι τι, τοῦτο δικαίως λέγοιτ' ἂν ἀγέννητον, οὐ τὸ δεύτερον· εἴτε συνυπάρχοι, τῇ πρὸς θάτερον κοινωνίᾳ τοῦ συνυπάρχειν ἑκάτερον ἀφαιρεθήσεται τὸ ἓν
15 μόνον εἶναι καὶ τὸ ἀγέννητον εἶναι, οἷα δὴ μετὰ τῆς οὐσίας ἀποκλήρωσίν τινα καὶ περιγραφὴν ἀμφοῖν συνεισαγόντων, συνθήκην τε αὖ καὶ τὸ τῆς συνθήκης αἴτιον, (11.) ᵃἀλλὰ μὴν οὐδ' ἐνυπάρχειν τι ταύτῃ δύνατον οἷον εἶδός φαμεν ἢ ὄγκον καὶ πηλικότητα, διὰ τὸ πάντη συνθήκης ἐλεύθερον εἶναι τὸν θεόν.

Εἰ δὲ τούτων καὶ τῶν τοιούτων μήτ' ἔστι μήτε ποτὲ γένοιτ'
5 ἂν εὐαγὲς ἐπινοῆσαι συμπεπλεγμένον τῇ οὐσίᾳ, ποῖος ἔτι συγχωρήσει λόγος πρὸς τὴν ἀγέννητον ὁμοιοῦν τὴν γεννητήν, τῆς κατ' οὐσίαν ὁμοιότητος ἢ συγκρίσεως ἢ κοινωνίας μηδεμίαν ὑπεροχὴν ἢ διαφορὰν καταλιπούσης, ἰσότητα δὲ σαφῶς ἐργαζομένης, μετὰ δὲ τῆς ἰσότητος ἀγέννητον
M 848 ἀποφαινούσης | τὸν ὁμοιούμενον ἢ συγκρινόμενον; οὐδεὶς δ' οὕτως
10 ἀνόητος καὶ πρὸς ἀσέβειαν τολμηρὸς ὥστε ἴσον εἰπεῖν τῷ πατρὶ τὸν υἱόν, αὐτοῦ τοῦ κυρίου διαρρήδην εἰπόντος, Ὁ πατὴρ ὁ πέμψας με μείζων μου ἐστίν,ᵃᵇ ἢ συζεῦξαι θατέρῳ τῶν ὀνομάτων θάτερον, ἀνθέλκοντος ἑκατέρου πρὸς ἑαυτὸ καὶ μηδ' ἑτέρου προσιεμένου τὴν πρὸς θάτερον κοινωνίαν, ἄν τε γὰρ ἀγέννητος οὐχ υἱός, ἄν τε υἱὸς οὐκ ἀγέννητος.

15 ᶜἈλλ' ὅτι μὲν εἷς ὁ τῶν ἁπάντων θεός, ἀγέννητος καὶ ἀσύγκριτος, πλειόνων ὄντων τῶν παραλελειμμένων, ἀποχρῆν ἡγοῦμαι καὶ τὰ ῥηθέντα πρὸς ἀπόδειξιν,ᶜ (12.) ὅτι δὲ ᵃκαὶ εἷς υἱός (μονογενὴς γάρ), ἐνῆν μὲν τὰς τῶν ἁγίων φωνὰς παραθεμένους δι' ὧν υἱὸν καὶ γέννημα καὶ

---

11. ᵃ⁻ᵃBasil, *Eun.* i.22 (560c-561b), cf. i.23 (564a-c); *GN* II (*J* i.238.18-19) ᵇJn. 14: 28, cf. 14: 24 etc. ᶜ⁻ᶜBasil, *Eun.* i.22 (561a/b), 26 (569a)
12. ᵃ⁻ᵃBasil, *Eun.* ii.1 (573a), cf. ii.5 (581a), 24 (628c)

13 ἀγέννητον IGB: ἀγένητον C   13-14 τῇ . . . κοινωνίᾳ C: τὴν . . . κοινωνίαν IGB   16 τὸ sic coniecit Migne: τοῦ codd.   11. 1 οὐδ' ἐνυπάρχειν IGB: οὐδὲν ὑπάρχειν C: οὐδὲ ἐνυπάρχειν *b*   ταύτῃ codd.: τῇ οὐσίᾳ τοῦ θεοῦ *b*   2 φαμεν codd.: om. *b*   καὶ codd.: ἢ *b*   4 τοιούτων codd.: τοιούτων τι *b* μήτ' codd.: μήτε *b*   ἔστι IGB*b*: ἔστιν C   μήτε ποτέ CGB: μήποτε I   5 συμπεπλεγμένον CGB*b*: συμπεπιπλεγμένον I   9 ἢ συγκρινόμενον C*b*: om. IGB δ' IGB: δὲ C*b*   15 ἁπάντων codd.: πάντων *b* (561b): ὅλων *b* var. (569a)   16 ἀποχρῆν CI*b*: ἀποχρῆναι GB   12. 2 ἐνῆν codd.: περὶ οὗ ἐνῆν *b*   παραθεμένους codd.: παραθέμενον *b*

common reckoning of mankind confirms them. It is not only impious, then, it is positively ridiculous for those who grant that there is one unique unbegotten being to say that anything else exists either before it or along with it. Indeed, if something else did exist before the Unbegotten, it is that which would properly have to be called 'unbegotten' and not the second. On the other hand, if some other individual existed along with the Unbegotten, then, by the very same association whereby each coexisted with the other, the qualities of being 'one and unique' and of being 'unbegotten' would be done away, because in conjunction with the essence the two entities would also introduce a kind of partitioning and circumscription. This in its turn would introduce composition along with the cause of the composition, (11.) and yet not even an attribute such as shape, say, or mass and size can exist in this essence because God is altogether free from composition.

But if it neither is nor ever could be lawful to conceive of these or anything like them as being joined to the essence of God, what further argument is there which will permit the likening of the begotten to the unbegotten essence? Neither the likening nor the comparison nor the association of the essence has left any room for a pre-eminence or a distinction but has manifestly yielded an equivalence, and along with that equivalence has shown that the thing likened or compared is itself unbegotten. But after all, there is no one so ignorant or so zealous for impiety as to say that the Son is *equal* to the Father! The Lord himself has expressly stated that 'the Father who sent me is greater than I.'[b] Nor is there anyone so rash as to try to yoke one name to the other![5] Each name pulls in its own direction and the other has no common meaning with it at all: if the one name is 'Unbegotten' it cannot be 'Son', and if 'Son' it cannot be 'Unbegotten'.

But now, even though the greater number of arguments have been passed over, I will take what has already been said as a sufficient demonstration that the God of all things is one and that he is unbegotten and incomparable. (12.) As for showing that the Son too is one, being only-begotten, we could rid ourselves of all care and trouble in that regard simply by quoting the words of the

[5] That is, to produce something like the 'Son-who-was-not-begotten' or 'Father-who-did-not-beget' ridiculed in chapter 14 below.

ποίημα καταγγέλλουσι[b] (ταῖς τῶν ὀνομάτων διαφοραῖς καὶ τὴν τῆς οὐσίας
παραλλαγὴν ἐμφαίνοντας) ἀπηλλάχθαι φροντίδος καὶ πραγμάτων, διὰ
5 μέντοι τοὺς σωματικὴν τὴν γέννησιν ὑπολαμβάνοντας καὶ ταῖς ὁμωνυμίαις
προσπταίοντας ἀναγκαῖον ἴσως καὶ περὶ τούτων διὰ βραχέων εἰπεῖν.[a] [c]γέν-
νημα τοίνυν φαμὲν τὸν υἱὸν κατὰ τὴν τῶν γραφῶν διδασκαλίαν, οὐχ ἕτερον
μὲν τὴν οὐσίαν νοοῦντες, ἕτερον δέ τι παρ' αὐτὴν τὸ σημαινόμενον,
ἀλλ' αὐτὴν εἶναι τὴν ὑπόστασιν ἣν σημαίνει τοὔνομα, ἐπαληθευούσης τῇ
10 οὐσίᾳ τῆς προσηγορίας,[c] [d]ταύτην δὲ γεγεννῆσθαι μὲν οὐκ οὖσαν πρὸ τῆς
ἰδίας συστάσεως, εἶναι δὲ γεννηθεῖσαν πρὸ πάντων γνώμῃ τοῦ θεοῦ καὶ
πατρός.[d]

13. [a]Εἰ δέ τῳ δοκεῖ τολμηρὸν εἶναι τὸ ῥηθέν, ἐπισκεφάσθω παρ'
ἑαυτῷ ὡς ἀληθὲς ὂν ἢ ψεῦδος. εἰ μὲν γὰρ τὸ πρότερον, ἀνυπαί-
τιος ἡ τόλμα κατὰ τὴν αὐτοῦ κρίσιν ἐπείπερ μηδὲν τῶν ἀληθῶν ἐν καιρῷ
καὶ μέτρῳ λεγόμενον ὑπαίτιον, εἰ δὲ ψεῦδος, ἀνάγκη δήπου πᾶσα τούτων
5 τοὐναντίον ἀληθὲς ἡγεῖσθαι. τοῦτο δ' ἐστίν, ὄντα γεγεννῆσθαι τὸν
υἱόν, ὅπερ οὐκ ἀτοπίας μόνον ἢ βλασφημίας, ἀλλὰ καὶ πάσης εὐηθείας
ὑπερβολὴν ἂν ἔχοι. [b]τῷ γὰρ ὄντι τί δεῖ γενέσεως[ab] εἰ μὴ πρὸς ἕτερόν τι
μεταρρυθμίζοιτο κατὰ τὴν ἐμφύχων τε καὶ ἀφύχων σωμάτων φύσιν, ἅπερ
γίνεσθαι λέγοιτ' ἂν ἀληθῶς, ὄντα μὲν ἅ ἐστιν, οὐκ ὄντα δὲ ἃ γίνεται;
10 οὔτε γὰρ τὸ σπέρμα ἄνθρωπος, οὔτε ὁ λίθος οἶκος, γίνεται δὲ τὸ μὲν
ἄνθρωπος, τὸ δὲ οἶκος. εἰ δὲ τούτων ἕκαστον (οἷς καὶ παραβάλλειν τὴν
υἱοῦ γένεσιν πάντων ἀσεβέστατον) οὐκ ὄντα γίνεται (οὐ γὰρ ἐκεῖνο γίνεται ὃ πρότερον ἦν), ποίαν δέξεται ἴασιν ὁ τὸν υἱὸν ὄντα γεγεννῆσθαι
λέγων;

---

[b]Prov. 8: 22, cf. 1 Cor. 1: 24   [c-c]Basil, *Eun.* ii.6 (584A), cf. 9 (588B)
[d-d]Basil, *Eun.* ii.11 (592B), 14 (597A)   13. [a-a]Cf. Basil, *Eun.* ii.14 (597B), 15
(601A)   [b-b]GN iii.vii (J ii.235.25-6)

---

3 καταγγέλλουσι IGB*b*: καταγγέλουσιν C   4 ἐμφαίνοντας codd.: ἐμφανίσαντας *b*,
an recte?   φροντίδος codd.: φροντίδων *b*   5 μέντοι codd.: δὲ *b*   7 φαμὲν
τὸν υἱὸν codd.: τὸν Υἱόν φαμεν *b*   8 μὲν codd.: μέν τι *b*   νοοῦντες *b*: νοοῦντας
codd.   αὐτὴν CI*b*: αὐτὸν GB   10 γεγεννῆσθαι IG*b*: γεγενῆσθαι CB
13. 1 δέ τῳ IG: δ' ὅτῳ CB   5 δ' IGB: δὲ C   γεγεννῆσθαι IGB*b*: γεγενῆσθαι C
7 γενέσεως codd.: γεννήσεως *b*   8 μεταρρυθμίζοιτο I: μεταρυθμίζοιτο C: μεταριθμί-
ζοιτο GB   9 γίνεσθαι IGB: γίγνεσθαι C   ἅ sic scripsi: ὅ codd.   11 ἕκαστον
IGB: ἕκαστος C   12 ἀσεβέστατον CI: εὐσεβέστατον GB   ἐκεῖνο IGB: ἐκείνω C
13 γεγεννῆσθαι CIG: γεγενῆσθαι B

saints in which they proclaim the Son to be both 'offspring' and 'thing made',[b6] since by distinguishing the names they show the difference in essence as well. However, because there are people who suppose that this generation is a bodily one and stumble at the use of equivocal terms, it will be necessary to discuss these words briefly also. We call the Son 'offspring', therefore, in accordance with the teaching of the Scriptures.[7] We do not understand his essence to be one thing and the meaning of the word which designates it to be something else. Rather, we take it that his substance is the very same as that which is signified by his name, granted that the designation applies properly to the essence. We assert, therefore, that this essence was begotten—not having been in existence prior to its own coming to be—and that it exists, having been begotten before all things by the will of its God and Father.

13. If this statement seems rash to anyone, let him ask himself whether it is true or false. If it is true, then in his own judgement the audacity is blameless since nothing that is true (when spoken at the proper time and in the proper measure) is blameworthy. If it is false, he will doubtless admit the necessity of accepting the opposite to be true: that the Son was begotten when he was already in existence. Now *that* would be not only the ultimate in absurdity or blasphemy, it would be completely ridiculous as well. What need of begetting has something which already exists unless it is transformed into something else after the manner of animate or inanimate bodies? Those might perhaps be properly said to be 'born' or 'come to be', since although they are in existence already, they are not what they are to become.[8] The seed is not the man, the stone is not the house, but each comes to be such, the one a man, the other a house. Now if each of these (to which in any case it is wholly impious to compare the begetting of the Son) becomes what it previously was not—it could not become what it already was— what cure is there for someone who still asserts that the Son was begotten when he was already in existence?

---

6 Basil, *Eun.* ii.2 (576A) refers this to Acts 2: 36, but Eunomius himself in *Apol. Apol.* iii (*J* ii.10.25–11.8) shows that the reference is to Prov. 8: 22 and 1 Cor. 1: 24.

7 Here, as in chap. 22, Eunomius' concern is to show that his teaching is consistent with the then current formula, 'similar . . . in accordance with the Scriptures'.

8 Eunomius' arguments here and in chap. 14 depend on γίγνομαι and γεννάω being synonymous. In English, the meanings of γίγνομαι, used here both for 'to come to be' and 'to be born', would be more clearly distinguished.

M 849 ᶜΕἰ γὰρ πρὸ τῆς γενέσεως ἦν, ἀγέννητος ἦν,ᶜ | (14.) ἀλλὰ
πάλαι γε καλῶς ὡμολόγηται μηδὲν ἕτερον ἀγέννητον εἶναι παρὰ τὸν θεόν.
ἢ τοίνυν μεταθέσθωσαν τῆς ὁμολογίας ταύτης, ἕτερον ἐπεισάγοντες ἀγέννητον, ἢ τούτοις ἐμμένοντες, παραιτείσθωσαν λέγειν ὄντα γεγεννῆσθαι
5 τὸν υἱὸν ἐπεὶ μηδὲ συγχωρεῖ τοῦ υἱοῦ καὶ τοῦ γεννήματος ἡ προσηγορία
πρὸς τὴν ἀγέννητον. πᾶσα γὰρ γένοιτο σύγχυσις ὀνομάτων τε καὶ πραγμάτων,
μιᾶς μὲν οὐσίας οὔσης τε καὶ λεγομένης ἀγεννήτου, ἐπεισαγομένης δὲ τῷ
λόγῳ πάλιν ἑτέρας, εἶτα ταύτης γεννητῆς ὀνομαζομένης, υἱοῦ τε μὴ γεν-
νηθέντος κατ' αὐτοὺς καὶ πατρὸς μὴ γεννήσαντος ὀνόματα, εἴγε μὴ γεννηθεὶς
10 ἦν. πλὴν εἰ μή τις (κατὰ τὸν λόγον, κακῷ κακὸν ἰώμενος, μείζονι τὸ
ἔλαττον) ᵃ αὐξητικὴν ἢ μεταβλητικὴν ἐπινοήσειε γένεσιν, πρὸς ἅπασι τοῖς
ἄλλοις μήτ' ἐκεῖνο καλῶς λογισάμενος, ὡς εἴτε αὐξάνοι τι, προσθήκῃ
τινὸς τῶν ἔξωθεν αὐξήσειεν ἄν. πόθεν οὖν τὸ προστεθὲν εἰ μὴ καὶ ἕτερον
ὑποθοίμεθα; ἀλλ' εἰ μὲν τοῦτο, πολλὰ τὰ ὄντα καὶ ἀγέννητα ⟨τὰ⟩ ὄντα
15 εἰς συμπλήρωσιν ἑνὸς ἐπινοεῖν ἀναγκαῖον. εἰ δ' ἐκ τοῦ μὴ ὄντος ἡ αὔξη-
σις, πότερον ἄμεινον ὁμολογεῖν πᾶν μὴ ὂν γεγεννῆσθαι γνώμῃ τοῦ παραγα-
γόντος, ἢ σύνθετον λέγειν τὴν οὐσίαν ἐξ ὄντος καὶ μὴ ὄντος; εἴτε μετα-
βάλλοιτο, μηδενὸς ὄντος εἰς ὃ μεταβληθείη, εἰς τὸ μὴ ὂν ἐξ ἀνάγκης μετα-
βληθήσεται. καὶ πῶς οὐκ εὔηθες (ἵνα μὴ λέγωμεν ἀσεβές) τὸ ὂν εἰς τὸ
20 μὴ ὂν κεχωρηκέναι λέγειν; δέον ἀφεμένους τῆς ἀμέτρου ταύτης εὐηθείας,
παρανοίας δὲ μᾶλλον, σωφρόνως παραδέξασθαι τἀληθές.

15. Ἀλλ' οὗτοι μὲν ταύταις καὶ πολλῷ πλείοσι τούτων ἀτοπίαις ὄντες
ὑπόδικοι λεληθασί σφας αὐτούς, οὐχ ἡμᾶς τόλμης εὐθύναις δικαίως ὑπάγον-
τες, ἀλλ' ἑαυτοὺς ἀσεβείας ἐγκλήμασιν· ᵃἡμεῖς δὲ τοῖς ὑπό τε τῶν ἁγίων
πάλαιᵇ καὶ νῦν ὑφ' ἡμῶν αὐτῶν ἀποδεδειγμένοις ἐμμένοντες, μήτε τῆς

ᶜ⁻ᶜBasil, *Eun.* ii.17 (608A)   14.ᵃAlthough this proverb is nowhere found as
such in the published collections of proverbs, it is alluded to frequently in other
literature, e.g. Aeschylus, *Fr.* 349 (Nauck 105); Sophocles, *Fr.* 77 (Pearson i.48 f.),
Ajax 362; Euripides, *Bacchae* 839; Herodotus iii.53.4; Thucydides v.65.2; Plato,
Protagoras 340D/E, etc.   15. ᵃ⁻ᵃBasil, *Eun.* ii.18 (608D–609A)   ᵇCf., e.g.
Arius, *Ad Eusebium Nicomediensem Epistolam* 4-5 (Opitz iii.2.9–3.8)

---

15 γενέσεως codd.*b* var.: γεννήσεως *b*   14. 2 ὡμολόγηται IGB: ὁμολόγηται C
4 γεγεννῆσθαι CIG: γεγενῆσθαι B   12 τι IGB: τῇ C   19 τὸ ὂν CGB: καὶ τὸ
ὂν I   15. 3-4 τοῖς ὑπό τε τῶν ἁγίων πάλαι codd.: τοῖς τε ὑπὸ τῶν ἁγίων καὶ πάλαι
b: ἁγίων Πατέρων *b* var.   4 ὑφ' codd.: ἐφ' *b*   αὐτῶν codd.: om. *b*
ἀποδεδειγμένοις codd.: ἀποδεικνυμένοις *b*

If he existed before his begetting, he was unbegotten; (14.) but it was already rightly conceded earlier that there is no unbegotten other than God. Let them therefore either retract this concession and bring in some other unbegotten, or else let them abide by what has been said and refuse to speak of the Son as being begotten after he was already in existence when there is no common ground between the designations 'son' and 'offspring' and that of 'unbegotten'. Indeed, if there were, there would be a complete confusion of both the names and their objects: there would be one essence which both is and is called 'unbegotten', yet there would be included within the scope of its definition still another essence, an essence designated 'begotten'. The names would then be, according to them, 'Son-who-was-not-begotten' and 'Father-who-did-not- beget' (if the Son, that is, was not begotten in a real sense). On the other hand, if someone were to understand this begetting as being by way of augmentation or transformation (curing one ill by another, as the saying is, the lesser by the greater),[a] he wouldn't have worked that argument out any better than he did the others, for if anything does grow by augmentation, it is by the addition of something from outside itself that it does so. And where is that addition to come from if we do not postulate the existence of some other being? But if that is so, then it is necessary to assume that many entities—entities themselves unbegotten—are required for the completion of just one! On the other hand, if the growth in question comes from a *non*-entity, that is, from that which does not exist, what is the better alternative? To admit that every non-existent thing has been begotten by the will of the one who brought it into existence? Or to say that this essence is made up of both the existent and the non-existent? Yet if we say that this essence is transformed, then of necessity it must be transformed into the *non*-existent! And how could the assertion that the existent has turned into the non-existent fail to be ridiculous, not to say irreligious? It is our duty to leave such unbridled nonsense (or rather, insanity) alone and soberly acknowledge the truth.

15. But these people—who are in fact liable to prosecution for these and many other more numerous absurdities—have forgotten all about themselves! They have not so much brought us into court for the correction of audacity as themselves on a charge of irreligion! Our practice has been to keep to the arguments used in

5 οὐσίας τοῦ θεοῦ προσιεμένης γένεσιν (ὡς ἀγεννήτου) μήτε διάστασιν ἢ
μερισμόν (ὡς ἀφθάρτου) μήτε μὴν ἑτέρας τινὸς ὑποκειμένης εἰς υἱοῦ
γένεσιν, μὴ ὄντα φαμὲν γεγεννῆσθαι τὸν υἱόν,[a] [c]οὐ κοινοποιοῦντες οὐδὲ
τοῦ μονογενοῦς τὴν οὐσίαν πρὸς τὰ ἐκ μὴ ὄντων γενόμενα, ἐπείπερ οὐκ
οὐσία τὸ μὴ ὄν, τῇ δὲ τοῦ ποιήσαντος γνώμῃ τὴν διαφορὰν τοῖς πᾶσιν
10 ὁριζόμενοι, τοσαύτην αὐτῷ νέμομεν τὴν ὑπεροχὴν ὅσην ἔχειν ἀναγκαῖον
τῶν ἰδίων ποιημάτων τὸν ποιητήν.[c] πάντα γὰρ δι᾽ αὐτοῦ γεγεννῆσθαι
κατὰ τὸν μακάριον Ἰωάννην ὁμολογοῦμεν,[d] συναπογεννηθείσης ἄνωθεν αὐτῷ
τῆς δημιουργικῆς δυνάμεως, ὥστ᾽ εἶναι θεὸν μονογενῆ πάντων τῶν μετ᾽
αὐτὸν καὶ τῶν δι᾽ αὐτοῦ γενομένων, [e]μόνος γὰρ τῇ τοῦ ἀγεννήτου δυνάμει
M 852 γεννηθεὶς καὶ κτισθείς, | τελειότατος γέγονεν ὑπουργὸς[e] πρὸς πᾶσαν δη-
μιουργίαν καὶ γνώμην τοῦ πατρός.

16. [a]Εἰ δ᾽ ὅτι πατὴρ καὶ υἱός, διὰ τοῦτο ἀνθρωπίνην καὶ σωματικὴν
χρὴ τὴν γένεσιν ἐννοεῖν, κἀκ τῶν ἐν ἀνθρώποις γενέσεων ἀναγομένους τοῖς
τῆς μετουσίας ὀνόμασι καὶ πάθεσιν ὑπάγειν τὸν θεόν,[a] [b]ἐπειδὴ καὶ δημιουργὸς ὁ θεός, ὕλην ὑποβάλλειν δεῖ πρὸς γένεσιν τῶν δεδημιουργημένων
5 κατὰ τὴν Ἑλληνικὴν πλάνην, ὁ γὰρ ἐκ τῆς ἰδίας οὐσίας γεννῶν ἄνθρωπος
οὐκ ἂν ὕλης χωρὶς δημιουργήσειεν.[b] εἰ δὲ τοῦτο παραιτοῖντο, μηδὲν τῆς
τῶν ὀνομάτων φροντίζοντες προφορᾶς, τὴν δὲ τῷ θεῷ περιπίπτουσαν ἔννοιαν
διασώζοντες ἐπιτρέποιεν ἐξουσίᾳ μόνῃ δημιουργεῖν, πῶς ἂν ἔχοι χώραν τὸ
τῆς μετουσίας πάθος ἐπὶ θεοῦ διὰ τὴν τοῦ πατρὸς προσηγορίαν; [c]τίς γὰρ
10 οὐκ ἂν ὁμολογήσειεν τῶν εὐφρονούντων ὅτι τῶν ὀνομάτων τὰ μὲν κατὰ τὴν
ἐκφώνησιν καὶ προφορὰν τὴν κοινωνίαν ἔχει μόνον, οὐκ ἔτι δὲ κατὰ τὴν
σημασίαν; ὡς ὀφθαλμὸς ἐπί τε ἀνθρώπου καὶ θεοῦ λεγόμενος, τοῦ μὲν γὰρ
σημαίνει τι μέρος, τοῦ δὲ ποτὲ μὲν ἀντίληψιν καὶ φυλακὴν τῶν δικαίων,

---

[c-c]Basil, *Eun.* ii.19 (613A)   [d]Jn. 1: 3   [e-e]Cf. Basil, *Eun.* ii.20 (631D),
21 (617A)   **16.** [a-a]Cf. Basil, *Eun.* ii.22 (620A-B), 23 (624B-C)   [b-b]Cf.
Basil, *Eun.* ii.22 (620B13-C4)   [c]Compare the following argument (up to 17.8)
with Basil's reply in *Eun.* ii.24 (625B-C), cf. also ii.23 (621C)

5 γένεσιν IGB: γέννεσιν C: γέννησιν *b*   5-6 (ὡς ἀγεννήτου ... ἀφθάρτου) om. *b*
7 γεγεννῆσθαι (γεγενῆσθαι C) τὸν υἱόν codd.: τὸν Υἱὸν γεγεννῆσθαι *b*   κοινοποιοῦντες codd.: κοινοποιοῦμεν *b*   οὐδὲ codd.: om. *b*   9-10 τῇ δὲ ... ὁριζόμενοι
codd.: ἀλλὰ *b*   11 τὸν IGB*b*: om. C   αὐτοῦ C: ἑαυτοῦ IGB   14 αὐτὸν
IGB: αὐτῶν C   **16.** 1 ἀνθρωπίνην codd.: ἀνθρωπικήν *b*   2 γένεσιν IGB:
γέννεσιν C: γέννησιν *b*   4 δεῖ IGB: δὴ C   γένεσιν IGB: γέννεσιν C
10 ὁμολογήσειεν CI: ὁμολογήσειε GB   12 ἐπί IGB: ἐπεί C

times past by the saints[b] and now again by us: we have not ascribed begetting to the essence of God (it is unbegotten); we have not ascribed separation or partition (it is incorruptible); we have not postulated some other underlying material for the begetting of the Son; rather, we assert that the Son was begotten when as yet he was not. We do not, however, include the essence of the Only-begotten among things brought into existence *out* of nothing, for 'no-thing' is not an essence. Rather, on the basis of the will of the one who made him we establish a distinction between the Only-begotten and all other things, affording him that same pre-eminence which the maker must necessarily have of his own products. For we acknowledge, in conformity with the blessed John, that 'all things were made through him',[d] since the creative power was begotten coexistentially in him from above; he is therefore the Only-begotten God of those things which came into existence after him and through him. Since he alone was begotten and created by the power of the Unbegotten, he became the perfect minister of the whole creative activity and purpose of the Father.

16. But if, because of the names 'Father' and 'Son', it is necessary to understand this begetting as a human and bodily one, and on the analogy of begetting among human beings to subject God to the names and passions of a communication of essence, then, since God is also 'Maker', it is necessary to presuppose matter for the production of the things made in accordance with the error of the pagans, for the same man who begets from his own essence is unable to make anything apart from matter. But if they reject this and pay no attention to the verbal expression of the words, holding rather to the meaning appropriate to God and ascribing the creative action to his power alone, how can the passion of a communication of essence have any place in God because of the designation 'Father'? What well-disposed person would not acknowledge that there are some words which have only their sound and utterance in common but not at all their signification? For instance, 'eye' is used of both human beings and God, but in the case of the one it signifies a certain bodily member while in the case of the other it means sometimes God's care and protection of the

ποτὲ δὲ τὴν τῶν πραττομένων γνῶσιν· (17.) ᵃτὰ δὲ πολλὰ κατὰ τὴν ἐκφώνησιν κεχωρισμένα τὴν αὐτὴν ἔχει σημασίαν, ὡς τὸ ὢνᵇ καὶ μόνος ἀληθινὸς θεός.ᵃᶜ

Οὐκοῦν οὐδὲ ὅταν λέγηται πατὴρ κοινὴν ἐννοεῖν χρὴ πρὸς ἀνθρώ-
5 πους τὴν ἐνέργειαν, ἐπ' ἀμφοῖν συνεπινοοῦντας ταύτῃ ῥεῦσιν ἢ πάθος,
ἐπείπερ ἡ μέν ἐστιν ἀπαθής, ἡ δὲ μετὰ πάθους, οὐδὲ ὅταν λέγηται πνεῦμαᵈ
κοινὴν ἔχει πρὸς τὰ λεγόμενα πνεύματα τὴν φύσιν, ἐν πᾶσι δὲ τὸ ἀνά-
λογον σώζοντας, ᵉμήτε τὸν υἱὸν ἀκούοντας ποίημα δυσχεραίνειν, ὡς
κοινοποιουμένης πάντως καὶ τῆς οὐσίας ὑπὸ τῆς τῶν ὀνομάτων κοινωνίας.ᵉ
10 ὁ μὲν γάρ ἐστιν ἀγεννήτου καὶ ἀποιήτου γέννημα καὶ ποίημα, οὐρανὸς
δὲ καὶ ἄγγελοι καὶ πᾶν ὅπερ ἐστιν ἄλλο ποίημα τούτου τοῦ ποιήματός
ἐστι ποιήματα, προστάγματι τοῦ πατρὸς δι' αὐτοῦ γενόμενα.ᶠ οὕτω γὰρ
ἂν ταῖς γραφαῖς τὸ ἀψευδεῖν φυλάττοιτο, ποίημα καὶ γέννημα λεγούσαις
τὸν υἱόν,ᵍ καὶ τῶν ὑγιαινόντων ἡμεῖς οὐκ ἐκστησόμεθα λογισμῶν, μήτε
15 μέρη τῷ θεῷ περιάπτοντες, μήτε μὴν πρὸς μὲν γένεσιν τὴν ἰδίαν οὐσίαν,
πρὸς δὲ κτίσιν ὕλην ὑποβάλλοντες, ἐξ ὧν ἡ τῶν ὀνομάτων διαφορὰ γίγνεσθαι πέφυκεν.

18. Εἰ δὲ μήτε γεννῶν ὁ θεὸς τῆς οἰκείας τῷ γεννωμένῳ μεταδίδωσι
φύσεως κατὰ τοὺς ἀνθρώπους (ἀγέννητος γάρ), μηδὲ κτίζων ὕλης ἐπιδεῖταί
M 853 τινος | (ἀπροσδεὴς ὢν καὶ δυνατός), ἀλόγιστος παντάπασιν ἡ τοῦ κτίσ-
ματος παραίτησις. ἐκ δὴ τούτων καὶ τῶν τοιούτων δεικνυμένους μήτε
5 πάντῃ τοῖς ὀνόμασι συνεξομοιοῦν πειρᾶσθαι τὰς σημασίας, μήτε μὴν παραλλάττειν παρηλλαγμένων, ταῖς δὲ τῶν ὑποκειμένων ἐννοίαις προσέχοντας
ἀκολούθως ἐφαρμόττειν τὰς προσηγορίας (ἐπεὶ μηδὲ ταῖς φωναῖς πέφυκεν

---

17. ᵃ⁻ᵃCf. Origen, *De Oratione* 24.2 (*GCS* ii.354.8-18)　　ᵇExod. 3: 14
ᶜJn. 17: 3　　ᵈJn. 4: 24　　ᵉ⁻ᵉBasil, *Eun.* ii.24 (628c)　　ᶠJn. 1: 3
ᵍProv. 8: 22

---

17. 2 τὴν αὐτὴν IGB: τοιαύτην C　　7 πνεύματα IGB: πνεῦμα C　　8 μήτε
codd.: μηδεὶς δὲ *b*　　9 πάντως καὶ codd.: om. *b*　　10-11 οὐρανὸς . . . ποίημα
IGB: om. C　　15 γένεσιν IGB: γέννεσιν C　　18. 4 ἐχρῆν ante μήτε coniecit
Fabricius (an recte?)　　5-6 παραλλάττειν IGB: παραλάττειν C

righteous, sometimes his knowledge of events. (17.) [a] On the other hand, the majority of words [referring to God] are different in their verbal expression but have the same meaning, as for instance, 'I AM',[b] and 'only true God'.[ac]

Accordingly, it is by no means necessary, when God is called 'Father', to understand this activity as having the same meaning that it does with human beings, as involving in both cases the idea of mutability or passion; the one activity is passionless, while the other involves passion. Again, when God is called 'Spirit'[d] this does not imply that he is of the same nature as other beings called 'spirits'. Rather, in each case we preserve the proportionate relationship, so we are not at all disturbed to hear the Son called 'thing made',[9] as though even his essence could be regarded as wholly comparable with those of others because they share the same names! The Son is the 'offspring' and 'thing made' of the Unbegotten and Unmade, while heaven and angels and every other 'thing made' whatsoever are things made by this 'thing made', 'made through him'[f] at the command of the Father. In this way the inerrancy of the scriptures can be preserved when they call the Son 'thing made' and 'offspring',[g] while we ourselves will not be moved from our own sound conclusions: we will neither ascribe bodily members to God, nor will we lay down either his own essence as the basis for begetting or matter for creation, for it is from these that the distinction in the use of these words inherently arises.[10]

18. Yet if in begetting God does not impart his own nature after the manner of human beings (for he is Unbegotten), and has no need of matter in creating (for he is without need and mighty), then the rejection of the word 'creature' in this context is altogether irrational. Once we have shown by these and other arguments that we need not try to conform meanings to words exactly or try to distinguish those of differing expressions, but must rather direct our attention to the concepts inherent in the underlying objects and accommodate the designations accordingly (for the natures of

[9] i.e. by Scripture; cf. the following remarks and n. 6 above.

[10] i.e. as above in *Apol.* 16.12 ff. it is the absence of matter or any other pre-existent substratum which distinguishes the meaning of ordinary words used in a divine context from that of their normal usage. Thus, in accepting Scripture's description of the Son as 'offspring' or 'thing made' Eunomius is no more obliged to ascribe bodily members (or parts) to God than he is by the use of the word 'eye' above. The absence of any pre-existent substratum distinguishes the words' usage,

ἀκολουθεῖν τῶν πραγμάτων ἡ φύσις, τοῖς δὲ πράγμασιν ἐφαρμόζεσθαι κατὰ
τὴν ἀξίαν ἡ τῶν ὀνομάτων δύναμις), καταμέμψαιτο δ' ἄν τις οὐχ ἧττον
10 καὶ τοὺς γέννημα μὲν καὶ ποίημα τὸν υἱὸν εἶναι πειθομένους, ἀγέννητόν
τε καὶ ἄκτιστον τὸν θεὸν συντιθεμένους, τῇ δὲ τῶν δευτέρων προσθήκῃ
καὶ τῇ κατ' οὐσίαν ὁμοιότητι ταῖς προλαβούσαις ὁμολογίαις ἐναντιουμέ-
νους. ᵃοὓς ἐχρῆν, εἰ μέν τις ἦν αὐτοῖς ἀληθείας φροντίς, παρηλλαγμένων τῶν ὀνομάτων παρηλλαγμένας ὁμολογεῖν καὶ τὰς οὐσίαςᵃ (ἡ γὰρ ἂν
15 οὕτως καὶ μόνως τὴν δικαίαν ἐφύλαττον τάξιν, ἑκατέρα τούτων τὴν
προσήκουσαν ἀποδιδόντες ὁμολογίαν), εἰ δὲ μὴ ταύτης ποιοῦνταί τινα
λόγον, τῆς γοῦν ἰδίας ἐπινοίας φυλάξαι τὴν ἀκολουθίαν, καὶ μὴ τῆς
αὐτῆς φύσεως παραχωροῦντας, ἀλλοτριοῦν τῆς ἁρμοζούσης ὀνομασίας, ἀπο-
δεδειγμένου διὰ πάντων ἡμῖν τῶν προλαβόντων αὐτῶν εἶναι τῶν οὐσίων
20 σημαντικὰς τὰς προσηγορίας.

19. Εἴποι δ' ἄν τις ἴσως πρὸς ἀντιλογίαν ἠκονημένος, ὡς εἴπερ δεῖ
τοῖς ὀνόμασι προσέχειν καὶ διὰ τούτων προσάγεσθαι ταῖς τῶν ὑποκειμένων
ἐννοίαις, καθὸ μὲν ἀγέννητον καὶ γεννητὸν παρηλλάχθαι φαμέν, καθὸ δὲ
φῶς καὶ φῶς, ζωή τε καὶ ζωή, δύναμις καὶ δύναμις ἐοικέναι.ᵃ πρὸς ὅν
5 φαμεν, οὐ βακτηρίᾳ χρώμενοι πρὸς τὴν ἐρώτησιν ἀντ' ἀποκρίσεως κατὰ τὸν
Διογένους ἐπαινέτηνᵇ (πολὺ γὰρ κυνισμὸς κεχώρισται Χριστιανισμοῦ), τὸν
δὲ μακάριον Παῦλον ἐζηλωκότες ὅς φησι δεῖν ἐν πολλῇ μακροθυμίᾳ παιδεύ-
ειν τοὺς ἀντιδιατιθεμένους,ᶜ ὅτι τὸ μέν ἐστιν ἀγέννητον φῶς, τὸ δὲ
γεννητόν. ᵈπότερον ἄλλο τι σημαίνει τὸ φῶς ἐπ' ἀγεννήτου λεγόμενον
10 παρὰ τὸ ‹ἀ›γέννητον, ἢ ταὐτὸν ἑκάτερον; εἰ μὲν γὰρ ἕτερόν τι καὶ
ἕτερον, εὔδηλον ὅτι καὶ σύνθετον τὸ ἐξ ἑτέρου καὶ ἑτέρου συγκείμενον,

---

18. ᵃ⁻ᵃBasil, *Eun.* ii.24 (629ᴀ)   19. ᵃThis passage addresses the problem of
the use by Scripture of identical words to describe both Father and Son; thus, (light)
1 Tim. 6: 16 (cf. Eun., *Apol. Apol.* iii (*J* ii.297.8–9))~Jn. 8: 12; (life) Jn. 5: 26;
(power) Matt. 26: 64~1 Cor. 1: 24. A very similar discussion of the words 'light' and
'life' is found in Origen, *Jo.* ii.xxiii.148–54 (*GCS* iv.79.26–80.36)   ᵇCf. Diogenes Laertius vi.32   ᶜCf. 2 Tim. 2: 25   ᵈ⁻ᵈBasil, *Eun.* ii.25 (629ᴄ)

10–11 ἀγέννητον . . . συντιθεμένους CGB: om. I   13 εἰ μὲν . . . αὐτοῖς codd.:
εἴπερ αὐτοῖς ἦν b   15 οὕτως CGB: οὕτω I   16 ἀποδιδόντες CGB: διδόντες
I   19. 8 ἀντιδιατιθεμένους CI: ἀντιτιθεμένους GB   9 λεγόμενον codd.: om. b
10 ‹ἀ›γέννητον sic recte coniecit Maran, *PG* 29.630ᴅ, n. 4: γεννητόν codd.b

objects are not naturally consequent on the verbal expressions; rather, the force of the words is accommodated to the objects in accordance with their proper status), we could find not a little fault with those who both accept that the Son is 'offspring' and 'thing made' and agree that God is unbegotten and uncreated, yet set themselves up against what they earlier acknowledged by adding qualifications and using the phrase 'similarity of essence'.[11] These people, if they really did have any concern for the truth, ought rather to have acknowledged that since the names are different, the essences are different as well (at any rate, that is the only way they could have kept the proper order and rendered to each essence the acknowledgement properly its own), or, if they took no notice of this, at least they ought to have kept to the logical sequence of their own supposition and not changed the language which fitted it by rejecting the phrase 'of the same nature' — not when we ourselves have shown throughout the preceding arguments that the designations in fact indicate the very essences.

19. But perhaps someone who has been goaded by all this into responding will say, 'Even granting the necessity of paying attention to the names and of being brought by them to the meanings of the underlying realities, still, by the same token that we say that the unbegotten is different from the begotten, we also say that "light" and "light", "life" and "life", "power" and "power" are alike with respect to both.'[a] Our reply is not to substitute the rod for an answer in the manner of the admirer of Diogenes[b] (for the philosophy of the Cynics is far removed from Christianity), but rather to emulate the blessed Paul who said that we must correct our opponents with great patience.[c] Our response, then, to such a person is to say that the one 'light' is unbegotten and the other begotten. When spoken of the Unbegotten, does 'light' signify an entity other than that signified by 'the Unbegotten', or does each word signify the same entity? If there are two separate entities, then it is obvious that the thing made up of these entities is also composite,

cf. R. Vaggione, 'Οὐχ ὡς ἓν τῶν γεννημάτων: Some Aspects of Dogmatic Formulae in the Arian Controversy', *Studia Patristica* 18 (1982), 181-7.

[11] Eunomius' reference, here and at 18.17-18, is to the so-called 'Semi-Arians' under Basil of Ancyra who at the Council of Ancyra held in Lent, 358 asserted that the Son is 'similar in essence' (ὅμοιος κατ' οὐσίαν) to the Father but rejected the doctrine of the identity of the essence, the *homoousios*.

τὸ δὲ σύνθετον οὐκ ἀγέννητον· εἰ δὲ ταὐτόν, ᵉὅσον παρήλλακται τὸ ἀγέννητον πρὸς τὸ γεννητόν, τοσοῦτον παρηλλάχθαι δεῖ καὶ τὸ φῶς πρὸς τὸ φῶςᵉ καὶ τὴν ζωὴν πρὸς τὴν ζωὴν καὶ τὴν δύναμιν πρὸς τὴν δύνα-
15 μιν,ᵈ ὁ γὰρ αὐτὸς κανὼν καὶ τρόπος πρὸς τὴν ἁπάντων τῶν τοιούτων διά-
λυσιν. εἰ τοίνυν πᾶν ὅπερ λέγεται τῆς τοῦ πατρός οὐσίας σημαντικόν, ἴσον ἐστὶ κατὰ τὴν τῆς σημασίας δύναμιν τῷ ἀγεννήτῳ διὰ τὸ ἀμερὲς καὶ ἀσύνθετον, κατὰ δὲ τὸν αὐτὸν λόγον κἀπὶ τοῦ μονογενοῦς αὐτὸ{ν} τῷ
M 856 γεννήματι. παρηλλάχθαι δὲ ταῦτά φασι καὶ αὐ|τοί· τίς ἔτι συγχωρήσει
20 λόγος τὴν τῆς οὐσίας ὁμοιότητα προσάγειν, ἤ τινι τὴν ὑπεροχὴν κατὰ τὸ μεῖζον ὁρίσασθαι, παντὸς μὲν ὄγκου, παντὸς δὲ χρόνου καὶ τῶν τοιούτων ἐξηρημένων, ἁπλῆς τε καὶ μόνης οὔσης τε τῆς οὐσίας καὶ νοουμένης;

20. ᵃἈρχὴν δὲ δοκοῦσιν ἡμῖν οἱ τὴν ἀδέσποτον καὶ πάσης μὲν αἰτίας κρείττονα, πάντων δὲ νόμων ἐλευθέραν οὐσίαν τῇ γεννητῇ καὶ νόμοις πατρικοῖς δουλευούσῃ συγκρῖναι τολμήσαντες μηδ᾽ ὅλως τὴν τῶν ὅλων ἐπεσκέφθαι φύσιν, ἢ μὴ καθαρᾷ τῇ διανοίᾳ τὰς περὶ τούτων ποιεῖσθαι
5 κρίσεις.ᵃ δυεῖν γὰρ ἡμῖν τετμημένων ὁδῶν πρὸς τὴν τῶν ζητουμένων εὕρεσιν, μιᾶς μὲν καθ᾽ ἣν τὰς οὐσίας αὐτὰς ἐπισκοπούμενοι, καθαρῷ τῷ περὶ αὐτῶν λόγῳ τὴν ἑκάστου ποιούμεθα κρίσιν, θατέρας δὲ τῆς διὰ τῶν ἐνεργείων ἐξετάσεως, ἣν ἐκ τῶν δημιουργημάτων καὶ τῶν ἀποτελεσμάτων διακρίνομεν, οὐδετέραν τῶν εἰρημένων εὑρεῖν ἐμφαινομένην τὴν τῆς οὐ-
10 σίας ὁμοιότητα δυνατόν. εἴτε γὰρ ἐκ τῶν οὐσίων ποιοῖτό τις τῆς ἐπισκέψεως τὴν ἀρχήν, ᵇἡ μὲν ἀνωτέρω βασιλείας καὶ πάντῃ γενέσεως ἀνεπίδεκτος οὖσα, τούτοις τε παιδεύουσα τὴν μετ᾽ εὐνοίας προσιοῦσαν

ᵉ⁻ᵉGN III.x (J ii.296.7-9)   20. ᵃ⁻ᵃBasil, Eun. ii.31 (644B)   ᵇ⁻ᵇBasil, Eun. ii.30 (641A-B)

12 παρήλλακται codd.b: διέστηκε g   12-13 τὸ ἀγέννητον πρὸς τὸ γεννητόν codd.: τὸ γεννητὸν πρὸς τὸ ἀγέννητον bg   13 παρηλλάχθαι δεῖ codd.: ἀνάγκη παρηλλάχθαι b   15 τρόπος IGB: τρόπως C sed corr.   18 αὐτὸ{ν} sic scripsi: αὐτόν codd.   19 αὐτοί IGB: αὐτ C   20 λόγος CI: λόγ GB   21 μεῖζον IG: μείζων C   20. 1 ἀρχήν codd.b var.: Τὴν ἀρχὴν b   δοκοῦσιν ἡμῖν codd.: δοκοῦσί μοι b   3 συγκρῖναι codd.: συγκρίνειν b   μηδ᾽ ὅλως C: μηδόλως I: μὴ δ᾽ ὅλως GB: ἢ μηδὲ ὅλως b   4 ἐπεσκέφθαι φύσιν codd.: φύσιν ἐπεσκέφθαι b   5 τετμημένων CGB: τετηρημένων I   11 ἐπισκέψεως C: σκέψεως IGB   ἡ μὲν IGBb: εἰ μὲν γὰρ C sed corr.   12 οὖσα codd.: om. b   τε codd.: om. b

and what is composite is not unbegotten! On the other hand, if both words signify the same entity, then, just as the unbegotten differs from the begotten, so 'the light' must differ from 'the light', and 'the life' from 'the life', and 'the power' from 'the power', for the same rule and method applies for the resolution of all such problems. If, then, every word used to signify the essence of the Father is equivalent in force of meaning to 'the Unbegotten' because the Father is without parts and uncomposed, by the same token that same word used of the Only-begotten is equivalent to 'offspring'. But even they admit that those words are to be distinguished! What argument is there, then, which will still permit a similarity of essence or allow God's pre-eminence to be circumscribed by something greater when all mass, all time, and everything of that kind has been excluded and this essence both is and is reckoned to be simple and alone?

20. Thus, to begin with, it seems to us that those who presume to compare the essence which is unmastered, superior to all cause, and unbound by any law to that which is begotten and serves the law of the Father, have neither really examined the nature of the universe, nor made judgements about these things with clear minds. There are two roads marked out to us for the discovery of what we seek: one is that by which we examine the actual essences and with clear and unadulterated reasoning about them make a judgement on each, the other is an enquiry by means of the actions, whereby we distinguish the essence on the basis of its products and completed works—and neither of the ways mentioned is able to bring out any apparent similarity of essence. For if anyone begins his enquiry from the essences, he finds that that essence which transcends all authority and is wholly incapable of undergoing generation—the essence that gives instruction in these things to the

60   LIBER APOLOGETICUS

διάνοιαν, ^cἀπωθεῖν ὡς πορρωτάτω παρακελεύεται νόμῳ φύσεως τὴν πρὸς
ἕτερον σύγκρισιν,^b ἀκόλουθον καὶ προσήκουσαν τῷ τῆς οὐσίας ἀξιώματι
15 παρέχουσα νοεῖν καὶ τὴν ἐνέργειαν·^{c d} εἴτ' ἐκ τῶν δημιουργημάτων σκοπούμενος, ἐκ τούτων ἐπὶ τὰς οὐσίας ἀνάγοιτο, τοῦ μὲν ἀγεννήτου τὸν
υἱὸν εὑρίσκων ποίημα, τοῦ δὲ μονογενοῦς τὸν παράκλητον, κἀκ τῆς
τοῦ μονογενοῦς ὑπεροχῆς τὴν τῆς ἐνεργείας διαφορὰν πιστούμενος, ἀναμφισβήτητον λαμβάνει καὶ τῆς κατ' οὐσίαν παραλλαγῆς τὴν ἀπόδειξιν,^d ἵνα
20 μὴ τρίτον λέγωμεν ὅτι πάμπολυ διενήνοχεν ὁ δημιουργῶν ἐξουσίᾳ τοῦ νεύματι πατρικῷ ποιοῦντος καὶ μηδὲν ἀφ' ἑαυτοῦ ποιεῖν ὁμολογοῦντος,^e ὅ τε
προσκυνούμενος τοῦ προσκυνοῦντος.^f

21. Εἰ μὲν οὖν μηδὲν ἄτοπον ἡγοῦνται τῶν αὐτῶν ἐπίσης ἑκατέρῳ
μεταδιδόναι τούτων, οἷον οὐσίας, ἐνεργείας, ἐξουσίας, ὀνόματος, ἀνελόντες τὰς τῶν ὀνομάτων καὶ πραγμάτων διαφοράς, δύο σαφῶς ἀγέννητα
λεγέτωσαν· εἰ δὲ τοῦτο προφανῶς ἀσεβές, μὴ δι' ἐπικαλύμματος ὁμοι-
5 ότητος ὀνόματι κατασκευαζέτωσαν τὸ πᾶσιν ὁμολογούμενον εἰς ἀσέβειαν.
ἀλλ' ἵνα γε μὴ δοκοίημεν κατὰ τὴν ἐπενεχθεῖσαν ἡμῖν καὶ παρὰ πολλοῖς
θρυλουμένην βλασφημίαν ἰδίοις πλάσμασι καὶ λόγοις ἐκβιάζεσθαι τὴν
M 857 ἀλήθειαν, ἐκ τῶν | γραφῶν αὐτῶν ποιησόμεθα τούτων τὴν ἀπόδειξιν. εἷς
ὑπὸ νόμου καὶ προφητῶν καταγγέλλεται θεός. οὗτος καὶ τοῦ μονογενοῦς
10 εἶναι θεὸς ὑπ' αὐτοῦ τοῦ σωτῆρος ὁμολογεῖται, Πορεύομαι γάρ, φησί,
πρὸς τὸν θεόν μου καὶ θεὸν ὑμῶν·^a μόνος ἀληθινὸς θεός,^b μόνος σοφός,^c
μόνος ἀγαθός,^d μόνος δυνατός, μόνος ἔχων ἀθανασίαν.^e θορυβείσθω δὲ
μηδείς, μηδὲ ταρασσέσθω τὴν διάνοιαν. οὐ γὰρ ἐπ' ἀναιρέσει τῆς τοῦ
μονογενοῦς θεότητος ἢ σοφίας ἢ τῆς ἀθανασίας ἢ τῆς ἀγαθότητος χρώμεθα
15 εἰρημένοις, ἀλλ' ἐπὶ διακρίσει τῆς τοῦ πατρὸς ὑπεροχῆς. μονογενῆ μὲν
γὰρ ὁμολογοῦμεν θεὸν^f καὶ τὸν κύριον ἡμῶν Ἰησοῦν, ἄφθαρτον καὶ ἀθάνα-
τον, σοφόν, ἀγαθόν, ἀλλ' αὐτῆς γε τῆς συστάσεως καὶ παντὸς ὅπερ ἐστὶ

---

^{c-c}Cf. Basil, *Eun.* ii.31 (644D-645A)   ^{d-d}Basil, *Eun.* ii.32 (645C-648A), cf.
33 (649B)   ^eJn. 5: 19   ^fBasil, *Eun.* ii.33 (649C) refers this passage to Jn.
16: 14, probably correctly.   **21.** ^aJn. 20: 17   ^bJn. 17: 3   ^cRom.
16: 27, 1 Tim. 1: 17 var.   ^dMk. 10: 18, cf. 1 Tim. 6: 15   ^e1 Tim. 6: 16
^fJn. 1: 18

15-16 σκοπούμενος codd.: σκοπούμενός τις *b*   17 εὑρίσκων IGB*b*: εὑρίσκον C
18 τοῦ om. B sed corr.   **21.** 1 ἑκατέρῳ sic scripsi: ἑκατέρων codd.   4 ἐπικαλύμματος IGB: ἐπικαλάμματος C   7 θρυλουμένην CGB: θρυλλουμένην I
8 ἀλήθειαν CI: ἀληθ' G: ἀληθίαν B   12 δὲ CI: om. GB   16 καὶ^z IGB: om. C

mind approaching them with good will—that essence commands him to reject any comparison with another as being wholly foreign to the law of its nature. As a consequence he is also brought to recognize that its action too conforms to the dignity of its nature. On the other hand, if he begins his study from the things which have been made, from them he is led up to the essences and discovers that the Son is the 'thing made' of the Unbegotten, while the Counsellor is that of the Only-begotten. Thus, having confirmed the difference in their activities from the pre-eminence of the Only-begotten, he accepts as indisputable the proof that their essences are distinct as well. And this is without even mentioning a third consideration, that he who creates by his own power is entirely different from him who does so at the Father's command and acknowledges that he can do nothing of his own accord,[e] just as the one who *is* worshipped is different from the one who worships.[f]

21. Hence, if they think it not ridiculous to ascribe the same qualities equally to both of them—essence say, or action, authority or name (thereby doing away with the differences between the names and their objects)—let them explicitly speak of two Unbegottens. But if that is manifestly irreligious, let them not twist what is acknowledged by everyone into an impiety under cover of the word 'similarity'! But now, lest we ourselves should seem to pervert the truth by our clever inventions and use of argument (such being the charge brought against us and commonly bandied about), we will establish the proof of these things from Scripture itself. There is one God proclaimed by both Law and Prophets. That this God is also the God of the Only-begotten is acknowledged by the Saviour himself, for he says, I am going 'to my God and your God'[a]—the Only true God,[b] the only wise God,[c] who alone is good,[d] alone mighty, who alone has immortality.[e] Now don't anyone interrupt or let his mind be troubled. We have not used these expressions in order to take away the godhead of the Only-begotten, or his wisdom, or his immortality, or his goodness, but rather to distinguish them with respect to the pre-eminence of the Father. For we confess that the Lord Jesus is himself 'Only-begotten God',[f] immortal and deathless, wise, good; but we say too that the Father is the cause of his actual existence and of all that he is,

τὸν πατέρα φαμὲν αἴτιον, οὐκ ἔχοντα τῆς ἰδίας οὐσίας ἢ τῆς ἀγαθότητος
αἴτιον ὡς ἀγέννητον, ταύτην ἡμῖν παρεχόντων τὴν ἔννοιαν τῶν προτε-
20 θέντων.

22. Οὐκοῦν εἰ μόνος μὲν ἀληθινὸς ὁ θεὸς καὶ σοφὸς ἐπειδὴ καὶ
μόνος ἀγέννητος, μονογενὴς υἱὸς ἐπειδὴ μόνος ἀγεννήτου γέννημα οὐκ
ἂν δέ τι μόνον εἴη, κοινοποιουμένης πρὸς ἕτερον δι' ὁμοιότητα τῆς
φύσεως. χρὴ τοίνυν τὴν κατ' οὐσίαν ὁμοιότητα ἀνελόντες, τὴν δὲ τοῦ
5 υἱοῦ πρὸς τὸν πατέρα δεξάμενοι κατὰ τὸν οἰκεῖον λόγον,[a] εἰς ἕνα καὶ
μόνον ἀληθῶς ἐνάγειν τὴν τῶν πάντων αἰτίαν τε καὶ ἀρχήν, ὑποτεταγμένου
δηλαδὴ τοῦ υἱοῦ τῷ πατρί, τὴν δὲ περὶ τούτων ἔννοιαν ἀκριβῶς διακαθαί-
ροντας καὶ τὸν τῆς ἐνεργείας τρόπον οὐκ ἀνθρώπειον νομίζειν, εὐμαρῆ δὲ
καὶ θεῖον, οὗτοι μερισμὸν ἢ κίνησίν τινα τῆς οὐσίας τὴν ἐνέργειαν ἡγουμένους,
10 ἅπερ ἐπινοεῖν ἀναγκαῖον τοὺς ὑπαγομένους τοῖς Ἑλλήνων σοφίσμασιν,
ἑνούντων τῇ οὐσίᾳ τὴν ἐνέργειαν καὶ διὰ τοῦθ' ἅμα μὲν τῷ θεῷ τὸν κόσμον ἀποφαινομένων, οὐδὲν δὲ μᾶλλον ἐκ τούτου τὴν ἀτοπίαν διαφευγόντων.
χρῆν γάρ τοι προς τὴν τῆς δημιουργίας παῦλαν ἀπιδόντας μηδὲν πρὸς τὴν
ἀρχὴν ἀνανεύειν, οὐδὲ γὰρ ἄν τι λήξειεν εἰς τέλος μὴ ἀπ' ἀρχῆς ὁρμώ-
15 μενον.[b]

23. Ἀλλ' οὗτοι μὲν μηθ' ὑγιαίνουσιν ὀφθαλμοῖς τὴν τῶν ὄντων
κατανενοηκότες διαφοράν, μήτε δίκαιοι κριταὶ γενόμενοι τῶν πραγμάτων
ἀφιέσθωσαν, διὰ κακόνοιαν ἐπικρυπτούσης αὐτοῖς τὴν ἀλήθειαν τῆς
δίκης· ἡμεῖς δὲ κατὰ τὰ μικρῷ πρόσθεν ῥηθέντα τὴν ἐνέργειαν ἐκ τῶν
5 ἔργων κρίνοντες,[a] οὐκ ἀσφαλὲς οἰόμεθα δεῖν ἑνοῦν τῇ οὐσίᾳ, τὴν μὲν
ἄναρχον ἁπλήν τε καὶ ἀτελεύτητον εἰδότες, τὴν δ' ἐνέργειαν οὐκ ἄναρχον
M 860 (ἢ γὰρ ἂν ἦν, καὶ τὸ ἔργον ἄναρχον), | οὔτ' ἀτελεύτητον, ἐπεὶ μηδὲ
οἷόν τε παυσαμένων τῶν ἔργων ἄπαυστον εἶναι τὴν ἐνέργειαν. λίαν γὰρ
μειρακιῶδες καὶ φρενὸς νηπίας ἀγέννητον καὶ ἀτελεύτητον λέγειν τὴν

22. [a] Cf. the formula adopted in 359 by the Synods of Ariminum (Hahn, no. 166),
Sirmium (Hahn, no. 163), Thracian Nike (Hahn, no. 164) and in 360 by the Synod
of Constantinople (Hahn, no. 167): ὅμοιον . . . κατὰ τὰς γραφάς, 'similar . . . in
accordance with the Scriptures'.   [b] As is apparent from *Apol. Apol* iii (*J*
ii.227.19-228.4), Eunomius is here thinking of God's resting from his works on the
seventh day in Gen. 2: 1-3; their cessation implies a beginning.   23. [a] See
Apol. 20.7-9 above

19 ἀγέννητον . . . ἔννοιαν IGB: om. C   22. 14 ἄν τι λήξειεν sic recte coniecit
v^m: ἀντιλήξειεν codd.   23. 4 πρόσθεν IGB: πρόσθε C   7 μηδὲ IGB: μηδ' C

for the Father, being unbegotten, has no cause of his essence or goodness. This is the understanding to which the preceding arguments have brought us.

22. If, then, God is the only true and the only wise God because only he is unbegotten, the Son, being only-begotten because he is the Unbegotten's only offspring, could not in fact be anything 'only' at all if his nature were made to share a common property with some other by means of a 'similarity'. Rejecting, therefore, any 'similarity of essence' and accepting the similarity of the Son to the Father in accordance with his own words,[a] we must mount up in very truth to the one and only font and source of all things, clearly having subordinated the Son to the Father. Again, having carefully refined our conception of these matters, we must understand that God's mode of action too is not human, but effortless and divine, and must by no means suppose that that action is some kind of division or motion of his essence. This is in fact what those who have been led astray by pagan sophistries do have to suppose, because they have united the action to the essence and therefore present the world as coeval with God. Yet even so they have not escaped the logical absurdity arising from this assertion: those who have once witnessed the cessation of the creative action have no need to look back toward its beginning — nothing could have come completely to an end which did not start from some beginning![b]

23. But these people really ought to give up! They have neither perceived the difference in the beings with wholesome eyes nor have they shown themselves right-minded judges of the actual objects — Judgement has hidden the truth from them on account of their ill-will. We ourselves, however, judge the action from its effects in accordance with the principles enunciated just a moment ago,[a] and do not consider it unhazardous to have to unite the action to the essence. We recognize that the divine essence is without beginning, simple, and endless, but we also recognize that its action is neither without beginning nor without ending. It cannot be without beginning, for, if it were, its effect would be without beginning as well. On the other hand, it cannot be without ending since, if the effects come to an end, the action which produced them cannot be unending either. It is therefore childish and infantile in the extreme to say that the action is unbegotten and unending (making it

10 ἐνέργειαν, ταὐτὸν τῇ οὐσίᾳ τιθεμένους, μηδενὸς τῶν ἔργων ἀγεννήτως
γίγνεσθαι δυναμένου μηδ' ἀτελευτήτως. ἐκ γὰρ τούτων συμβαίνει δυοῖν
θάτερον, ἢ τὴν ἐνέργειαν ἄπρακτον εἶναι τοῦ θεοῦ ἢ τὸ ἔργον ἀγέννητον.
εἰ δ' ἑκάτερον τούτων ὁμολογουμένως ἄτοπον, ἀληθὲς τὸ λειπόμενον, ἀρ-
χομένων τε τῶν ἔργων μὴ ἄναρχον εἶναι τὴν ἐνέργειαν, παυομένων τε μὴ
15 ἄπαυστον. οὐ χρὴ τοίνυν πειθομένους γνώμαις ἑτέρων ἀνεξετάστοις
ἑνοῦν τῇ οὐσίᾳ τὴν ἐνέργειαν, ἀληθεστάτην δὲ καὶ θεῷ πρεπωδεστάτην
ἐνέργειαν ἡγεῖσθαι τὴν βούλησιν, ἀρκοῦσαν πρός τε τὸ εἶναι καὶ σώζεσθαι
τὰ πάντα, μαρτυρούσης καὶ προφητικῆς φωνῆς, Πάντα γὰρ ὅσα ἠθέλησεν
ἐποίησεν.[b] οὐ γὰρ ἐπιδέεταί τινος πρὸς τὴν ὧν βούλεται σύστασιν, ἀλλ'
20 ἅμα τε βούλεται καὶ γέγονεν ὅπερ ἠθέλησεν.

24. Οὐκοῦν εἰ τὴν μὲν βούλησιν ἀπέδειξεν ὁ λόγος ἐνέργειαν, οὐκ
οὐσίαν δὲ τὴν ἐνέργειαν, ὑπέστη δὲ βουλήσει τοῦ πατρὸς ὁ μονογενής, οὐ
πρὸς τὴν οὐσίαν, πρὸς δὲ τὴν ἐνέργειαν (ἥτις ἐστὶ καὶ βούλησις) ἀποσώ-
ζειν τὴν ὁμοιότητα τὸν υἱὸν ἀναγκαῖον. ἐξ ὧν προσαγομένους δεῖ τὸν
5 ἀληθῆ τῆς εἰκόνος διασώζειν λόγον. αὐτὸς ὁ μακάριος Παῦλος ἐξηγήσατο
εἰπών, Ὅς ἐστιν εἰκὼν τοῦ θεοῦ τοῦ ἀοράτου, πρωτότοκος πάσης κτίσεως,
ὅτι ἐν αὐτῷ ἐκτίσθη τὰ πάντα τά τε ἐν οὐρανῷ καὶ ἐπὶ γῆς, ὁρατὰ καὶ
ἀόρατα.[a] διὰ τοῦτ' εἰκών, πάντα δὲ τὰ ἐν αὐτῷ κτισθέντα μετὰ τοῦ
πρωτοτόκου οὐ τὴν ἀγέννητον οὐσίαν χαρακτηρίζει (οὐ γὰρ κατὰ ταῦτα ἡ
10 οὐσία), τὴν δὲ ἐνέργειαν δι' ἧς ὁ υἱὸς ἐν ᾧ τὰ πάντα. οὐ πρὸς τὴν
οὐσίαν φέροι ἂν ἡ εἰκὼν τὴν ὁμοιότητα, πρὸς δὲ τὴν ἐνέργειαν ἐναποκει-
μένην ἀγεννήτως τῇ προγνώσει, καὶ πρὸ τῆς πρωτοτόκου συστάσεως καὶ τῶν
ἐν αὐτῷ κτισθέντων. τίς γὰρ αὐτόν τε τὸν μονογενῆ γινώσκων, καὶ πάντα
τὰ δι' αὐτοῦ γενόμενα καταμαθών,[b] οὐκ ἂν ὁμολογήσειεν ⟨ἐν⟩ αὐτῷ θεω-
15 ρεῖσθαι πᾶσαν τὴν τοῦ πατρὸς δύναμιν; πρὸς ὅπερ ἀπιδὼν ὁ μακαριώτατος

[b] Ps. 113: 11 (115: 3)   24. [a] Col. 1: 15-16   [b] Jn. 1: 3

11 συμβαίνει CI: συμβαίνοι GB   15 πειθομένους IG: πειθομέναις C   ἑτέρων
CI: ἑτέροις GB sed corr.   24. 8 τοῦτ' IGB: τοῦτο C   13 αὐτόν τε CGB:
αὐτόν τε καὶ I   14 ⟨ἐν⟩ sic conieci: codd. om.

identical with the essence) when not one of its effects is capable of being produced either unbegottenly or unendingly! Indeed, on these premises only one of two conclusions can follow: either the action of God is unproductive or its effect is unbegotten. If both of these are admittedly ridiculous, then the remaining possibility must be correct: that granted the effects had a start, the action is not without beginning, and granted the effects come to an end, the action is not without ending. There is no need, therefore, to accept the half-baked opinions of outsiders and unite the action to the essence. On the contrary, we must believe that the action which is the truest and the most befitting God is his will, and that that will is sufficient to bring into existence and to redeem all things, as indeed the prophetic voice bears witness: 'Whatever he willed to do, he did.'[b] God needs nothing in order to bring what he intends into existence; rather, at the same moment he intends it, whatever he willed comes to be.

24. Accordingly, if this argument has demonstrated that God's will is an action, and that this action is not essence but that the Only-begotten exists by virtue of the will of the Father, then of necessity it is not with respect to the essence but with respect to the action (which is what the will is) that the Son preserves his similarity to the Father. Going forward on the basis of these conclusions, we must also safeguard the real meaning of the word 'image'. The blessed Paul has explained this meaning himself when he says, 'He is the image of the invisible God, the first-born of all creation, because in him all things were created, in heaven and on earth, visible and invisible.'[a] This is the reason for 'image', but the mention of 'all the things created in him' along with 'the first-born' points not to the unbegotten essence (for that essence has nothing in common with these things), but to the action through which the Son 'in whom are all things' came to be. The word 'image', then, would refer the similarity back, not to the essence of God, but to the action unbegottenly stored up in his foreknowledge prior to the existence of the first-born and of the things created 'in him'. Indeed, what person who knew the Only-begotten himself and then perceived 'all the things made through him'[b] would not acknowledge that 'in him' he had seen all the power of the Father?

Παῦλος οὐ Δι' αὐτοῦ φησὶν ἀλλ' Ἐν αὐτῷ, καίτοι προσθεὶς τὸ Πρωτότοκος ἵνα τοῖς δι' αὐτοῦ γενομένοις καὶ αὐτὸς συμπαραληφθεὶς πᾶσι γνωρίζῃ τοῖς ταῦτα συνορᾶν δυναμένοις τὴν τοῦ πατρὸς ἐνέργειαν. εἰκόνα τοίνυν φαμὲν οὐχ ὡς ἀγεννήτῳ γέννημα παραβάλλοντες (ἀνάρμοστον γὰρ τοῦτό γε
20 καὶ τοῖς πᾶσιν ἀδύνατον), ἀλλ' υἱὸν μονογενῆ καὶ πρωτότοκον πατρί, τῆς
M 861 μὲν υἱοῦ προσηγορίας τὴν οὐσίαν δηλούσης, τῆς δὲ πατρὸς τὴν τοῦ | γεννήσαντος ἐνέργειαν. εἰ δέ τις φιλονείκως τοῖς οἰκείοις ἐμμένων μὴ προσέχοι τοῖς ῥηθεῖσι τὸν νοῦν, ἐκβιάζοιτο δὲ τὴν πατρὸς προσηγορίαν οὐσίας εἶναι σημαντικήν, μεταδιδότω καὶ τῷ υἱῷ καὶ τῆς ὁμοίας φωνῆς
25 ᾧ προλαβὼν μετέδωκε καὶ τῆς ὁμοίας οὐσίας, μᾶλλον δὲ ἀμφοῖν ἑκατέρῳ, τῷ τε πατρὶ τῆς υἱοῦ καὶ τῷ υἱῷ τῆς πατρός· ἡ γὰρ τῆς οὐσίας ὁμοιότης ταῖς αὐταῖς ὀνομάζειν προσηγορίαις ἀναγκάσει τοὺς ταύτην περὶ αὐτῶν ἔχοντας τὴν δόξαν.

25. ᵃἈρχούντων δὲ ἡμῖν τοσούτων καὶ περὶ τοῦ μονογενοῦς, ἀκόλουθον ἂν εἴη καὶ περὶ τοῦ παρακλήτου λοιπὸν εἰπεῖν, οὐ ταῖς ἀνεξετάστοις τῶν πολλῶν ἀκολουθοῦντες δόξαις, τὴν δὲ τῶν ἁγίων ἐν ἅπασι φυλάττοντες διδασκαλίαν, παρ' ὧν τρίτον αὐτὸ ἀξιώματι καὶ τάξει μαθόντες,ᵇ τρίτον
5 εἶναι καὶ τὴν φύσιν πεπιστεύκαμεν,ᵃ οὐκ ἐπαμειβομένων ταῖς φύσεσι τῶν ἀξιωμάτων κατὰ τὴν ἐν ἀνθρώποις ἐκ πολιτείας μεταβολήν, οὔτ' ἐνηλλαγμένης τῆς τάξεως κατὰ τὴν δημιουργίαν ἐναντίως ταῖς οὐσίαις, ἀλλ' εὐαρμόστως ἐχούσης πρὸς τὴν φύσιν, ὡς μήτε τὸ πρῶτον τῇ τάξει δεύτερον εἶναι τὴν φύσιν, μήτε μὴν τὸ φύσει πρῶτον δευτέρας ἢ τρίτης λαχεῖν
10 τάξεως. οὐκοῦν εἴπερ ἥδε τῆς τῶν νοητῶν· δημιουργίας ἀρίστη τάξις, τρίτον ὂν τὸ πνεῦμα τὸ ἅγιον τὴν τάξιν, οὐκ ἂν πρῶτον εἴη τὴν φύσιν, ὅπερ ἐστὶν ὁ θεὸς καὶ πατήρᶜ (ἢ γὰρ ἂν εὔηθες καὶ περιττὸν τὸν αὐτὸν ποτὲ μὲν πρώτην, ποτὲ δὲ τρίτην ἐπέχειν χώραν, ἔν τε ἄμφω εἶναι, τό τε

25. ᵃ⁻ᵃBasil, *Eun.* iii.1 (653A)   ᵇHere as in *Apol.* 12.1-7 above Eunomius means the Scriptures; despite Basil's sarcastic demand for the location of the passage (*Eun.* iii.1-2 (653B-660A)) he is probably right in supposing it to be Matt. 28: 19 (*Eun.* iii.2 (657B-660A))   ᶜCf. Rom. 15: 6, 2 Cor. 1: 3, 11: 31, Gal. 1: 3, etc.

28 τὴν δόξαν CGB: δόξαν I   25. 1 Hic habent codd. adnotationem in marg.: ση(μείωσ)αι CGB: περὶ τοῦ ἁγίου πνεύματος I   καὶ codd.: om. *b*   3 ἀκολουθοῦντες codd.*b* var.: ἀκολουθοῦντας *b*   φυλάττοντες codd.: φυλάσσοντες *b* var.: φυλάσσοντας *b*   4 αὐτὸ *b*: codd. om.   5 τὴν φύσιν codd.: τῇ φύσει *b* 6 μεταβολὴν CI: περιβολὴν G sed corr. in marg.: μεταβολὴν B sed περι- inter lineas 13 ἐπέχειν C: ἔχειν IGB

It was because the most blessed Paul recognized this that he said not 'through him' but 'in him', though he also added the title 'first-born' so that by including the Only-begotten himself along with the things made through him he could make known to all those capable of comprehending these things the action of the Father. We use the word 'image', therefore, not as comparing the Offspring to the Unbegotten (which in any case is both incongruous and impossible for any creature), but as comparing the only-begotten Son and first-born to the Father, for the designation 'Son' makes his own essence clear, while that of 'Father' manifests the action of the one who begot him. However, if there is anyone who still holds contentiously to his own opinions and, paying no attention to what has been said, still insists that the designation 'Father' is indicative of the essence, let him give this same designation to the Son also, since he previously gave him a similar essence! Indeed, let him give each of them a share in both these names—the Father in that of the Son, and the Son in that of the Father—for the idea of a similarity of essence will force those who hold such an opinion about them to give the same designations to both.

25. However, if these arguments have sufficed us for what concerns the Only-begotten, logical order requires us in what remains to say something about the Counsellor as well, not following the thoughtless opinions of the multitude, but holding to the teaching of the saints in all things. Since from them we learn that he is third in both dignity and order,[b] we believe that he is third in nature as well, for the dignities of the natures have not been bestowed on each in turn the way political office is among human beings, nor is the order of their creation the reverse of that of their essences. Rather, the order of each conforms harmoniously to its nature, so that the first in order is not second in nature and the first in nature is certainly not allotted second or third place in the order. Now if this order is in fact the best as regards the creation of the intelligible beings, and the Holy Spirit is third in the order, he cannot be first in nature since that 'first' is 'the God and Father'[c] (for surely it would be both ridiculous and silly for the very same thing to occupy first place at one time and third at another, and for

προσκυνούμενον καὶ ἐν ᾧ προσκυνεῖται, καθὰ φησὶν ὁ κύριος, Πνεῦμα ὁ
15 θεός, καὶ τοὺς προσκυνοῦντας αὐτὸν ἐν πνεύματι καὶ ἀληθείᾳ δεῖ προσ-
κυνεῖν),[d] οὐδὲ μὴν ταὐτὸν τῷ μονογενεῖ (οὐ γὰρ ἂν ὑπηριθμήθη τούτῳ ὡς
ἰδίαν ἔχον ὑπόστασιν, ἀρκούσης καὶ πρὸ τούτων τῆς τοῦ σωτῆρος φωνῆς
δι' ἧς ἕτερον[e] ἔφη σαφῶς τὸν ἀποσταλησόμενον εἶναι πρὸς ὑπόμνησιν καὶ
διδασκαλίαν τῶν ἀποστόλων),[f] [g]οὐδ' ἕτερον μὲν ἀριθμῷ παρὰ τὸν θεόν,
20 ἀγέννητον δὲ (εἷς γὰρ καὶ μόνος[h] ἀγέννητος ἐξ οὗ τὰ πάντα γέγονεν),[i] ἢ
ἄλλο μὲν παρὰ τὸν υἱόν, γέννημα δέ (εἷς γὰρ καὶ μονογενὴς ὁ κύριος ἡμῶν
Δι' οὗ τὰ πάντα,[j] κατὰ τὸν ἀπόστολον), ἀλλὰ [k]τρίτον καὶ φύσει καὶ
τάξει, προστάγματι τοῦ πατρός, ἐνεργείᾳ δὲ τοῦ υἱοῦ γενόμενον, τρίτῃ
χώρᾳ τιμώμενον ὡς πρῶτον καὶ μεῖζον πάντων καὶ μόνον τοιοῦτον
25 τοῦ μονογενοῦς ποίημα, θεότητος μὲν καὶ δημιουργικῆς δυνάμεως ἀπολει-
πόμενον,[gk] ἁγιαστικῆς δὲ καὶ διδασκαλικῆς πεπληρωμένον.

Τοὺς γάρ τοι πεπιστευκότας ἐνέργειαν εἶναί τινα τοῦ θεοῦ τὸν
παράκλητον, εἶτα ταῖς οὐσίαις ὑπαριθμοῦντας,[l] ὡς λίαν εὐήθεις καὶ πολὺ
τῆς ἀληθείας ἀπεσχοινισμένους, νῦν διελέγχειν μακρᾶς ἂν εἴη σχολῆς, |
M 864 (26.) ἀλλ' ἵνα μὴ τῷ μήκει τῶν λόγων ἀποκνήσωμεν τοὺς ἀκούοντας, πᾶσαν
ἐν βραχεῖ τῶν ῥηθέντων περιλαβόντες τὴν δύναμιν φαμὲν ἕνα καὶ μόνον
ἀληθινὸν[a] εἶναι τὸν τῶν πάντων θεόν,[b] ἀγέννητον, ἄναρχον, ἀσύγκριτον,
πάσης αἰτίας κρείττονα, πᾶσι τοῖς οὖσι τοῦ εἶναι αἴτιον, οὐκ ἐκ κοινω-
5 νίας τῆς πρὸς ἕτερον τὴν τῶν ὄντων δημιουργίαν συστησάμενον, οὐ τῇ τάξει
τὸ πρῶτον, οὐ συγκρίσει τὸ κρεῖττον κατὰ πάντων ἀποφερόμενον, ἀλλὰ καθ'
ὑπεροχὴν ἀσύγκριτον οὐσίας καὶ δυνάμεως καὶ ἐξουσίας, γεννήσαντα καὶ
ποιήσαντα πρὸ πάντων μονογενῆ θεὸν[c] τὸν κύριον ἡμῶν Ἰησοῦν Χριστόν, δι'
οὗ τὰ πάντα γέγονεν,[d] εἰκόνα καὶ σφραγῖδα τῆς ἰδίας δυνάμεως καὶ ἐνερ-
10 γείας, μήτε τῷ γεννήσαντι κατὰ τὴν οὐσίαν συγκρινόμενον, μήτε τῷ δι'

[d]Jn. 4: 24   [e]Cf. Jn. 14: 16   [f]Cf. Jn. 14: 26   [g-g]Cf. Basil, *Eun.*
iii.6 (665D-668A)   [h]Cf. Jn. 17: 3   [i]Cf. 1 Cor. 8: 6, Jn. 1: 3   [j]Cf.
1 Cor. 8: 6, Jn. 1: 18   [k-k]Basil, *Eun.* iii.5 (665A-B)   [l]Cf. Origen, *Jo.*,
Fr. 37 (*GCS* iv.513.17)   **26.** [a]Jn. 17: 3   [b]Eph. 4: 6 var.   [c]Jn. 1: 18
[d]Cf. 1 Cor. 8: 6, Jn. 1: 3

14 κύριος IGB: υἱὸς C   16 ὑπηριθμήθη CI: ὑπηρηθμήθη GB   17 ἔχον GB:
ἔχων CI   19 οὐδ' ἕτερον CI: οὐδέτερον GB   22 ἀλλὰ IGB: ἀλλὰ καὶ C
22-3 καὶ φύσει καὶ τάξει codd.: (καὶ) τάξει καὶ φύσει *b*   23 prost?agmati codd.:
προστάγματι μὲν *b*   24 μεῖζον *b*: μείζων C: μείζω IGB   πάντων codd.:
ἁπάντων *b*   τοιοῦτον IGB*b*: τοιοῦτο C   25 μὲν codd.: om. *b*   **26.** 1 τῶν
λόγων IGB: τοῦ λόγου C   ἀποκνήσωμεν CGB: ἀποκναίσωμεν I   4 τοῦ CI:
τὸ GB

both the one worshipped and the one 'in whom' he is worshipped to be identical, that is, in accordance with the Lord's own statement, 'God is spirit, and those who worship him must worship in spirit and truth'),[d] nor is he identical with the Only-begotten (otherwise he would not have been numbered after him as possessing his own substance, since the Saviour's own voice is sufficient proof of these things, when he expressly says that the one who would be sent to bring to the Apostles' remembrance all that he had said and to teach them[f] would be 'another'),[e] nor is he something numerically other than God but nevertheless unbegotten (for the Unbegotten 'from whom all things'[i] came to be is 'one and only'),[h] nor yet is he some other distinct from the Son but nonetheless an 'offspring' (for our Lord, 'through whom are all things', as says the Apostle, is 'one' and 'only-begotten'),[j] rather, he is third both in nature and in order since he was brought into existence at the command of the Father by the action of the Son. He is honoured in third place as the first and greatest work of all, the only such 'thing made' of the Only-begotten, lacking indeed godhead and the power of creation, but filled with the power of sanctification and instruction.

But as for those who believe that the Counsellor is some kind of action of God but include him in the order along with the essences none the less,[l] they are so completely ridiculous and so wholly debarred from the truth that to refute them at this time would undoubtedly require a lengthy discourse; (26.) but so as not to weary our audience by the length of our arguments, we will encompass the whole force of our discussion in a few words: We assert that 'the God of all things'[b] is the one and 'only true God',[a] unbegotten, without beginning, incomparable, superior to all cause, himself the cause of the existence of all existing things, but not accomplishing the creation of those things by an association with any other. His primacy is not taken away by the order nor is his superiority to all things done away by a comparison, but being, in accordance with his pre-eminence, incomparable in essence, power, and authority, he begot and created before all things as Only-begotten God[c] our Lord Jesus Christ, through whom all things were made,[d] the image and seal of his own power and action. This Only-begotten God is not to be compared either with the one who

70   LIBER APOLOGETICUS

αὐτοῦ γενομένῳ ἁγίῳ πνεύματι, τοῦ μὲν γὰρ ἐλάττων ἐστὶν ὡς ποίημα, τοῦ
δὲ κρείττων ὡς ποιητής. τοῦ μὲν οὖν πεποιῆσθαι μάρτυς ἀξιόπιστος ὁ
παρ᾽ αὐτοῦ τοῦ κυρίου μαρτυρηθεὶς ἐκ θεοῦ τὴν γνῶσιν ἔχειν Πέτρος[e] εἰπών,
Ἀσφαλῶς οὖν γινωσκέτω πᾶς οἶκος Ἰσραὴλ ὅτι κύριον αὐτὸν καὶ χριστὸν
15 ὁ θεὸς ἐποίησε,[f] καὶ ὁ ἐκ προσώπου τοῦ κυρίου λέγων, Κύριος ἔκτισέ με
ἀρχὴν ὁδῶν αὐτοῦ,[g] τοῦ δὲ πεποιηκέναι τὸ πνεῦμα τὸ ἅγιον ὅ τε εἰπών,
Εἷς θεὸς ἐξ οὗ τὰ πάντα, καὶ εἷς κύριος Ἰησοῦς Χριστὸς δι᾽ οὗ τὰ
πάντα,[h] καὶ ὁ μακάριος Ἰωάννης φήσας, Πάντα δι᾽ αὐτοῦ ἐγένετο καὶ
χωρὶς αὐτοῦ ἐγένετο οὐδὲ ἕν,[i] ἐξ ὧν ἀκολουθοίη ἂν ἢ ἀγέννητον λέγειν
20 (ὅπερ ἀσεβές), ἢ εἴπερ γέγονε, δι᾽ αὐτοῦ γεγονέναι.

Μόνον γὰρ ὑπὸ τοῦ πατρὸς ὁμολογοῦμεν γεγεννῆσθαι τὸν υἱόν,
ὑποτεταγμένον οὐσίᾳ καὶ γνώμῃ (ζῆν τε γὰρ διὰ τὸν πατέρα[j] καὶ μηδὲν ἀφ᾽
ἑαυτοῦ ποιεῖν[k] αὐτὸς ὁμολογεῖ), μήτε μὴν ὁμοούσιον ⟨μηδὲ ὁμοιούσιον⟩,
ἐπείπερ τὸ μὲν γένεσιν καὶ μερισμὸν σημαίνει τῆς οὐσίας, τὸ δὲ ἰσότητα,
(27.) οὔτε δὲ γεννητὸς ὁ πατήρ, οὔτε ἀγέννητος ὁ υἱός, ἀλλ᾽ ὅπερ ἐστὶν
ἀτελευτήτως τοῦτο καὶ λεγόμενον ἀληθῶς, γέννημα, υἱὸν ὑπήκοον, ὑπουργὸν
τελειότατον πρὸς πᾶσαν δημιουργίαν καὶ γνώμην πατρικήν, ὑπηρετήσαντα
πρὸς τὴν τῶν ὄντων σύστασιν καὶ διαμονήν, πρὸς νομοθεσίαν ἀνθρώπων,
5 πρὸς οἰκονομίαν καὶ πᾶσαν πρόνοιαν, ὑπηρέτῃ χρώμενον τῷ παρακλήτῳ πρὸς
ἁγιασμόν, πρὸς διδασκαλίαν, πρὸς βεβαίωσιν τῶν πιστῶν, [a]ἐπ᾽ ἐσχάτων τῶν
M 865 ἡμερῶν γεννηθέντα ἐκ τῆς ἁγίας παρθένου, νόμοις ἀνθρωπίνοις πολιτευ-
σάμενον ὁσίως,[a] σταυρωθέντα, ἀποθανόντα, ἀναστάντα τῇ τρίτῃ τῶν ἡμερῶν,
ἀνελθόντα εἰς οὐρανόν, ἐρχόμενον κρῖναι ζῶντας καὶ νεκροὺς κατὰ δικαίαν
10 ἀνταπόδοσιν πίστεώς τε καὶ ἔργων, βασιλεύοντά τε εἰς τοὺς αἰῶνας, σῳζο-
μένης ἐν ἅπασι πάντοτε τῆς ὑπεροχῆς τοῦ θεοῦ καὶ μοναρχίας, ὑποτεταγμένου δηλαδὴ τοῦ πνεύματος τοῦ ἁγίου τῷ Χριστῷ μετὰ πάντων, αὐτοῦ τοῦ
υἱοῦ καὶ τῷ θεῷ καὶ πατρί,[b] κατὰ τὴν τοῦ μακαρίου Παύλου διδασκαλίαν,

[e]Matt. 16: 17   [f]Acts 2: 36   [g]Prov. 8: 22   [h]1 Cor. 8: 6   [i]Jn. 1: 3
[j]Jn. 6: 57   [k]Jn. 5: 19   27. [a-a]Cf. the creed found in the *Apostolic
Constitutions* (Hahn, no. 129)   Cf. Rom. 15: 6, 2 Cor. 1: 3, 11: 31, Gal. 1: 3, etc.

12 κρείττων CI: κρεῖττον GB   15 ἐποίησε IGB: ἐποίησεν C   ἔκτισε IGB:
ἔκτισεν C   20 γέγονε IGB: γέγονεν C   21 γεγεννῆσθαι CI: γεγενῆσθαι G (sed
corr.)B   23 ⟨μηδὲ ὁμοιούσιον⟩ sic coniecit Fabricius, ut videtur, recte: codd. om.
27. 1 ὁ υἱός IGB: υἱός C   13 καὶ[l] C: om. IGB

begot him or with the Holy Spirit who was made through him, for he is less than the one in being a 'thing made', and greater than the other in being a maker. And indeed, a trustworthy witness of the fact that he was made is Peter, of whom the Lord himself bore witness that he had received his knowledge from God,[e] for Peter said, 'Let all the house of Israel therefore know assuredly that God has made him both Lord and Christ',[f] and still another witness to this is the one who spoke in the Lord's own person saying, 'The Lord created me as the beginning of his ways.'[g] But the one who bears witness to the fact that the Holy Spirit, on the other hand, was also made is the one who said, 'There is one God from whom are all things, and one Lord Jesus Christ through whom are all things',[h] to which also the blessed John bore witness when he said, 'All things were made through him and without him not one thing was made.'[i] From these passages it must follow either that the Holy Spirit is unbegotten (which is blasphemous), or that, if he was made, he was made 'through him'.

For we confess that only the Son was begotten of the Father and that he is subject to him both in essence and in will (indeed, he himself has admitted that he 'lives because of the Father'[j] and that he can 'do nothing of his own accord'),[k] believing him to be neither *homoousios* nor *homoiousios*, since the one implies a generation and division of the essence and the other an equality; (27.) we neither believe that the Father is begotten or that the Son is unbegotten, but that what the Son is everlastingly is what he is also rightly called: Offspring, obedient Son, most perfect Minister of the whole creation and will of the Father, ministering for the maintenance and preservation of all existing things, for the giving of the Law to mankind, for the ordering of the world and for all providential care. He makes use of the Counsellor as his servant for the sanctification, instruction, and assurance of believers. [a]In these last days he was born of the holy Virgin, lived in holiness in accordance with human laws,[a] was crucified, died, rose again the third day, and ascended into heaven. He will come again to judge both the living and the dead by a righteous retribution of both faith and works, and he will reign as king forever. In all these things the pre-eminence and sole supremacy of God is preserved, for the Holy Spirit is clearly subject to Christ, as are all things, while the Son himself is subject to his 'God and Father'[b] in accordance

ὅς φησιν, "Οταν γὰρ ὑποταγῇ αὐτῷ τὰ πάντα, τότε καὶ αὐτὸς ὁ υἱὸς ὑπο-
15 ταγήσεται τῷ ὑποτάξαντι αὐτῷ τὰ πάντα, ἵνα ᾖ ὁ θεὸς τὰ πάντα ἐν πᾶσι.ᶜ

Τούτων δὴ πάντων εὐκρινῶς μὲν καὶ πλατύτερον ἐν ἑτέροις
ἡμῖν ἀποδεδειγμένων, ἐν βραχεῖ δὲ νῦν πρὸς ὑμᾶς ὡμολογημένων, εὐχόμεθα
τούς τε παρόντας ὑμᾶς καὶ πάντας τοὺς τῶν αὐτῶν ἡμῖν μυστηρίων κοινω-
νοῦντας, μὴ φόγον ἀνθρώπων δεδοικότας, μήτε σοφίσμασιν ἀπατωμένους
20 ἢ κολακείαις ὑπαγομένους, κατὰ τὴν ἀληθῆ καὶ δικαίαν κρίσιν ἐπιψηφίσασ-
θαι τοῖς εἰρημένοις, κρατούσης δηλαδὴ παρὰ πᾶσι τῆς βελτίονος μοίρας,
τόν τε λογισμὸν τῶν ἐνοχλούντων προστησαμένους, πάντα θήρατρα καὶ
δίκτυα διαφυγεῖν ἃ τῷ διαβόλῳ κατ' ἀνθρώπων μεμηχάνηται, πολλοὺς
φοβεῖν ἢ δελεάζειν μεμελετηκότι τοὺς μὴ πρὸ τῶν ἡδέων τὸ συμφέρον
25 αἱρουμένους, ἢ τὰ παρόντα τῶν μελλόντων ἀσφαλέστερα λογιζομένους· εἰ
δ' ἄρα καὶ παρά τισι νικήσει τὰ χείρω (ἀποστρέψαι δὲ ὁ θεὸς τοῦ λόγου
τὴν πεῖραν), πρὸς μὲν τὸ ψεῦδος τῶν πολλῶν συμπνεόντων, πρὸς δὲ τὴν
ἀλήθειαν διϊσταμένων, τῶν τε ἀρεσκόντων τῷ θεῷ καὶ κοινῇ συμφερόντων
τὴν πρὸς τὸ παρὸν ἀσφάλειαν καὶ δόξαν περὶ πλείονος ποιουμένων, τοὺς
30 γοῦν ἑπομένους ἀσάλευτον καὶ παγίαν διαφυλάξαι τῷ παραδεδωκότι τὴν
πίστιν, περιμένοντας τὸ τοῦ σωτῆρος ἡμῶν Χριστοῦ κριτήριον, οὗ τῦφος
μὲν καὶ δόξα καὶ ψεῦδος πρόρριζος ἠφάνισται, γυμνοὶ δὲ πάσης ἀρχῆς ἢ
θεραπείας ἢ κολακείας οἱ κρινόμενοι, πολυχειρία δὲ καὶ πλοῦτος ἀσθενὴς πρὸς δυσώπησιν, κἂν ᾖ λίαν παρ' ἀνθρώποις εὐδόκιμος. ἀνδρῶν
35 γὰρ ἐνδόξων πλῆθος ἑνὸς πένητος εὐσεβοῦς οὐκ ἀντάξιον εἰς παραίτησιν
παρ' ἀληθείᾳ δοκιμαζούσῃ, συναγωνιζομένης μὲν εὐσεβείας κατὰ δικαίαν
ἀμοιβὴν τῶν νῦν δι' αὐτὴν καὶ τὸ θανεῖν κέρδος ἡγουμένων,ᵈ ἀποδιδόντος
δὲ τὰ τῶν ἀγώνων ἆθλα τοῦ πάλαι καὶ νῦν ἀθλοθετοῦντος Χριστοῦ, τοῖς
μὲν ὑπὲρ ἀληθείας πονέσασι τὴν ἀληθινὴν ἐλευθερίαν καὶ βασιλείαν οὐ-
40 ρανῶν, τοῖς δὲ διὰ κακόνοιαν ταύτην ἀτιμάσασι τιμωρίας ἀπαραιτήτους.
ταῦτ' εἰρήσθω μὲν ἀμφότερα πρὸς ὑμᾶς, ἐκβαίη δὲ πρὸς τὴν βελτίω μοῖ-
ραν τὸ τέλος.

ᶜ1 Cor. 15: 28   ᵈCf. Phil. 1: 21

14 καὶ IGB: om. C   16 δὴ IGB: δὲ C   πλατύτερον IGB: πλάττερον C
18 ὑμᾶς sic recte scripsit Cave et Fabricius: ἡμᾶς codd. sed corr. G alia manu
19 ἀπατωμένους IGB: ἀπατομένους C   22 θήρατρα IG marg.: θήρατα CGB
23 κατ' IGB: κατὰ C   24 φοβεῖν CI: φυγεῖν GB   33–4 ἀσθενὴς IGB:
ἀσθενεὶς C   34 παρ' IGB: παρὰ C

with the teaching of the blessed Paul who said, 'When all things are subject to him, then the Son himself will also be subjected to him who put all things under him, that God may be everything to everyone.'[c]

Since we gave a clearer and more extensive demonstration of all this in the other parts of our discourse and have now gone over it for you again by way of summary, we beseech not only those who are present, but all who have shared with us in the same sacraments: don't be afraid of human censure; don't be deceived by their sophistries or led astray by their flatteries. Give a true and just verdict on the issues of which we've spoken; show that the better part has clearly won out among you all. Let right reason prevail over these troublemakers and flee all the traps and snares laid for us by the devil; he has made it his business either to terrify or entice the many who fail to put what is right before what is pleasurable, and who account things present more certain than things to come. But if, because the majority have agreed in a lie and fought against the truth, preferring their present safety and reputation to what is pleasing to God and commonly reckoned fitting, the worse part should triumph among some (and may God for] 'd the fulfillment of these words!), I beseech my own followers, at least, to preserve the faith unshaken and steadfast for the one who gave it to them, awaiting the judgement seat of Christ our Saviour. For from that tribunal all pretence, conjecture, and falsehood have been done away, and those who are judged are stripped of all power, attendance, and flattery. There, indeed, neither a numerous retinue nor wealth are a sufficient appeal, be they never so esteemed by human beings, for a whole crowd of distinguished men is not the equal in intercession of a single poor and religious man when Truth itself is judge: religion joins its plea with his in conformity with the recompense due those who now count even death a gain in its behalf.[d] The rewards of those contests are given by Christ, who both in ages past and in the present offers his rewards: to those who have laboured for the truth, the genuine liberty and kingship of heaven; to those who through ill-will have dishonoured it, inexorable punishment. Let these two alternatives be mentioned before you but once, and may the outcome go to the better part.

Confessio Eunomiana ad calcem manuscriptorum transmissa

M 868   **28.** Εἷς ἔστι θεός, ἀγέννητος καὶ ἄναρχος, οὔτε πρὸ ἑαυτοῦ ἔχων
τινὰ ὄντα (οὐδὲν γὰρ πρὸ τοῦ ἀγεννήτου εἶναι δύναται), οὔτε σὺν αὐτῷ
(εἷς γὰρ καὶ μόνος θεὸς ὁ ἀγέννητος), οὔτ' ἐν αὐτῷ (ἁπλοῦς γὰρ καὶ
ἀσύνθετος). εἷς δὲ ὢν καὶ μόνος ὢν καὶ ἀεὶ ὁ αὐτὸς ὤν,ᵃ πάντων ἐστὶ
5 θεὸς καὶ κτίστης καὶ δημιουργός, πρώτως μὲν καὶ ἐξαιρέτως τοῦ μονογενοῦς, ἰδίως δὲ τῶν δι' αὐτοῦ γενομένων, τὸν μὲν γὰρ υἱὸν πρὸ πάντων
καὶ πρὸ πάσης κτίσεως μόνον τῇ ἑαυτοῦ δυνάμει καὶ ἐνεργείᾳ ἐγέννησέ
τε καὶ ἔκτισε καὶ ἐποίησεν, οὐδὲν τῆς ἑαυτοῦ ὑποστάσεως μεταδοὺς τῷ
γεννηθέντι (ἄφθαρτος γὰρ καὶ ἀδιαίρετος καὶ ἀμέριστος ὁ θεός, ὁ δ'
10 ἄφθαρτος τῆς ἑαυτοῦ οὐσίας οὐ μεταδίδωσιν), οὔτε καθ' ἑαυτὸν ἄλλον
ὑποστησάμενος (μόνος γὰρ αὐτὸς ἀγέννητος, κατὰ δὲ τὴν ἀγέννητον οὐσίαν
γεννηθῆναι ἀδύνατον), οὔτε οὖν τῇ ἑαυτοῦ οὐσίᾳ ἀπεχρήσατο, ἀλλὰ τῇ
βουλήσει μόνῃ, οὔτε κατὰ τὴν ἑαυτοῦ οὐσίαν, ἀλλ' οἷον ἐβουλήθη ἐγέννησε. καὶ διὰ τούτου πρῶτον μὲν πάντων καὶ μεῖζον τὸ πνεῦμα τὸ ἅγιον
15 ἐποίησεν, ἐξουσίᾳ μὲν ἰδίᾳ καὶ προστάγματι, ἐνεργείᾳ δὲ καὶ δυνάμει
τοῦ υἱοῦ, μετὰ δὲ τοῦτο τὰ λοιπὰ πάντα τὰ ἐν οὐρανῷ καὶ ἐπὶ γῆς, ὁρατά
τε καὶ ἀόρατα, καὶ σώματά τε καὶ ἀσώματα διὰ τοῦ υἱοῦ ἐποίησεν. Εἷς
γὰρ θεὸς ἐξ οὗ τὰ πάντα, κατὰ τὸν ἀπόστολον, καὶ εἷς κύριος Ἰησοῦς
Χριστός, δι' οὗ τὰ πάντα.ᵇ εἷς οὖν θεός, ἀγέννητος, ἄκτιστος, ἀποίη-
20 τος, καὶ εἷς κύριος Ἰησοῦς Χριστός, ὁ υἱὸς τοῦ θεοῦ, ᶜγέννημα τοῦ
ἀγεννήτου (οὐχ ὡς ἓν τῶν γεννημάτων), κτίσμα τοῦ ἀκτίστου (οὐχ ὡς ἓν
τῶν κτισμάτων), ποίημα τοῦ ⟨ἀ⟩ποιήτου (οὐχ ὡς ἓν τῶν ποιημάτων),ᶜκαθὼς
εἴρηται ὑπὸ τῆς ἁγίας γραφῆς, Κύριος ἔκτισέ με ἀρχὴν ὁδῶν αὐτοῦ, πρὸ
τοῦ αἰῶνος ἐθεμελίωσέ με, πρὸ δὲ πάντων βουνῶν γεννᾷ με.ᵈ καὶ ἓν πνεῦ-
25 μα ἅγιον, πρῶτον καὶ μεῖζον πάντων τοῦ μονογενοῦς ἔργων, προστάγματι
μὲν τοῦ πατρός, ἐνεργείᾳ δὲ καὶ δυνάμει τοῦ υἱοῦ γενόμενον.

28. ᵃThe repeated use of ὤν here may be an allusion to the Divine Name in Exod.
3: 4 (LXX)   ᵇ1 Cor. 8: 6   ᶜ⁻ᶜCf. Arius, *Ep. ad Alex.* 2 (Opitz
3.1.12.9–10), and the second formula of the Synod of Antioch in 341 (Hahn, no.
154)   ᵈProv. 8: 22, 23, 25b

---

28. 5 πρώτως IGB: πρῶτος C   7 ἐγέννησε IGB: ἐγέννησεν C   8 ἔκτισε
IGB: ἔκτισεν C   13 ἐγέννησε IGB: ἐγέννησεν C   17 ἐποίησεν CIB: ἐποίσεν G
22 ⟨ἀ⟩ποιήτου sic recte coniecit Fabricius: ποιήτου codd.   23 ἔκτισέ IGB:
ἔκτισέν C   24 ἐθεμελίωσέ IGB: ἐθεμελίωσέν C   25 ἔργων sic recte coniecit Cave:
ἔργον codd.   26 Post γενόμενον add. B *explicit* sequentem: τέλος τοῦ Εὐνομίου

*A Eunomian Confession of Faith
appended to the manuscripts of the Apology*

28. God is one, both unbegotten and without beginning, admitting of no being prior to himself (for nothing can exist prior to the Unbegotten), nor with himself (for the Unbegotten is one, and only he is God), nor in himself (for he is simple and uncompounded). Because he is one and only and always the same,[a] he is the God, creator, and maker of all things, primarily and in a special sense of the Only-begotten, but also in a sense appropriate to himself of the things made through the Only-begotten,[b] for he begot and created and made only the Son by his own power and action prior to all things and prior to the whole creation. He did not, however, share out anything of his own substance with the one begotten (for God is immortal, undivided, and indivisible, and what is immortal cannot share out its own essence), nor did he establish any other like himself (for only he is unbegotten, and nothing can be begotten which is like the unbegotten essence), nor, indeed, did he make use of his own essence in begetting, but of his will only, or beget anything like his own essence, but rather, what he willed, such he begot. It was through the Son that he made the Holy Spirit, the first and greatest of all his works, creating him by his own authority and commandment, but by means of the action and power of the Son. After the Holy Spirit, he made through the Son all the other things which are in heaven and upon earth, things seen and unseen, corporeal and incorporeal. 'There is one God from whom are all things,' as says the Apostle, 'and one Lord, Jesus Christ, through whom are all things.'[b] Hence, there is 'one God', unbegotten, uncreated, unmade, and 'one Lord, Jesus Christ', the Son of God, [c] the offspring of the Unbegotten (but not like any other offspring), the creature of the Uncreated (but not like any other creature), the 'thing made' of the Unmade (but not like any other 'thing made'),[c] just as Holy Scripture proclaims: 'The Lord created me as the beginning of his ways, before eternity he set me up, before all the hills he brought me forth.'[d] There is also one Holy Spirit, the first and greatest of all the Only-begotten's works, made at the command of the Father by the action and power of the Son.

EUNOMII APOLOGIA APOLOGIAE
AN APOLOGY FOR THE APOLOGY

INTRODUCTION

I. THE ORIGINAL EXTENT OF THE WORK

As we already noted in our General Introduction,[1] all the surviving
works of Eunomius are offshoots of a single great controversy; this is
no less true of the work now under consideration. Eunomius' first
effort, the *Liber Apologeticus*, was answered promptly by St Basil
in his treatise, *Adversus Eunomium*. Basil was answered in his turn
(though not so promptly) by Eunomius in his *Apologia Apologiae*,
his 'Apology for the Apology'. Unfortunately, this work has come
down to us only in the more or less extensive quotations of it by
Gregory of Nyssa, who answered it in what proved to be the final
riposte of this phase of the controversy.

Because we do not possess the treatise as a whole, therefore, there
is some question as to its original size. Both Gregory of Nyssa[2] and
Photius[3] seem to assert that the work consisted of three books, while
the Eunomian historian Philostorgius speaks of five.[4] It is certain
that we now possess the fragments of only three books, but the
question remains open as to whether there were not once two more.
Let us look at the evidence.

When St Basil wrote his refutation of Eunomius' first apology, he
did so by quoting from it and answering each section in turn. It is
because Gregory of Nyssa adopted a similar policy with regard to
the second that its surviving fragments have come down to us.
Eunomius' practice in the matter was little different from that of his
adversaries; there are any number of instances in which his own
comments are directly based on those of Basil.[5] If with this in mind
we examine the instances where his argument is a response to that
of his adversary, we find that the latest passage refuted is that
beginning in chapter twenty-five of Basil's second book.[6] This

---

[1] See pp. 3 f. above.

[2] Apart from the mentions of the books found in the manuscript titles of the
books of Gregory, see *GN* II (*J* i.226.2, 10-11, 16; 227.22), III.i (*J* ii.3.6-16; 4.19).

[3] Photius, *Cod.* 138 (Henry ii.106.12).

[4] Philost., *HE* viii.12 (*GCS* 114.3, 24).

[5] See pp. 6-9 above.   [6] See pp. 126-7 below.

leaves the last five to eight chapters of this book and all of book three unanswered. Unless we are prepared to believe, then, that Eunomius replied to Basil only in part, some portion of his work must be missing. The question is, how much? In trying to find an answer, let us look at the direct evidence, beginning with that of Photius.

It seems almost inescapable that Photius did not himself possess a copy of this apology; all his information about it derives from Gregory of Nyssa. A comparison of the two authors' statements shows not only that Photius has very little which cannot be found in Gregory, but that there are striking verbal parallels as well.[7] The conceptual parallels are even more striking: the simile of the children of Babylon dashed against the rock of Christ;[8] the mention of the secrecy with which the work was produced[9] and the joy with which it was received by Eunomius' intimates;[10] the (slightly different) pictures of Basil's ascent to his true home in heaven.[11] The only passages in Photius which are actually new are the use of the simile of Kronos devouring his children,[12] and the statement that Eunomius published his work only after the death of Basil.[13] This last assertion is not made by Gregory in any of the places where he discusses the matter, but since it does appear in the title given in the manuscripts of his first book,[14] and might be deduced from a hasty reading of what he actually does say,[15] there is no reason to suppose any additional source for Photius' statements. We can take it as virtually certain, then, that Photius derived all of his information about Eunomius' book from Gregory. Our problem thus reduces itself to a simple opposition between the statements made by Gregory and those made by Philostorgius. Let us see if this opposition is as absolute as has been supposed.

Important to an understanding of our problem is the realization that Gregory nowhere states that there were *not* five books; he

---

[7] Photius, *Cod.* 138 (Henry ii.106.15-16) ~ *GN* I (*J* i.26.6-7); Photius, *Cod.* 138 (Henry ii.106.18-19) ~ *GN* I (*J* i.24.8-10); Photius, *Cod.* 138 (Henry ii.106.19-20) ~ *GN* I (*J* i.24.8, 10-11).

[8] Photius, *Cod.* 137 (Henry ii.106.7-9) ~ *GN* I (*J* i.24.10-17).

[9] Photius, *Cod.* 138 (Henry ii.106.16-18) ~ *GN* I (i.24.7-8).

[10] Photius, *Cod.* 138 (Henry ii.106.29-30) ~ *GN* I (*J* i.26.4-6).

[11] Photius, *Cod.* 138 (Henry ii.106.27-8) ~ *GN* I (*J* i.24.26-25.3).

[12] Photius, *Cod.* 138 (Henry ii.106.23-5).

[13] Ibid. (Henry ii.106.25-30). [14] *GN* I (*J* 1.22.3).

[15] e.g., ibid. (*J* i.24.19-25.6), cf. also Grg. Nyss., *Ep.* 29 (*J* VIII.ii.87.22-88.8).

simply makes it clear that he himself did not possess more than three. How is this to be explained? Part of our problem is resolved if we take into consideration that Eunomius' work did not appear as a complete whole, but that the various books were issued individually or in groups over a period of time. Both Philostorgius[16] and Gregory[17] state specifically that the first two books came out together.[18] The third book appeared at a somewhat later date, as is implied by some statements of Gregory.[19] Furthermore, the work was not readily available to the general public, at least to begin with; Gregory had some difficultly in obtaining a copy of the first two books,[20] and some of his other statements suggest that initially the work was confined to circles likely to be sympathetic.[21] It thus becomes understandable that Gregory might know of some parts of the work without having heard of (or at any rate seen) others. Moreover, there is every reason to believe that Philostorgius would have known the work intimately. He was himself a member of the Eunomian Church, had written an encomium of Eunomius,[22] and had even as a young man seen him personally.[23] It is almost impossible to believe that Philostorgius might have been mistaken in a case like this or that he would have accepted a lengthy spurious addition to the work practically within the lifetime of its reputed author. It seems, then, that the opposition between Philostorgius and Gregory is not so absolute as it might at first appear, and that we may accept as almost certain Philostorgius' statement that in its finished form Eunomius' second apology consisted of five books.

---

[16] Philost., *HE* viii.12a (*GCS* 114.25).

[17] Grg. Nyss., *Ep.* 29 (*J* viii.ii.87.8-9, 14-15).

[18] Though this does not mean that Gregory answered them together. Because of the short time he was allowed to keep the book by the person who loaned it to him (17 days), he was then able to reply only to Eunomius' first book, *Ep.* 29 (*J* viii.ii.87.8-15); later, urged on by his brother Peter, *Ep.* 30 (*J* viii.ii.90.13-25), he brought out his answer to the second book in the second book of his own treatise.

[19] *GN* iii.i (*J* ii.3.5-12; 4.18-19); there is no evidence, however, to support Jaeger's assertion that Eunomius was moved to produce the rest of his refutation *because* of Gregory's treatise (*J* ii, p. ix).

[20] Grg. Nyss., *Ep.* 29 (*J* viii.ii.87.9-15).

[21] *GN* i (*J* i.24.10-11; 26.4-6, 15-16), all referring to the joy of Eunomius' adherents on the appearance of this work.

[22] Philost., *HE* iii.21 (*GCS* 49.1-2).

[23] Ibid., x.6 (*GCS* 128.10-20), quoted above, pp. xiv-xv.

II. DATE AND OCCASION

If we have successfully gauged the extent of Eunomius' work, the problem that now faces us is the date of the book's appearance and the occasion that warranted it. That Eunomius' reply had appeared only some years after Basil launched his attack is sufficiently obvious from the comments of Gregory of Nyssa, who jeers that Eunomius slaved over it for long years,[24] that he passed many olympiads in its production,[25] that, indeed, the whole thing took longer than the Trojan War![26] Fortunately, we are in a position to date the work with more precision than this and can assert with some assurance that it appeared around the time of the death of Basil the Great (1 January 379). Whether it was before or after that event is more problematic. Philostorgius implies that it appeared before Basil's death, for he tells us that on reading the first two books Basil died of despair![27] On the other hand, both an early editor of Gregory of Nyssa's *Contra Eunomium* and Photius understood Gregory to mean that it appeared only after Basil's death, since the title of the one[28] and the direct statement of the other[29] assert this to be the case. Gregory himself, however, does not say this. All he says is that his own justification for writing is that the great and holy Basil is now dead.[30] This, presumably, is the source of Photius' statement and of that in the title of the *Contra Eunomium*. Although this is one possible interpretation of Gregory's statements, it is far from being the only one. Most attempts to solve this problem have been based on the statements found in the *Contra Eunomium*, but Gregory in fact makes a much more precise statement elsewhere. In the letter to his brother Peter to which we have already referred several times,[31] Gregory mentions that he received Eunomius' work at the time of Basil's death (κατ' αὐτὴν τοῦ ἁγίου Βασιλείου τὴν κοίμησιν), and that his natural reaction at such a time to the slanders contained in it accounts for the harshness of tone in his own work.[32] Since Gregory

---

[24] *GN* I (*J* i.24.5-10).   [25] Ibid. (*J* 1.26.6-8).
[26] *GN* II (*J* i.263.3-6).   [27] Philost., *HE* viii.12 (*GCS* 114.2-4, 24-6).
[28] *GN* I (*J* i.22.3).   [29] Photius, *Cod.* 138 (Henry ii.106.25-30).
[30] *GN* I (*J* i.24.19-25.6).   [31] nn. 15, 17, 18, 20, above.
[32] Grg. Nyss., *Ep.* 29 (*J* VIII.ii.87.22-88.8), as already noted by Fr. Diekamp, 'Literargeschichtliches zu der Eunomianischen Kontroverse', *BZ* 18 (1909), 9-10.

had only just heard of it, it cannot have appeared any long while prior to Basil's death, but since he also mentions various 'threats' accompanying its production,[33] it must have been an open secret that it was forthcoming. Books one and two, then, of the *Apologia Apologiae* must have been published sometime during the last few months of 378 with the rest of the work appearing at intervals in the years following.

If we have sufficiently resolved the problem of the date of the book's appearance, the next question which must be considered is the occasion of its publication and why it appeared so long after the work it was intended to refute. The years immediately following the publication of Eunomius' first apology were sufficiently eventful, both for him personally and for the world at large, to provide a sufficient explanation as to why he did not answer his attacker immediately, but a consideration of the events surrounding the appearance of his second work should enable us to explain the reasons for its publication at that particular time. Philostorgius tells us that Eunomius was exiled to *Naoxia* (almost certainly Naxos)[34] after Modestus had replaced Auxonius as Praetorian Prefect.[35] Modestus became *Praefectus Praetorio per Orientem* in 369. There is, however, some possibility that Eunomius was not exiled until 370, when Demophilus succeeded Eudoxius as bishop of Constantinople; Demophilus is singled out by Philostorgius as particularly hostile to the Eunomians.[36] We have no direct information about Eunomius' recall, but just prior to the entry of Theodosius into the city (24 November 380) we find him at Constantinople, feared by the Orthodox as the hope of the Arian party.[37] If we take this information together with the date previously established for the publication of the second apology, we can reconstruct some of the reasons that moved Eunomius to bring out this work when he did.

In the aftermath of the battle of Adrianople (9 August 378), the

---

[33] *GN* I (*J* i.24.7-8).

[34] Cf. the medieval forms of the island's name: *Naxia, Nacsia, Nicsia*, etc., *P-W* 16.2081.3-9.

[35] Philost., *HE* ix.11 (*GCS* 120.4-7).

[36] Ibid., ix.14 (*GCS* 122.2-3); though it may be questioned how much difference the death of his old protector would have made to Eunomius' situation, since he had broken with him some time previously, and had even been involved in an attempt to consecrate a rival bishop of Constantinople! Philost., *HE* ix.4 (*GCS* 117.1-3).

[37] Soz., *HE* vii.6 (*GCS* 307.13-15).

Emperor Gratian is said by Socrates[38] and Sozomen[39] to have recalled the exiles and to have permitted all religious groups to assemble freely with the exception of the Manichaeans, Photinians, and Eunomians.[40] That there was such a decree granting toleration (said to have been a *rescriptum* issued from Sirmium) is sufficiently proved by another decree of Gratian withdrawing it, given at Milan nearly a year later (3 August 379);[41] the actual decree itself has perished. Moreover, while both Socrates and Sozomen make it clear that toleration was not extended to Manichaeans, Photinians, or Eunomians, they also indicate that the recall from exile was not so restricted, but applied to all. This, taken together with the date established for the publication of Eunomius' work, suggests that Eunomius too took advantage of the decree to return to Constantinople, probably to Chalcedon, where he had had a house and a garden prior to his exile.[42] At a slightly later date we find him living in 'Bithynia near Constantinople'.[43] This gives us the information necessary to construct a possible scenario explaining Eunomius' actions with regard to the production of this book: during his exile Eunomius made good use of his enforced leisure to work on

[38] Soc., *HE* v.2 (*PG* 67.568A-B).

[39] Soz., *HE* vii.1 (*GCS* 302.10-15).

[40] Note, however, that Rufinus, *HE* xi [ii].13 (*PL* 21.522C) ascribes this recall to a repentant Valens just after the Gothic invasion and does not mention Gratian's law at all.

[41] *Cod. Theod.* xvi.5.5 (Mommsen i, pars posterior, p. 856); all ministers of such 'perverse superstitions' (apparently Arians and Donatists) are to cease holding assemblies and the earlier decree is to apply only to Catholics. That the decree referred to must be one issued by Gratian and not an earlier emperor is sufficiently shown in *Gothofredus* vi.116-17. As for other possible references, there is nothing to indicate what is meant by the mention of a 'special rescript obtained by fraud' in *Cod. Theod.* xvi.5.6 (Mommsen i, pars posterior, p. 856), but it seems unlikely that it could refer to the decree of Gratian, as implied by a note in the *GCS* edition of Sozomen, *HE* vii.1 (*GCS* 302.10-15).

[42] Philost., *HE* ix.4 (*GCS* 117.6-9).

[43] Soz., *HE* vii.6 (*GCS* 307.17-19). Although Sozomen apparently knew nothing of an exile to Naxos and visualized Eunomius' residence in Bithynia as extending from his eviction from Cyzicus until the arrival of Theodosius in Constantinople in 380, he clearly implies that the heresiarch was there at the latter date since it was the crowds going out to hear him there who first drew the Emperor's attention to him. Sozomen may not, of course, have had Chalcedon in mind, since at a later date Eunomius is described simply as 'living in the suburbs', *HE* vii.17 (*GCS* 324.17-18), but Chalcedon, though separated by the Bosporus, was only 7 stades from the city (something under a mile) and thus well within the definition of 'suburb'.

a rebuttal of Basil's charges and had completed, or very nearly completed, the first and second books of it when news of his release reached him in late September or October of 378 (allowing a certain amount of time for Gratian's decree to be promulgated and disseminated). Hastening to Constantinople, he published (at first to sympathetic circles) his *Apologia Apologiae* sometime during November or early December 378, so that a copy (or at least word of it) would have reached Gregory about the time of Basil's death on 1 January 379. After this first installment, subsequent volumes appeared over the next few years.

If this provides us with a scenario explaining this apology's late appearance, we must still ask ourselves not only what Eunomius hoped to accomplish by it, but also the reasons for its continued publication in a rapidly changing political situation and the uses to which it was put. To answer this, we must return to a consideration of the events surrounding the appearance of this apology. The initial result of Gratian's decree must have been a considerable amount of confusion if not actual chaos. Leaders of the Church did not need the events at Antioch[44] to warn them of the damage that might be done to the Church from the competition of several returned bishops for the same see, and some at least tried to compose their differences with their rivals in an attempt to remedy the situation.[45] These efforts, however, seem to have been of little avail, and Constantinople in particular (whither Eunomius had immediately gone) is described as a hot-bed of competing sects.[46] Although the established Arian Church of the previous reign was still officially in power there, and was, indeed, much the largest religious body in the city,[47] the various other parties took advantage of their new freedom to reinforce their positions and gain converts. Thus the Macedonians, for instance, used this opportunity to repudiate their previous alliance with the homoousians,[48] while among those attempting to rally their flocks in the city we find not only Eunomius, but at a slightly later date (early 379) Gregory of Nazianzus as well.[49] Moreover, there were rumours of a meeting of

---

[44] Soc., *HE* v.5 (*PG* 67.569C-572B), Soz., *HE* vii.3 (*GCS* 304.1-21), Thdt., *HE* v.3 (*GCS* 279.10-282.8).

[45] Soz., *HE* vii.2 (*GCS* 303.18-30).   [46] Ibid., vii.4 (*GCS* 305.8-12).

[47] Ibid., vii.5 (*GCS* 306.1-12), 6 (*GCS* 307.9-13).

[48] Soc., *HE* v.4 (*PG* 67.569B-C).

[49] Grg. Naz., *Carm. Vit.* 562-82 (*PG* 37.1068-9).

Apollinarian bishops,[50] and other groups were also active.[51] Eunomius himself was not only engaged in building up his followers in Constantinople, but even went on an organizing tour of the East, putting the affairs of the Churches in order.[52] Gregory has given us a vivid picture not only of the divisions which split the capital,[53] and the zeal with which religious controversy was pursued,[54] but also of the inherent violence of the situation—he himself was actually mobbed in the course of the Easter celebrations of 379.[55] It is not without significance that during this period Gregory preached two sermons on Peace,[56] and one on Moderation in Disputes![57]

The problem which now faces us is how we are to place Eunomius in all this. It is significant that during this period an apparent change seems to have come over his approach. To begin with, as we have seen, he was extremely cautious and took care to restrict his new work to sympathetic circles. By the latter part of 380, however, we find him openly drawing large crowds to hear him speak.[58] Since we are also told that one of his usual means of instruction was the public recitation of his writings,[59] it is difficult not to connect a *magnum opus* produced at just this period with this activity. But how are we to account for this apparent change? Let us look again at the progress of events during this period.

When Eunomius first returned to Constantinople, Gratian was still sole Emperor, but on 3 January 379 he invested Theodosius with the purple as his eastern colleague. While no one would have been under any illusions as to the probable religious tendencies of a westerner chosen by an Orthodox Emperor, Theodosius' delay in entering his capital city as well as his preoccupation with fighting the barbarians must have permitted the initial chaotic conditions to continue for some time. By the summer of 379, however, things had already begun to change. Quite apart from the repeal of the edict of toleration by the Emperor Gratian (3 August 379),[60] we find that

---

[50] Ibid., 609-30 (*PG* 37.1071-2).   [51] Ibid., 631-51 (*PG* 37.1072-4).

[52] Philost., *HE* ix.18 (*GCS* 125.2-6).

[53] Grg. Naz., *Carm. Vit.* 652-720 (*PG* 37.1074-9).

[54] Grg. Naz., *Or.* 27.2 (Mason 3.5-11).

[55] Grg. Naz., *Ep.* 77.1-3 (*GCS* 66.10-19), 78.1-4 (*GCS* 68.15-28).

[56] Grg. Naz., *Or.* 22 (*PG* 35.1132A-1152A), 23 (*PG* 35.1152B-1168A).

[57] Grg. Naz., *Or.* 32 (*PG* 36.173A-212C).

[58] Soz., *HE* vii.6 (*GCS* 307.17-20).

[59] Soc., *HE* v.20 (*PG* 67.620B-C), Soz., *HE* vii.17 (*GCS* 324.17-20).

[60] *Cod. Theod.* xvi.5.5 (Mommsen i, pars posterior, p. 856).

Gregory of Nazianzus had already begun to account the Emperors as members of his own party:

σὺ τὸν σὸν βασιλέα, κἀγὼ τοὺς ἐμούς· σὺ τὸν Ἀχαάβ, ἐγὼ τὸν Ἰωσίαν.[61]

You have your Emperor, and I have my Emperors; you have Ahab, I Josiah.

If in the summer of 379 it might still have been possible to take such allusions lightly, the events of the following year were enough to cause second thoughts. In a law dated 27 February 380 and addressed specifically to the people of Constantinople, Theodosius commanded all peoples to follow that faith delivered by the Apostle Peter to the Romans and now followed by Damasus of Rome and Peter of Alexandria. Further, he declared that only these were to be designated by the title 'Catholic Christians'.[62] The baptism of Theodosius shortly thereafter by Ascholius, the Orthodox bishop of Thessalonica, must have made things even clearer.[63] While the practical effects of this edict may have been for the moment negligible, it made crystal clear which way things were going. It is fortunate, therefore, that we possess an account of the Arian party's reaction to these events:

Ἔτι δὲ ᾽οὗτοι, πλῆθος ὄντες ἐκ τῆς Κωνσταντίου καὶ Οὐάλεντος ῥοπῆς, ἀδεέστερον συνιόντες περὶ θεοῦ καὶ οὐσίας αὐτοῦ δημοσίᾳ διελέγοντο καὶ ἀποπειρᾶσθαι τοῦ βασιλέως ἔπειθον τοὺς ὁμόφρονας αὐτοῖς ἐν τοῖς βασιλείοις. ἡγοῦντο γὰρ ἐπιτεύξεσθαι τῆς ἐπιχειρήσεως τὰ ἐπὶ Κωνσταντίου συμβάντα σκοποῦντες. τοῦτο δὲ αὐτὸ καὶ τοῖς ἀπὸ καθόλου ἐκκλησίας φροντίδας καὶ φόβον ἐκίνει· οὐχ ἥκιστα δὲ περιδεεῖς ἦσαν λογιζόμενοι τὴν ἐν ταῖς διαλέξεσιν Εὐνομίου δεινότητα.[64]

These (Arians), however, still numerous on account of the influence of Constantius and Valens, were continuing to meet without fear and discoursing publicly about God and his essence. They persuaded some of their co-religionists at court to make an attempt to win over the Emperor. Indeed, looking for precedent to what happened under Constantius, they thought they might really succeed in their undertaking, a possibility which caused heart-searchings and fear among the Catholic party, not the least

---

[61] Grg. Naz., Or. 33.2 (PG 36.216c); dated to the period after Easter 379 by P. Gallay, La vie de St. Grégoire de Nazianze (Lyons/Paris: Emmanuel Vitte, 1943), pp. 145-6. The reference to Josiah is enough to show what Gregory's expectations were, even if at this point they may have been as much pious hope as sober thinking.

[62] Cod. Theod. xvi.1.2 (Mommsen i, pars posterior, p. 833).

[63] For the baptism after the decree and the literature, see N. Q. King, The Emperor Theodosius and the Establishment of Christianity (London: SCM, 1961), p. 30 n. 3.　　　　　　　　　　　　　　[64] Soz., HE vii.6 (GCS 307.9–15).

part of whose apprehension came from their recognition of Eunomius' formidable skill in debate.

That such a plan might have succeeded was not an entirely forlorn hope. Contemporaries did not have our own knowledge of Theodosius' subsequent policies, and at this early date he was inclined to be conciliatory, to judge from Gregory of Nazianzus' evident dissatisfaction with him.[65] The fear that the reigning monarch might be won over by a heretical body seems to have been one of the abiding anxieties of late Roman life. We may note that even at a much later period, when the Eunomian Church was in manifest decline, the Emperor Anastasius is said to have been publicly rebuked by the populace for Eunomian leanings, a story which, however unlikely as fact, fully reveals the reality of the concern.[66] In the present instance, indeed, the plan seems to have come very near to succeeding, for Eunomius' preaching attracted the attention of the Emperor and, until dissuaded by the Empress Flacilla, he actually expressed a desire to meet him personally.[67] The fact that the plan was ultimately foiled need not lessen its interest for our own purposes, for it shows Eunomius an apparent participant in a plan sponsored by the 'official' Arian party, a party headed by that same Demophilus who had perhaps been responsible for his exile and who was certainly his bitter opponent.[68] Seemingly, then, between the time of Eunomius' cautious arrival in the city and these last desperate efforts of the Arian party to retain its hold on power, a reconciliation had taken place, even if it was to prove only a temporary one.[69]

This conclusion leaves us with a tantalizing possibility. For while the fragmentary state of the evidence makes it inevitably somewhat conjectural, it can (if true) enable us to understand some of Eunomius' purposes in writing this, his second apology. The main

[65] Grg. Naz., *Carm. Vit.* 1279-1304 ff. (*PG* 37.1117-8).

[66] *Excerpta Valesiana*, pars posterior 13.78.

[67] Soz., *HE* vii.6 (*GCS* 307.19-23).   [68] Philost., *HE* ix.11 (*GCS* 120.4-7).

[69] Although Sozomen was obviously ignorant of Eunomius' exile, he was clearly aware that a break had existed between Eunomius and the 'official' Arians during the time of Eudoxius, *HE* vi.26 (*GCS* 273.10-17). He is not, therefore, likely simply to have confused the two groups. However, he also describes Demophilus and Eunomius as leaders of the Arian and Eunomian parties respectively at Theodosius' 'Council of Heresies', *HE* vii.12 (*GCS* 316.1-2); whatever *modus vivendi* may have been established, therefore, must have been short-lived.

purpose, of course, was the ostensible one, the defence of his own position against a hostile attack. In addition to being a step-by-step rebuttal of Basil's treatise, however, it was also a fairly systematic presentation of Eunomius' own theology.[70] In this guise, there is every reason to suppose that it was one of the works used in Eunomius' public meetings as part of his attempt to spread his influence and gain converts,[71] an endeavour in which he was not wholly unsuccessful, for he was even able to gain supporters at the Imperial court.[72] It is possible, indeed, that this explains why he was able to continue publishing his book, and was not immediately exiled. But if Eunomius' apology was directed in part at high court officials as well as the general public, we must ask ourselves if they were the only ones whom he hoped to influence. His earlier work was, as we have seen, most probably addressed to the Council of homoean bishops assembled at Constantinople in 360, while the immediate cause of that exile during which he wrote the first part of the *Apologia Apologiae* was the hostility of those same homoean bishops under Valens. If after his return from exile and the publication of his book we find him reconciled, if only briefly, with these bishops, we must ask ourselves why. While it is easy to fall into the fallacy of *post quod, propter quod*, it seems not unlikely that one of the purposes of this work was his own rehabilitation in the eyes of the ruling 'orthodoxy', a purpose certainly begun during his exile and partially consummated on his recall. While in view of the nature of the evidence this conclusion is inevitably speculative, it none the less provides us with a framework within which we may understand both Eunomius' actions and some of the aims and purposes which moved him to write this, his second apology.

III. THE QUOTATIONS OF GREGORY OF NYSSA

We have already noted that this work has come down to us only in fragments preserved by Gregory of Nyssa. The next problem which faces us is one which arises directly out of that fact. We must ask ourselves how accurate Gregory's quotations are, and to what extent he has conformed them to his own purposes; still more

---

[70] Cf., e.g., the lengthy systematic résumé of Eunomius' teaching found in *Apol. Apol.* i (*J* i.71.28-73.15).

[71] See the references in n. 59 above.

[72] Philost., *HE* x.6 (*GCS* 127.23-128.3).

importantly we must ask how confidently we can use them ourselves. We may note in this regard that Gregory was perfectly prepared to accuse Eunomius of misquoting,[73] and shows an awareness that his own accuracy might be called in question.[74] Moreover, Gregory specifically states that at least in some respects he is following the practice of Basil,[75] and the latter's treatment of the text, while far from cavalier, is none the less very selective and often paraphrastic.[76] Beyond this, Gregory's frequent use of sarcastic misapprehension[77] must be taken into consideration, and we have already seen that he is not above 'economizing' the truth on occasion.[78] The question of accuracy, therefore, is a real one, and must be faced before we can treat the text with any confidence.

When we do look at Gregory's treatment of Eunomius, we find that at least on the surface there is good reason to believe that he does not deliberately misquote him (as opposed to interpreting him tendentiously!). We find that he several times refers his readers to the original or assumes that they have access to it and are in a position to check him.[79] Moreover, when we examine his manner of citation in detail, we find that he frequently gives quite specific indications of the accuracy of his quotations. He makes a careful distinction between those cases where he is reproducing the text of Eunomius with *verbatim* accuracy,[80] and those where he is

[73] GN I (J i.187.19–188.13), II (J i.404.24–7).
[74] GN III.vii (J ii.228.5–9), viii (J ii.251.16–18), ix (J ii.287.8–11).
[75] GN I (J i.29.15–20).
[76] Compare Basil's highly paraphrastic treatment of Eunomius at *Eun.* ii.14 (597B) ~ *Apol.* 13.1–7, and *Eun.* ii.33 (649B) ~ *Apol.* 20.15–19.
[77] Cf., e.g., GN I (J i.156.4–160.2; 216.23–217.25), II (J i.282.29–286.7; 401.10–402.18), etc.
[78] See the discussion in *Liber Apologeticus*, Introduction, section II, above.
[79] GN II (J i.385.1–11; cf. 388.25–9), III.v (J ii.168.5–8), ix (J ii.287.8–11), x (J ii.310.28–311.3); cf. also GN III.vi (J ii.251.16–18) where he shows that he is aware that he may be charged with συκοφαντία.
[80] He expresses this in various ways, most frequently by ἐπὶ λέξεως, GN I (J i.71.25–6; 142.27–143.2; 216.15–16), II (J i.262.28–263.3; 311.28–30; 366.16–18; 374.2 (Basil); 379.32–380.2),˙III.i (J ii.111.27; 129.13–14), vi (J ii.200.25–6), ix (J ii.271.28–272.1; 272.16–17), and κατὰ (αὐτὴν τὴν)λέξιν, GN I (J i.164.1; 165.20), II (J i.303.6; 315.31; 318.15–16), III.ii (J ii.52.3–4; 82.6–7), viii (J ii.250.23–4); other less widely used phrases are (κατ') αὐτὰ τὰ ῥήματα GN I (J i.145.20–2), II (J i.406.26–7), III.ix (J ii.276.22), ἐπὶ ῥημάτων, GN II (J i.347.3–4), αὐτοῖς . . . τοῖς ῥήμασι, GN III.i (J ii.44.7–8), αὐτὴν . . . τὴν ῥῆσιν, GN III.ii (J ii.76.6–7), αὐτὰ τὰ γεγραμμένα, GN II (J i.60.11–12; 216.15–16), αὐτὴν τὴν λέξιν, GN I (J i.145.8–9), αὐταῖς , , , ταῖς . . . φωναῖς, GN II (J i.271.16–17), τοῖς σοῖς λόγοις, GN II (J i.408.32).

epitomizing him or merely giving the general sense[81] while using his own style and vocabulary.[82] In so far as he gives reasons for paraphrasing, it is generally because he says that to quote verbatim would be too tiring for himself or for his readers,[83] or because he wants to eliminate abusive language,[84] or so that he need not subject his readers to the roughness and verbosity of Eunomius' style.[85] We note, too, that where he says that his paraphrase is intended to make the meaning clearer, it is generally after he has already quoted the passage in full elsewhere.[86] Thus, while we have no way of checking him and may be sure that he was prepared to put Eunomius in the worst light possible, at least on his own say-so Gregory did not substantially distort the text by reworking it. While Gregory may not always give us Eunomius' exact words, we may count on him to give us the thought they represent. Any other policy, indeed, would have undermined his whole purpose in writing a refutation.

If we may be confident, therefore, about the substantial veracity of Gregory when he actually quotes Eunomius, we cannot help wondering how much he has given us out of a work said to have extended to 'many thousands of lines' (ἐπῶν).[87] Gregory was presenting a lawyer's case, not a dispassionate disquisition, and it is only natural to suppose that he selected those passages for quotation which were most damaging to his adversary. He was obviously aware of the problem of selectivity and found himself torn between a desire to avoid excessive length and the need to consider all the arguments.[88] There is no question but that he eliminated a great

---

[81] Usually expressed by the word διάνοια, e.g. *GN* I (*J* i.165.16-20), II (*J* i.347.3-4), III.ii (*J* ii.73.14-16), but also by κατασκευή in opposition to τῇ ἐμαυτοῦ λέξει, *GN* II (*J* i.366.30-367.1), and by τὸν νοῦν τῶν εἰρημένων, *GN* III.ii (*J* ii.53.5-6).

[82] Thus, e.g., in addition to those mentioned in the preceding note we find *GN* I (*J* i.181.12-18), II (*J* i.282.15-18; 302.27-8; 372.5-6; 391.14-17), III.iii (*J* ii.116.29-117.5; 124.18-20).

[83] *GN* II (*J* i.262.28-263.3), III.ii (*J* ii.73.14-15).

[84] *GN* I (*J* i.181.12-18), II (*J* i.302.27-8).

[85] *GN* I (*J* i.282.15-18; 372.5-6); cf. E. Norden, *Die antike Kunstprosa* ii (Leipzig/Berlin: Teubner, 1909), pp. 558 ff.

[86] *GN* I (*J* i.165.16-20; cf. 71.25-6), III.ii (*J* ii.53.5-6), iii (*J* ii.116.29-117.5).

[87] *GN* II (*J* i.325.24). The lines referred to, however, may be those of Gregory's refutation rather than Eunomius' apology.

[88] *GN* II (*J* i.324.30-325.28), III.ix (*J* ii.279.24-280.17).

deal.[89] Fortunately, he has given us a description of his policy:

ἐπειδὴ τοίνυν δύο προκειμένων ἡμῖν, τοῦ τε διὰ πάντων τὸν λόγον ἐλθεῖν καὶ τοῦ τοῖς ἀναγκαιοτέροις μόνοις ἐπιδραμεῖν. τὸ μὲν ἐπαχθὲς τοῖς ἀκούουσι, τὸ δὲ τοῖς διαβάλλουσιν ὕποπτον, καλῶς ἔχειν φημὶ μέσην τινὰ τραπόμενον ἐκφυγεῖν ἑκατέρωθεν ὡς οἷόν τε τὸ ὑπαίτιον. τίς οὖν ἡ μέθοδος; πάντων τῶν κατὰ τὸ μάταιον πεπονημένων αὐτῷ συντεμόντες ὡς οἷόν τε τὸν πολὺν συρφετὸν δι' ὀλίγων ἐπιδραμούμεθα κεφαλαιωδῶς τὰ νοήματα, ὡς μήτε τοῖς ἀνοήτοις ἐμβαθύνειν εἰκῇ μήτε τι τῶν εἰρημένων περιϊδεῖν ἀνεξέταστον.[90]

Two roads, then, lie before us: either to go over the work in complete detail, or to touch only on its stronger points—the one burdensome to the hearers, the other an opening for critics. I think, therefore, a kind of middle way the best, as putting to flight, so far as possible, the accusations of either side. What then is to be our method? Clearing aside as far as we can all the rubbish of his useless productions, we shall briefly touch on the main points of his arguments. Thus we shall neither rashly plunge ourselves into his nonsense, nor pass over any saying unexamined.

Thus, while attempting to deal with the work as a whole (if not always in order), Gregory will take up only its more important arguments in detail, and will pass over those of lesser significance.

On the whole Gregory's statement is supported by the evidence of his work itself. It is clear that in general he discusses each part of Eunomius' apology in turn. For example, he occasionally gives indications of the structure of the work, and mentions the preface[91] or the end[92] of a book. He frequently draws attention to the fact that his quotations are consecutive by the use of such phrases as 'the following' (ἀκολουθία),[93] or 'after a little he adds',[94] or 'immediately following'.[95] However, if we can be fairly sure that Gregory follows Eunomius grosso modo, the same cannot always be said in detail. Quite apart from the fact that the sheer number of omissions sometimes makes it difficult to follow the train of Eunomius'

[89] Thus, e.g., GN II (J i.341.22-6), III.v (J ii.182.19-21), viii (J ii.247.14-20), ix (J ii.279.24-280.3).

[90] GN II (J i.325.28-326.5).

[91] (Bk. I) GN I (J i.27.11-12; 28.27; 29.25; 42.18; 163.28); (Bk. III) GN III.i (J ii.4.18-19).

[92] (Bk. II) GN II (J i.404.22).

[93] GN I (J i.121.4-5; 140.3), II (J i.356.28-9), III.i (J ii.41.21), ii (J ii.91.4; 105.5), vi (J ii.185.14-15).

[94] GN I (J i.121.5, 11), II (J i.274.26-7), III.iv (J ii.149.6-8), v (J ii.171.21-2), ix (J ii.283.11-16).

[95] GN I (J i.146.20-1).

thought, it is clear that Gregory occasionally rearranges the argument or cites it only in random fragments. Thus, in his refutation of the opening section of Eunomius' first book, he asks the point of going over the whole thing in order (κατὰ τὴν τοῦ λόγου τάξιν).[96] Indeed, between Gregory's very allusive manner of quotation and the fact that he apparently went over the same material several times (a phenomenon also visible in several other passages), it is now virtually impossible to restore the original order with any confidence. Elsewhere we find several instances of places where Gregory rearranged the order to suit his own convenience.[97] Thus, while we may be sure that Gregory follows the main lines of Eunomius' arguments, this assurance must not be pressed too far.

When we turn to Gregory's omissions, we find that we can place them under a number of headings. Apart from his frequent use of paraleipsis,[98] we find that he passes over sections because they are unimportant, stupid, or vain,[99] because they are too ridiculous to bother refuting,[100] because they do not contribute to the argument,[101] or might weary his readers,[102] because he needs to get on to more important matters,[103] or sees no reason to repeat something already refuted,[104] because he fears to revolt his readers,[105] or (most often) does not wish to retail abuse.[106] A varied list, but sufficient to show us the extent of Gregory's omissions as well as the possibility of distortion which may arise from them. It seems, then, that the greatest problems in dealing with the *Apologia Apologiae* will arise not from what Gregory gives us, but from what he does not. Within limits we can accept the passages which Gregory does quote as substantially accurate; what we frequently cannot do is judge those quotations within their context, and this must inevitably give rise to distortions. In dealing with this

[96] *GN* I (*J* i.29.21-2).
[97] e.g. *GN* III.i (*J* ii.6.3-6, omitted passage given at ii.27.21-2; 47.21-5), iii (*J* ii.119.4-9), vii (*J* ii.217.13-16).
[98] e.g. *GN* II (*J* i.311.18-23; 345.25-346.6; 398.4-6; 399.16-400.1).
[99] *GN* I (*J* i.29.11-15), II (*J* i.339.8-15; 342.15-21; 403.5-10), III.ii (*J* ii.122.5-9).
[100] *GN* II (*J* i.363.13-16; 385.1-11), III.v (*J* ii.166.24-167.2), vi (*J* ii.205.9-12).
[101] *GN* II (*J* i.380.10-12).   [102] *GN* II (*J* i.323.16-23; 324.19-29).
[103] *GN* I (*J* i.71.3-17).
[104] *GN* II (*J* i.356.17-20; 378.14-16), III.vi (*J* ii.185.3-10), viii (*J* ii.247.14-20).
[105] *GN* II (*J* i.393.1-13), III.v (*J* ii.168.8-11).
[106] *GN* I (*J* i.49.24-50.2; 53.11-13; 164.5-10; 164.28-165.2), II (*J* i.313.10-14; 356.6-7; 357.9-15; 359.14-18; 406.16-18, 23-6; 407.16-28), III.iii (*J* ii.117.15-17).

most important of Eunomius' surviving works, then, while we may be generally confident in the text Gregory gives us, we must always be conscious of the great deal he does not, and, since we frequently cannot judge their context, that many of the surviving fragments have been chosen purely for their damaging potential. Despite this, we cannot but be grateful that Gregory chose to refute his opponent so thoroughly, for without him a work which was perhaps Eunomius' *magnum opus* would have disappeared without a trace.

IV. STRUCTURE AND CONTENTS

As has already been noted, Eunomius' second apology is a step by step refutation of Basil's *Adversus Eunomium*; its structure therefore is largely based on his and, indirectly, on that of the *Liber Apologeticus*. No outline less detailed than that given below with the list of fragments is likely to prove useful here, but we can give a brief general summary of the contents of each book.

Book I is a defence of the first seven chapters of the *Liber Apologeticus* against Basil's attack in *Eun.* i.1-5 (*PG* 29.497A-520B). Apart from the preface, this defence is divided into two parts. The first is historical, a defence of Eunomius' claim to have presented his apology at a real trial before real judges; the second is more properly theological. Eunomius rejects Basil's claim that he should have begun his treatise with a flat assertion of 'the Unbegotten' and then proceeds to a defence of *Apol.* 7.3-15, his first arguments for the absolute and unbegotten nature of God.

Book II undertakes the defence of Eunomius' assertion in *Apol.* 8 (and following) that God's very essence is to be unbegotten and that this unbegottenness is not in name only but in reality and in very truth — apart from and prior to any human word or concept. Basil had attacked this in *Eun.* i.5-14 (*PG* 29.520C-544B) by asserting that the titles and names of God, even those in holy scripture, are predicated of him through the exercise of a God-given human mental faculty (κατ' ἐπίνοιαν). Even when they are divinely inspired, therefore, they cannot give us any direct knowledge of the essence of God, for that remains unknowable. In Eunomius' view this was blasphemous, for it seemed to undermine the possibility of any real knowledge or revelation of God.[107] In order to guarantee

---

[107] See the fragments listed below under Bk. II sections ii-iii.

the reality of God's revelation, therefore, and in particular to guarantee the real separate identities of the divine persons as revealed by their names,[108] Eunomius developed an elaborate theory of language ultimately based on that found in the *Cratylus* of Plato.[109] According to this theory words are directly expressive of the essences to which they refer and have their origin in the divine creative act recorded in Genesis.[110] The divine names thus refer directly to the divine essences and manifest the separate identities of each. Book II is largely devoted to the development of this theory. Its first part is devoted to the refutation of Basil's theory and to the scriptural defence of his own. The second part defends the unity of the eternal divine life against Basil's contention that its eternity is perceived through a comparison with the temporal order. The third part undertakes the defence of Eunomius' discussion of 'privation' in *Apol.* 8.7-18 against the attacks of Basil.

The third and final surviving book is a defence of Eunomius' doctrine of the generation of the Son as found in *Apol.* 11.15 and following. After a discussion of the nature of generation, Eunomius goes on to defend his contention that the Son was begotten 'when as yet he was not'; the final argument takes up the defence of Eunomius' discussion of the differing senses of 'light' in *Apol.* 19.1-16. At this point the surviving fragments cease and the remainder is lost.

V. EDITIONS

Christ. Henr. Georg. Rettberg, *Marcelliana. Accedit Eunomii ΕΚΘΕΣΙΣ ΠΙΣΤΕΩΣ Emendatior* (Gottingae: sumptibus Vandenhoek et Ruprecht, 1794), pp. 125-48.

---

[108] The antecedents of Eunomius' theory are not easy to determine, but at least one of the concerns behind it is that expressed in the so-called Second Creed of Antioch (Hahn, no. 154, pp. 185-6) regarding Matt. 28: 19: '. . . the names not being given without meaning or effect, but denoting accurately the peculiar subsistence, rank and glory of each that is named . . .' (translation of J. N. D. Kelly, *Early Christian Creeds* (London: Longman, 1950), p. 269). This is one of the points at which Eunomius differed sharply from Arius, who regarded God as ἀκατάληπτος, cf. Philost., *HE* ii.3 (*GCS* 14.1-3), i.2 (*GCS* 6.1-5).

[109] As first recognized by J. Daniélou, 'Eunome l'arien et l'exégèse néo-platonicienne du Cratyle', *REG* 69 (1956), 412-32. In Eunomius' own view, of course, he was merely presenting the authentic teaching of scripture, cf. the fragments of Bk. II section ii below.   [110] Cf. Bk. II section ii below.

This edition by C. H. G. Rettberg (1736-1806) is the only known attempt, even if partial, to publish the fragments of Eunomius' *Apologia Apologiae* apart from the *Contra Eunomium* of Gregory of Nyssa.[111] While Rettberg made no attempt to produce a complete edition, he did publish fifteen of the most important fragments, chiefly from Gregory's third book (*vulgate* books iii-xii). His comments on these fragments are highly perceptive and in many cases still retain their usefulness.

J   Werner Jaeger, ed., *Gregorii Nysseni Opera* (Leiden: E. J. Brill, 1921, second edition, 1960), vols. i and ii, *Contra Eunomium Libri*.

Although Jaeger never fulfilled his intention of bringing out a separate edition of the fragments of Eunomius,[112] he took a first step in this direction by italicizing these fragments as they occur in the text of Gregory. This, together with the fact that he restored the original order of Gregory's books (and hence of Eunomius' fragments), accounts for his mention here. The passages selected for italicization are generally reliable, but there is some inconsistency in detail. At some points isolated words quoted from longer fragments are italicized every time they occur, while at other points they are ignored. At times passages which are largely summaries of the argument by Gregory are italicized while similar passages elsewhere are ignored. There are also on occasion errors in gauging the precise extent of fragments. Most of these problems arise less from any carelessness on Jaeger's part than from the difficulties inherent in Gregory's editorial technique. While these problems must be kept in mind, we must also recognize the great service which Jaeger has performed not only in enabling us to read Eunomius' fragments in sequence, but in making them genuinely available to us.

L. Abramowski, 'Eunomios', *Reallexikon für Antike und Christentum* (Stuttgart: Anton Hiersemann, 1966), vol. vi, cols. 940-2.

---

[111] Note also that on pp. 119-24 of this work there are a number of highly perceptive notes on the *Liber Apologeticus*.

[112] Cf. *J* ii, p. vii. Apparently it was because he intended to publish the fragments separately that his apparatus did not give passages of scripture cited by Eunomius.

H. C. Brennecke, 'Nachtrage zum Reallexikon für Antike und Christentum: Stellenkonkordanz zum artikel 'Eunomios' (RAC 6 [1966] 936/47)', in *Jahrbuch für Antike und Christentum* 18 (1975), 202–5.

In her excellent article on Eunomius in the *Reallexikon für Antike und Christentum* Professor Abramowski did not attempt to present the text of Eunomius' lost work; rather, she listed in order each of the fragments as they occur in the first edition of Jaeger's text of the *Contra Eunomium* (1921). Although she based her work on the fragments italicized by Jaeger, she did not list separately those fragments which appear several times. In 1975 H. C. Brennecke brought her article up to date by publishing her original listings together with the corresponding passages in Jaeger's second edition of 1960.

VI. THE PRESENT EDITION

The present edition follows in the footsteps of that of L. Abramowski in that its fundamental component is a list of the surviving fragments. Considerations of space and the very diverse nature of the fragments as presented by Gregory have made it impossible to give the actual text. In order to make it as easy as possible for the reader to follow the main lines of the work, we have organized our edition as follows:

1. The volume, page, and line numbers of each fragment are given as in Jaeger's second edition (1960) of the *Contra Eunomium* (= *J*) on the left hand side of the page. The fragments are listed in their original order so far as this can be determined; where this differs from Gregory's order the fragment is indented.

2. An English summary is given with each fragment. This is not a translation but is intended to give the main points of the fragment and to relate it to its context. Read consecutively, the summaries (with the notes) give a general idea of the main lines of the work.

3. At the end of each summary the page, column, and line numbers are given for the only English translation of the *Contra Eunomium*, that in *The Nicene and Post-Nicene Fathers*, second series, vol. v.[113]

[113] We have included this with some reluctance as there is no easy way to refer to specific passages, and the translation, being designed to convey Gregory's

4. Words of theological or other importance have been listed in the *Index Verborum* at the end of all.

5. The passages of Basil's *Adversus Eunomium* being refuted are listed as sub-headings in the text and a summary of the relevant portions is given in the notes.

It is our hope that in presenting the fragments in this manner, we will have to some extent made up for the loss of this interesting and important ancient work.

understanding of a passage, often does less than justice to that of Eunomius. It is, however, the only English translation, is readily available, and will be of use to the English reader. Some of the very short passages have not been included.

ΥΠΕΡ ΤΗΣ ΑΠΟΛΟΓΙΑΣ ΑΠΟΛΟΓΙΑ[1]
AN APOLOGY FOR THE APOLOGY

BOOK I[2]

i. ἐν προοιμίοις[3]

a. Opening paragraph[4]

J i: 27.4-5[5]

27.16-17

28.27-29.13[a]   Eunomius is hated by his enemies for the truth's sake (37b.11-28).[6]

29.25-30.2   He gives a lengthy account of a dream.[7]

b. ἡ ἱστορία: a reply to Basil, Eun. i.2 (501B-505B)[8]

1. Events surrounding the Council of Ancyra (358)

30.6-9   Eunomius' tribulations.

30.14-31.2   His encounter with Basil of Ancyra and Eustathius of Sebaste; his condemnation by the Council (38a.6-20).[9]

---

[a]28.28-29.2 ~ 42.17-18; 28.28 ~ 44.21-2, 47.21

---

[1] Title: *GN* I (*J* i.29.26; 42.24-43.1), cf. II (*J* i.392.7-10).

[2] Cf. *GN* II (*J* i.226.6) and I (*J* i.22.4).

[3] So *GN* I (*J* i.27.11/12, 28.27, 29.25, 42.18). The reconstruction of this opening section is rendered appreciably more difficult by the fact that Gregory chose not to go over it 'in order' (*J* i.29.21-2).

[4] Cf. *GN* I (*J* i.28.27, 29.25): εὐθύς.

[5] Though some of Eunomius' language seems to be preserved here, this fragment may in fact be only Gregory's mocking imitation of his 'Sotadean' style (*J* i.27.13).

[6] The number in parentheses at the end of the longer fragments represents page, column, and line in *The Nicene and Post-Nicene Fathers*, second series, vol. v.

[7] Unfortunately not repeated by Gregory; the mention of a μακρὰν τοῦ ὀνείρου . . . διήγησιν (30.1-2) seems to allude to some such experience as that recorded of Aetius in Philost., *HE* iii.15 (*GCS* 46.19-21).

[8] So *GN* I (*J* i.30.13, 31.14, 16, 21, 32.3, 41.9-10); Basil had claimed that Eunomius' first apology was only a literary fiction and that it had never been presented publicly in the context of a real trial. Eunomius' response was to give an account of the events leading up to the presentation of his defence.

[9] So *GN* I (*J* i.41.7-9), though the names are not actually given; a clearer account, which may in fact be based on this passage, is to be found in Philost., *HE* iv.8 (*GCS* 61.17-62.24).

J i: 31.7-12   He is accused of complicity in the revolt of the
                             Caesar Gallus in 354 (38a.26-33).[10]

32.6-8, 18-33.1   Abuse of Basil and Eustathius.

33.6-8, 13-16[b]   Eunomius is exiled to Phrygia (38b.32-44).[11]

                             2. Eunomius' early life[12]

33.17-34.3,[c]   Eunomius' youth and upbringing (38b.44-
  cf. 39.3-23   39a.6).

34.5-7

34.12-17   His increasing notoriety (39a.16-22).

40.16-21   (?) Eunomius' baptism (40b.35-45).[13]

41.15

         3. Events surrounding the Councils of Seleucia (359) and
                         Constantinople (360)[14]

49.9-22   The council gathers; Eunomius flees home
                             (43b.7-20).[15]

50.4-10   The importance of the council and its partici-
                             pants (43b.27-35).[16]

  [b] 33.13-14 = 43.15-16   [c] 33.20-34.3 ~ 56.15-18

---

[10] Aetius had in fact been a confidant of Gallus and to some extent of Julian (Philost., *HE* iii.27 (*GCS* 52.18-53.10)); it was inevitable that he should have been suspected of complicity and that Eunomius should have been involved in his teacher's downfall, cf. Philost., *HE* iv.8 (*GCS* 61.17-62.5).

[11] Apparently at this point Eunomius mentioned Aetius, who was also exiled at this time, and thus called forth the unflattering discussion by Gregory of the latter's life and background in *GN* I (*J* i.34.18-39.2).

[12] This autobiographical digression appears to be part of Eunomius' lament over the disgrace of exile, cf. *GN* I (*J* i.41.19-24).

[13] These lines are not italicized by Jaeger and yet clearly reflect something in the text Gregory had before him; they apparently formed part of a larger account of Eunomius' relationship with Aetius, cf. *GN* I (*J* i.39.24-41.2). Since the reference to baptism itself is clear enough, the logical assumption is that the baptism referred to is Eunomius' own.

[14] Eunomius did not give the actual name of the council at which he was condemned (cf. *GN* I (*J* i.49.8-11)), but the fragments preserved clearly allude to the language used by Basil of Seleucia and Constantinople (see the following notes), and this is the sense in which they were taken by Gregory (*GN* I (*J* i.50.18-23)). There is also evidence from the *Contra Eunomium* of Theodore of Mopsuestia that the affair of Cyril of Jerusalem and Acacius of Caesarea was discussed at this point, see R. P. Vaggione, 'Some Neglected Fragments of Theodore of Mopsuestia's *Contra Eunomium*', *JTS* 31 (1980), 456-7.

[15] Cf. Basil, *Eun.* 1.2 (*PG* 29.504c5-7).

[16] *J* i.50.4-5 = Basil, *Eun.* i.2 (*PG* 29.504c7-8), 50.13-14 = ibid. (*PG* 29.504c9-10)

50.13-14		Basil of Caesarea, though present (at Constantinople?), shrank from the struggle (43b. 38-41).[17]
51.17-21 =	44.4-7, 10	Eunomius was condemned by default (44a.32-7).[18]
	44.15-18	His jury were the prosecutors (42a.3-7).
	45.18-20[d]	= *Apol.* 2.2-3.[19]
	46.12-13	= *Apol.* 6.6.[20]
	47.8-11	Eunomius was driven over land and sea (42b.43-8).
54.6-17[e] ~	47.22-7	Abuse of Basil of Caesarea.
57.14-16[f]		Abuse of Basil of Caesarea.[21]
57.20-1		Basil had wrongly called Eunomius a Galatian though he was in fact a Cappadocian.[22]
60.1		
51.23-8		Basil's own words show that Eunomius' apology was not a literary fiction (44a.41-6).[23]
60.12-16,[g] cf. 6-11		Basil admits that Eunomius received the bishopric of Cyzicus as the 'prize' in a real contest (46b.36-42).[24]
63.2-10[h]		Basil is accused of cowardice (47b.1-10).[25]

[d]45.19-20 = 48.17-18, cf. 55.16-20   [e]54.6-7 = 55.14-15; 54.7-8 = 55.15-16; 54.8-9, 10 = 55.23-5; 54.10-11 = 56.15-16, 56.12/13 = 56.15   [f]57.14-15 = 58.4   [g] 60.12-13 = 61.16-18   [h]63.2 = 66.2-3, 68.17 (cf. 70.11); 63.2-3 = 70.12-13; 63.7 ~ 66.3; 63.5-6 = 66.4; 63.6 = 68.18

---

[17] Cf. Philost., *HE* iv.12 (*GCS* 64.5-7) and Eunomius' own comments at *J* i.63.2-10; presumably this episode was introduced to provide a justification for Eunomius' allowing himself to be condemned by default at Seleucia. On the role of Basil at this council, see S. Giet, 'Sainte Basile et le concile de Constantinople de 360', *JTS* 6 (1955), 94-9.   [18] Cf. Basil, *Eun.* i.2 (*PG* 29.504c11).

[19] Quoted by Basil, *Eun.* i.3 (*PG* 29.505B-508A).

[20] Not quoted by Basil and perhaps, therefore, quoted by Eunomius himself.

[21] This and the preceding string of abusive epithets may have been provoked by Basil's own shorter list in *Eun.* i.1 (*PG* 29.501B).

[22] In Basil, *Eun.* i.1 (*PG* 29.500c). Gregory, *GN* I (*J* i.58.1-3) claims not to have found this phrase in his copy. Eunomius was in fact from a border region.

[23] This fragment is clearly out of place in its present location in Gregory; it is most logically seen as the preface to the quotation of Basil given in 60.12-16.

[24] Quoting Basil, *Eun.* i.2 (*PG* 29.505A15-B1).

[25] It is not impossible that *GN* I (*J* i.70.13-17) also reflects something of Eunomius' language. The matter intervening between this and the next section has been omitted according to *GN* I (*J* i.53.11-13).

ii. ὁ περὶ τοῦ δόγματος λόγος.[26]

a. *A reply to Basil,* Eun. *i.4 (512B)*[27]

J i:

71.28-73.15[i]

Our whole doctrine is summed up in the highest and principal essence, in the essence which exists through it but before all others, and in the essence which is third in terms of origin and the activity which produced it. This same order is revealed whether we consider the essences themselves or approach them through their characteristic activities (50a.13-b.16).[28]

156.4-8[j]

The argument turns from providence to the manner of the (divine) begetting (76b.7-13).[29]

---

[i]71.28-72.7 = 73.20-6; 71.28-72.1 = 75.14-15; 72.1 = 76.23, 78.1, 137.17; 72.1-2 = 75.18-19, 76.6-7, 78.7, 81.23-4, 96.29, 97.2/3, 137.19, 146.4-5, 148.16-17, 151.21, 159.23; 72.2-4 = 82.6-8; 72.6-7 = 82.17; 72.7-10 = 86.17-19; 72.9 = 86.22, 87.3, 8, 20/1, 88.11; 72.10 = 74.24-5, 82.2, 86.25-6, 217.6; 72.10-18 = 91.20-92.1; 72.10-12 = 92.18-20; 72.10-11 = 92.3-4, 94.15-17, 95.20; 72.11 = 96.4; 72.11-12 = 96.14-15; 72.12 = 96.16, 25; 72.12-18 = 97.24-98.1; 72.12-13 = 98.5-6, 9; 72.13, 14, etc. = 88.18, 89.8, 90.26, 149.27; 72.13-15 = 98.16-18 (cf. 99.4-5); 72.14-15 = 150.3-4; 72.15-17 = 101.12-14 (cf. 92.9-10, 109.15-16); 72.15-18: cf. 121.5-10; 72.16-17 = 112.23-4; 72.18-73.3 = 121.11-21; 72.19-20 = 122.2-3; 72.20-3 = 123.2-4; 72.23-4 = 125.3-4, 128.8, 17, 133.3/4, 134.6, 137.15/16, 139.26; 72.24 = 139.27; 72.23-6 = 122.15-19, 124.19-22; 72.26-73.3 = 140.3-7; 72.26-73.1 = 140.8-9, 25-6, 141.29-142.1; 73.1-3 = 143.9-11, 144.16-17; 73.3 = 146.3; 73.3-13 = 145.10-20; 73.4-5 = 146.21-3, 28-30, 147.2-3; 73.6 = 147.3-4, 8; 73.8-12: cf. 159.18-19; 73.11-12 = 153.3-4   [j]156.7-8 = 156.11-12, 17-18, 157.7-8, 15-16, 25, 158.4, 9-11, 16-18, 27-8; 156.8 = 157.28-158.1, 159.14-15.

---

[26] So *GN* i (*J* i.42.16, cf. 53.13).

[27] The whole of the following argument is designed to refute Basil's claim (ad loc.) that if Eunomius had really intended to 'lay out unveiled the naked truth' (*Apol.* 3.4-5), he would have begun with a flat assertion of the *agenneton* and the *anomoion*.   [28] = Rettberg, *Frag.* 1 (pp. 125-7).

[29] This is apparently a reiterated portion of a larger fragment lost to us through a lacuna in the manuscripts of Gregory, cf. *J* i.154.1-4 and Jaeger's comments ad loc. The missing section doubtless dealt with the activities of the various essences as revealed in divine providence (cf. *J* i.72.20-73.12); having completed this, Eunomius tries to show the impossibility of begetting in the proper sense within these essences.

160.11-13 = 161.7-8	The manner of the begetting is shown by the status of the begetter (77b.46-8).
164.1-5ᵏ	As against Basil, it is not necessary to begin with a flat assertion of *agennesia* and the difference in the essences (79a.17-22).[30]
164.10-27ˡ 165.24-5	Begetting within the divine essence is a contradiction in terms (79a.29-50).[31]

b. *A reply to Basil*, Eun. *i.5 (516D-517A)*[32]

182.2-6ᵐ = 182.9-12	The folly of Basil's rejection of 'Unbegotten' in favour of 'Father' (85a.41-7).
189.4-11ⁿ	He might better have kept silent altogether (87b.49-54).
186.3-10ᵒ	A *reductio ad absurdum*: If 'Father' is the same as 'Unbegotten', then 'Father' means 'from nothing', not 'begetter of the Son' (86b.31-8).[33]
192.20-193.1ᵖ	But if God is 'Father' because he begot the Son, and 'Father' is equivalent to 'Unbegotten', then God was not unbegotten before he begot the Son (89a.9-14).

ᵏ164.3 = 163.16/17, 173.24, 174.15   ˡ164.13-17 = 166.2-6; 164.16-17 = 168.18-20; 164.24-7 = 168.24-8   ᵐ182.2-3 = 183.16-17   ⁿ189.7-11 = 185.26-8   ᵒ186.3-10: cf. 188.27-189.3; 186.6-8: cf. 189.22-3 ᵖ192.20-193.1: cf. 195.7-10; 192.20-2 = 193.10-11; 192.22-193.1: cf. 199.24-5; 192.23-193.1 = 193.20-3; 192.24-193.1 = 193.30-194.1

---

[30] Gregory here omits a lengthy section of the work because of its abuse of Basil, *GN* I (*J* i.164.5-10, 28-165.2).

[31] At *J* i.165.10-16 Gregory gives a paraphrase of this passage in his own words, *GN* I (*J* i.165.16-20).

[32] Basil had contended that, however true in itself, the use of the word 'Unbegotten' ought to be discontinued in favour of the word 'Father' on the grounds that it was not found in scripture and had been abused by Eunomius. Gregory, *GN* I (*J* i.181.12-182.1), complains that in quoting this passage Eunomius had left off a crucial qualification.

[33] It is clear from Gregory's statement at *GN* I (*J* i.199.18-28) that this fragment and the two following (*J* i.192.20-193.1, 201.26-202.5) are to be taken as part of the same argument, preceded by that at *J* i.189.4-11 (cited in part earlier at 185.26-8).

J i:

198.27

201.26–202.5[q] Another *reductio ad absurdum*: If 'Father' is equivalent to 'Unbegotten', then we ought to be able to say things such as, 'The Unbegotten is the Unbegotten of the Son' (92a.10–15).

201.3–5[r] What sensible person would suppress the natural meaning of a word in favour of a secondary meaning (91b.41–3)?

c. *A reply to Basil,* Eun. *i.5 (517B–520B)*[34]

214.6–10 Basil's ineptitude and failure to understand Eunomius' meaning (96a.35–8).[35]

214.21–2, 215.13–14 = *Apol.* 7.10–11.[36]

215.16–17 = *Apol.* 7.10.

216.12–13

216.16–22[s] In the face of Basil's criticism, Eunomius clarifies his meaning (97a.22–31).[37]

[q]201.26–202.5 = 199.4–10, 203.10–15; 201.27–202.2: cf. 199.26–8; 202.2–3 = 200.30; 202.3–5 = 200.1–2; 202.4–5 = 200.10–11 [r]201.4–5 = 201.11–13 [s]216.17–18 = 216.23–4, 25; 216.21–2 = 217.10–12

[34] This section, only fragmentarily preserved, is a reply to Basil's critique of the assertion in *Apol.* 7.10–11 that 'what follows from this is the Unbegotten, or rather, that he is unbegotten essence.'

[35] The burden of this passage seems to have been that Basil (deliberately?) misunderstood Eunomius' meaning, cf. *GN* I (*J* i.214.25–214.12); it was in this context that Eunomius referred to or quoted the following passages from the *Liber Apologeticus*.

[36] The use of (*παρ*)*έπεσθαι* here shows that Gregory at any rate (and perhaps Eunomius) is quoting the version of this passage given by Basil in *Eun.* i.5 (*PG* 29.517C–520A) and not the *Liber Apologeticus* directly.

[37] *J* i.216.16/17 = *Apol.* 7.11; 216.18 = *Apol.* 7.10/11. Basil had claimed that Eunomius' statement that 'the Unbegotten' 'followed' from his arguments meant that God's unbegottenness was adventitious and secondary; Eunomius replies that his statement applied only to our manner of expression, not to God's being.

BOOK II[1]

i. *A reply to Basil*, Eun. *i.5-6 (520C-524B)*[2]

J i:

[233.11-17[a]]	A summary by Gregory of Eunomius' argument that 'Unbegotten' designates the nature of God (252b.10-18).[3]
238.11-12	Cf. *Apol.* 8.16-18.
238.15-16	Cf. *Apol.* 8.15.
238.18-19	Cf. *Apol.* 11.1-3.
238.26-9	Cf. *Apol.* 8.1-5.
245.1-5[b]	= *Apol.* 8.14-18.[4]
270.1-4[c]	Basil rejoices in God's life by means of invented names; God rejoiced in it before the creation of anyone to invent them (265b.3-6).
271.11-16	Eunomius will dispel Basil's ignorant understanding of his meaning (266a.3-9).
271.17-22[d]	He notes the real context of his statement in *Apol.* 8.3-7 (266a.11-15).[5]

[a]233.13/14, 15 = 233.18; 233.17 = 234.2, 235.7, 12   [b]245.5: cf. 317.6-7
[c]270.1-2 = 270.25-6; 270.1 = 270.15-16, 271.9-10, 272.31; 270.2 = 270.16, 18, 21; 270.3-4 = 270.5-6   [d]271.11-16, 17-22: cf. 272.13-16, 274.7-10; 271.18-19 = 286.7; 271.21-2: cf. 273.16-17, 276.12-13

---

[1] Title: cf. *GN* II (*J* i.226.10; 230.11-12; 245.16; and Gregory's own transmitted title, 226.2).

[2] As Gregory sarcastically indicates in *GN* II (*J* i.229.29-230.14), this book is almost wholly consecrated to the refutation of Basil's contention that (scriptural) names and titles can be and are predicated of God by means of human invention (κατ' ἐπίνοιαν), cf. also *J* i.240.10-12.

[3] The introduction to this book appears to be wholly lost. The present fragment (in brackets) is part of Gregory's summary of Eunomius' position in contradistinction to that of the Orthodox, just gone over in outline, *GN* II (*J* i.230.15-18); since the passages which follow are all paraphrases of the *Liber Apologeticus*, it is not impossible that the same is true of the first, in which case it would summarize the whole of *Apol.* 8 and *Apol.* 8.1-3, 14-18 in particular. There is, of course, no way to be sure.

[4] This quotation appears to have been made by Eunomius himself, cf. *GN* II (*J* i.244.28-245.1).

[5] Basil had quoted this passage in *Eun.* i.5 (*PG* 29.520c) and then given an interpretation of it, ibid. i.6 (*PG* 29.521A); Eunomius complains that he had only quoted part of it and gives the complete text.

J i:

274.25-30, cf. 268.20-4	The folly of thinking that invented names are older than those who invent them (267a.22-8).[6]
276.22-9	Genuine invented names are mental constructs (267b.49-57).[7]

ii. *A reply to Basil,* Eun. *i.6 (524B-C)*[8]

281.25-7	Basil's eisegesis; his shrinking from the witness of scripture (269b.19-22).
282.1-14	By introducing pagan philosophy into his analysis he has denied providence and rejected the scriptures which portray God as using names before the existence of human beings (269b.27-270a.10).[9]
282.26-7 = 302.26-7	Basil is the advocate of a perverted (linguistic) usage.[10]

---

[6] Though not italicized by Jaeger, *J* i.268.20-4 seems to contain a portion of the present argument. Eunomius' point appears to be that Scripture portrays God as making use of names before the existence of human beings (cf. *J* i.303.1-6); if as Basil contends these words are based on human invention, they must be older than those who invented them!

[7] Replying to Basil, *Eun.* i.6 (*PG* 29.521B, 524A). Basil, taking up Eunomius' contention in *Apol.* 8.3-5 that invented words 'have their existence in name and utterance only', argued that all human conceptions would therefore be completely arbitrary and fictional, like centaurs or pygmies; Eunomius responded by admitting that conceptions of this kind do exist, but asserted that they are the exception rather than the rule.

[8] According to *GN* II (*J* i.281.27-282.1), immediately following the fragment which begins this section (281.25-7) Eunomius quoted Basil, *Eun.* i.6 (*PG* 29.524B-C). In this passage Basil discussed the analytical powers of the human mind by using the word 'grain' as an example and analysing it into the concepts (ἐπίνοιαι) 'fruit', 'seed', and 'food'. Though this was clearly not Basil's intention (cf. his comment on taking up a new argument in *Eun.* i.7 (524C), καὶ παρὰ τοῦ θείου δεδιδάγμεθα λόγου), Eunomius understood him to be referring to holy scripture and in particular to Gen. 1: 11-12. This explains his accusing Basil of adulterating the witness of scripture and his own exegesis of the opening chapters of Genesis which immediately follow.

[9] *J* i.282.12-14: cf. Gen. 1: 11-12. This fragment is a paraphrase of Gregory's (cf. *GN* II (*J* i.282.15-18)) and seems in large part to be a summary of the argument developed in the following fragments.

[10] Eunomius here takes up Basil's use of the word συνήθεια in *Eun.* i.6 (*PG* 29.521C4, 524B6).

284.30-285.3[e]   In the creation narrative, Moses shows that God himself used words in creating (270b. 48-56).[11]

303.1-6[f]   Moses bears witness that God gave human beings the use of both the things named and their names, and that the names are older than those who use them (277a.11-17).[12]

342.21-9   If our first parents had not been taught the names of things by God, they would have been irrational and dumb, unable to make use of creation (290a.49-58).[13]

344.8-13[g]   The Creator's greatness is shown in the fitting bestowal of names as well as in the things made (290b.48-52).

345.12-16   From these things it is clearly shown that God made names conformable to natures (291a.36-40).[14]

311.24-8[h]   Basil thinks human thought is more important than the providence of God (279b.49-53).

345.25-9   His doctrine of 'invention' is equivalent to

---

[e]284.30-285.3: cf. 282.30-283.2, 284.1-4   [f]303.2-4 = 303.9-10, cf. 317.24
[g]344.12 = 345.23   [h]311.24 = 310.8; 311.24-6 = 312.2-3

---

[11] J i.284.31-2: Gen. 1: 3; 284.32: Gen. 1: 6; 285.1: Gen. 1: 9; 285.2a: Gen. 1: 11; 284.2b: Gen. 1: 20.

[12] J i.303.1-6: cf. Gen. 2: 19-20. Gregory, GN II (J i.311.18-24), seems to indicate an omission at this point, presumably of Eunomius' further exegesis of Genesis (see the fragments cited out of sequence immediately below). It is not clear how far this exegesis went but Gregory's own arguments in GN II (J i.300.27-302.24) suggest that it may have included the assertion that the original language was Hebrew.

[13] J i.342.21-9: cf. Gen. 2: 19-20. Gregory tells us in GN II (J i.342.15-21) that he will now return to deal with some material found ἔκ τινων τῶν κατὰ τὸ μέσον. It is clear enough that this involves the partial repetition of the preceding argument, but the precise locations of the individual fragments within the argument are more difficult to determine. In what follows we have indented the fragments listed out of sequence but have not attempted to show more than their general place in the argument.

[14] Because the passage is cited by Gregory out of context, it is not clear what 'these things' refers to; the most likely supposition is that it is the preceding argument from scripture.

J i: the teaching of Epicurus (291b.10-15).[15]
346.4-11   In asserting it, Basil agrees with Aristotle in
                                denying providence (291b.22-31).
346.12-15   Basil is challenged either to deny the creation
                                of the world by God or admit it and not
                                reject the bestowal of names (291b.32-5).
346.20-347.1   God's providence combined the transmission
                                of names with the knowledge and use of
                                things (291b.43-51).[16]

iii. *A reply to Basil*, Eun. *i.7 (524c-d)*[17]

312.30-313.3   Basil not only perverts scripture, but even
                                defames God (280a.39-41).
313.16-18[i]   Which of the saints ever said that the titles of
                                Christ were applied to him by way of human
                                invention (280b.1-3)?
315.31-316.3   Contrary to the teaching of the apostles and
                                evangelists, Basil derives these titles from
                                human invention (281a.41-5).
316.6-11[j]   To ascribe what are in fact equivocal terms
                                based on analogy to human invention is to
                                pervert scripture (281a.48-b.2).
318.10-15[k]   God (in scripture) has allowed the lowest things
                                to share the names of the most honourable, but
                                without any interchange of rank (282a.30-6).
323.23-6   Human inventiveness has not been given
                                authority over names (283b.57-60).[18]

---

[i] 313.16-18: cf. 317.3-4   [j] 316.7: cf. 316.23-4; 316.8-11: cf. 320.23-5
[k] 318.10-13 = 318.24-7, cf. 322.12-13; 318.10-11; cf. 319.26-7, 320.28-9;
318.13 = 323.14

---

[15] Though not italicized by Jaeger, this passage clearly contains fragments of Eunomius' language.

[16] Gregory has here omitted other similar passages, *GN* II (*J* i.347.1-3).

[17] In this passage Basil raised the issue of the application of the scriptural terms 'door', 'way', 'bread', 'vine', 'shepherd', 'light', etc., to Christ; since these words could hardly refer to his nature, they must be applied by way of 'invention'. Gregory tells us that Eunomius quoted this passage immediately following the first fragment of this section, *GN* II (*J* i.313.4-10).

[18] It is apparent from *GN* II (*J* i.323.16-22) that there has been an omission at this point.

347.4-6	The invention of new words is not to be ascribed to poets (291b.56-8).[19]
347.18-21	The saints are not said by scripture to have invented new words (292a.11-15).
348.6-10	Since God has not refused to speak with his servants, it must be supposed that from the beginning he has given them proper words with which to do so (292a.30-33).
324.1-5	The Creator, by means of relationship, activity, and analogy, has apportioned names suitable to each thing (284a.9-13).
350.6-9	David bears witness that God calls the stars by their names (292b.48-52).[20]
326.14-18	Basil says that our first act of thought about something is analysed in a second stage which is called 'invention' (284b.49-52).[21]
326.19-22	But where there are not two stages of thought there can be no such 'invention' (284b.54-8);
327.9-12	If an apostle or prophet had used the titles under discussion of Christ, Basil would have a case (285a.23-6),
328.21-5[1]	But as the Lord has used them of himself, there are not two stages of thought and therefore no 'invention' (285b.21-5).
329.26-8	Such names are not bestowed upon the Lord by another (286a.5-7).

[1] 328.21-5: cf. 328.8-14

---

[19] In this and the following fragments Gregory has given the sense rather than the exact words of the argument, *GN* II (*J* i.347.3-5).

[20] *J* i.350.8-9: Ps. 146(147): 4. Eunomius seems to have given a more extensive scriptural proof at this point, including an explanation of the name of Adam, cf. *GN* II (*J* i.356.4-10).

[21] The argument found here and in the following fragments is given only κεφαλαι-ωδῶς, *GN* II (*J* i.325.30-326.5). It refers back to Basil's statement in *Eun.* i.6 (*PG* 29.524B7 ff.) on the stages of human thought (see n. 8 above) and relates it to his discussion of the titles of Christ: since these titles were revealed by Christ himself and not deduced by the apostles they cannot be 'inventions' in the sense meant by Basil.

iv. *A reply to Basil,* Eun. *i.7 (525B-C)*[22]

J i:

331.17-21[m]	Basil blasphemes the God who is over all (286b.7-10).[23]
356.20-4	The grain of Valentinus is stored up in his soul (295a.22-5).[24]
332.7-10	After having speculated about 'wheat' and the titles of Christ, Basil even declares that the essence of God admits of a variety of invented notions (286b.31-5).[25]
332.18-22	He had already said that the Only-begotten God can admit of such notions (286b.45-50),[26]
332.23-4 = 332.29-333.1	But what a ridiculous blasphemy it is to compare the Unbegotten to such things (286b. 52-287a.1)![27]
357.9-14	Abuse of Basil (295a.43-8).
359.19-20, cf. 360.1-3	It is from the Aeons that Basil lends God his superiority (296a.21-2).
360.3-4	He divides the Aeons in two (past and future) (296a.40-4)!
361.27-8	What does he think the Aeons are?

[m] 331.19-20 = 331.22; 331.20 = 331.23-4

---

[22] It is clear from *GN* II (*J* i.331.3-17) that a new argument began at this point. Eunomius now turned to a discussion of Basil's application of his idea of 'invention' to God himself.

[23] *J* i.331.18: Rom. 9: 5; this may be based on Basil's use of τοῦ Θεοῦ τῶν ὅλων in *Eun.* i.7 (*PG* 29.525B11).

[24] *J* i.356.20-1: Matt. 13: 25-6. Gregory has omitted a good deal here (cf. *GN* II (*J* i.356.17-20)) but it is clear enough that Eunomius profited by Basil's earlier analysis of the word 'wheat' to bring in an allusion to the parable of the tares and the wheat. The reference to Valentinus is explained by the discussion of the 'aeons' later in the argument.

[25] Gregory gives a general outline of this argument in *GN* II (*J* i.333.14-24; 339.16-340.4). [26] *J* i.332.18-19: cf. Jn. 1: 18.

[27] Although it is no longer clear at what precise point he did so, in the course of this argument Eunomius quoted Basil's remark about God's incorruption and unbegottenness in *Eun.* i.7 (*PG* 29.525B-C). Basil had said that if we look back at God's infinite life in the aeons which preceded us, we speak of 'unbegotten'; if we look forward to the aeons yet to come, we speak of 'incorruptible'. It is of these remarks that the following is a detailed refutation, cf. *GN* II (*J* i.356.29-357.9).

362.7-11   If you say that the Aeons are eternal, you are
                  pagans, Valentinians, barbarians; if you say
                  that they are not, then God is not un-
                  begotten (297a.6-10),

362.23-5   For if it is by comparison with the Aeons that
                  God is without beginning, then, if the Aeons
                  do not exist, neither does the one compared
                  to them (297a.27-30).

v. *A reply to Basil,* Eun. *i.8 (528B-529C)*[28]

363.16-18[n]   The divine life which is without beginning
                  and without ending is one (297b.12-15).

364.1-8 ⎫   But if there is a single divine life, every name
367.9-14 ⎭   applied to it must effectively signify the same
                  divine essence (297b.29-37, 298b.38-40).

368.6-18[o]   This single divine life must have a single
                  inner meaning, even if the names expressing
                  it are different; real meanings are deter-
                  mined on the basis of the underlying objects,
                  so that (if their names are different) either
                  the reference is to a different object or there
                  is no difference in meaning (299a.10-25).[29]

370.20-3   All designations used of the divine nature
                  agree in meaning with one another in

[n] 363.16-18: cf. 363.27-8   [o] 368.6-18: cf. 367.2-6; 368.6-7 = 368.21;
368.6-9: cf. 370.20-3; 368.7-9 = 368.22-4; 368.9-16 = 366.18-25; 368.13-18
= 368.24-369.1; 368.14-15 = 369.31-370.2

[28] Basil, after ridiculing the idea that all names referring to God, because they
refer to the same subject, must signify the same thing, goes on to say that this very
argument in fact leads to the conclusion that the Father and Son are one because
they share the same attributes: how could the single attribute 'unbegottenness' show
a difference in essence when there are so many others to show identity? The following
is Eunomius' attempt to reply to this attack by defending his basic contention; in the
course of it he refers back to some of Basil's earlier statements.

[29] There is some question about the order at this point but it seems likely that
J i.368.6-18 belongs after 367.9-14, and that the portion cited before it (366.18-25
is identical with 368.9-16) was quoted by Gregory out of order.

J i:	accordance with the thing signified (299b. 40-3).[30]
334.23-4p	God is not 'incorruptible' and 'unbegotten' in the same way that he is 'Father' and 'creator' (287b.27-30).[31]
370.14-19	'Father' is more recent than God's other names, for he became 'Father' from begetting (299b.33-9).
371.5-9q	The names 'Father' and 'creator' are applied to God on the basis of his activities (300a. 7-12).
337.14-16r	It is in terms of the essence itself that God is incorruptible and unbegotten, for he is simple and unmixed (288b.16-18).
373.10-13s	But if we must use a more detailed argument, according to them even the essence itself is not unmixed (300b.35-9),[32]
373.16-23 = 380.2-10t	For if God is incorruptible and unbegotten only because his life is without beginning or ending, then in so far as he is not incorruptible he is corruptible, and not unbegotten he is begotten; thus, on the side of

p 334.23-4: cf. 333.25-6   q 371.8 = 371.13, 16   r 337.14 = 336.22-3;
337.14-15: cf. 337.1-2   s 373.11 = 373.24   t 373.16-20 = 375.1-5;
373.21-3 = 376.23-6

---

[30] It is possible that this fragment is part of an earlier section of the argument, cf. *GN* II (*J* i.370.19-20); on the other hand, it may be Gregory's own summary of the preceding fragment.

[31] This seems to be the sense of the argument; it is difficult to be certain because Gregory has quoted very little of the context. The connection of this argument with that in *J* i.370 ff. is shown by the mention of τῆς τοῦ πατρὸς καὶ τοῦ δημιουργοῦ προσηγορίας at *J* i.371.6-7. *J* i.333.25-6 is apparently Gregory's paraphrase of this passage as the use of the word 'Father' there is his. It appears, too, that it was in the course of this argument that Eunomius made the assertion alluded to by Gregory at *J* i.339.22-4 that the most fitting αἰτία for God to beget the Son was his unmastered power (cf. *J* i.339.8-11).

[32] Immediately preceding this fragment, Jaeger has italicized *J* i.371.31-372.5. Since Gregory himself, however, has described this as a paraphrase given in his own words (*J* i.372.5-6) and since it reproduces the order of ideas found in the succeeding fragments, it is apparently a summary of the argument by Gregory and not a fragment in its own right.

	beginninglessness he will be Unbegotten and corruptible, on the side of endlessness, incorruptible and begotten (300b.41-9).
382.11-12	But God is unbegotten by nature, not by comparison with the Aeons (303b.52-4).
382.22-6 ⎫ 383.10-12 ⎭	God's single life, beginninglessly incorruptible and endlessly unbegotten, is uncomposed and incomparable (304a.10-14, 32-5).
340.9-11	God was not given his name by the Son or by the intelligible beings made through him (289b.14-16).[33]
341.23-6	The madness of asserting that God's name is based on invention (290a.14-17).
385.11-13	God's status is higher and older than Basil's 'invention' (305a.3-4).
385.21-4	A law of nature teaches us that the status of names derives from the things named, not from the authority of the one who does the naming (305a.15-18).
386.5-7	It is in accordance with the law of Providence that words are bestowed upon things from above (305a.15-18).
386.18-20	The Provider, by a law of creation, has sown them in our souls (305a.53-6).
388.2-7	On Basil's theory there are two possibilities: either the invention is older than its inventors or words belonging naturally to God before creation are later than man (305b.50-6).
388.29-30	God's essence itself is incorruptibility and immortality (306a.27-8).[34]

[33] It is difficult to identify the locations of this and the following fragment in the argument. Gregory gives little of their context and is here preparing to go over the same material a second time; it may be that these two fragments are in fact parallel with materials found at *J* i.274 ff. and *J* i.284 ff. and belong with that. On the other hand, they are at the end of a series of fragments dealing with Basil, *Eun.* i.8 (*PG* 29.529A-B) and fit in well with them; indeed, it may be that the μανία of the second fragment (*J* i.341.23) picks up the charge of μανία made by Basil in *Eun.* i.8 (*PG* 29.529A). In any case we may note that Gregory has omitted a good deal at this point, *GN* II (*J* i.341.22-3).

[34] Gregory may be summarizing Eunomius' position rather than quoting directly.

vi. *A reply to Basil,* Eun. *i.9 (532A-533C)*[35]

J i: 391.19-27	The folly of those who assert that God is un-begotten by way of privation (307a.26-36).
392.11-19[u]	In his perplexity, Basil accuses us of using pagan learning, and claims a monopoly of the Holy Spirit (307b.2-10).[36]
395.25-6	
398.7-11[v]	Basil thinks more of the forms of words than the things they designate (309b.13-17).[37]

vii. *A reply to Basil,* Eun. *i.10 (533C-536C)*[38]

399.4-8	'Privation' is not used indiscriminately: it refers to privation of the good, not the bad (310a.12-16).[39]
399.14-16 = 402.29-31	Basil neither understands how to distinguish the actual objects nor how to use their names (310a.25-7).[40]
399.23-5	We do not think it right for the forms of words to be twisted into inappropriate inventions (310a.37-43).

[u] 392.13-14: cf. 391.20-2   [v] 398.9-10 = 398.14-15

---

[35] As is clear from the introductory remarks of Gregory (*GN* II (*J* i.391.9-11)), the following fragments mark the beginning of Eunomius' defence of his assertion in *Apol.* 8.7-14 that, though privative in form, 'unbegotten' is not privative in meaning. His argument, however, is only given by Gregory διὰ συντομίας ἐπὶ κεφαλαίῳ, *GN* II (*J* i.391.14-17).

[36] *J* i.392.17-18: cf. Basil, *Eun.* i.9 (*PG* 29.532A-B).

[37] *J* i.398.7-11: cf. Basil, *Eun.* i.9 (*PG* 29.532B-C). At this point Eunomius introduced a discussion of Scriptural passages showing the distinction between the word 'immortality' as used of angels and of human beings, so *GN* II (*J* i.398.24-8).

[38] Basil's main contention in this chapter is that words applied to God (by 'invention') are of two kinds: those which are negative and assert that God does *not* possess a certain quality, and those which are positive and assert that he does. In neither case is there any single word which expresses directly the nature of God.

[39] The fragments in this section appear designed to refute Basil, *Eun.* i.10 (*PG* 29.533C-536A). In this passage Basil argued that words such as 'incorruptible' are not only privative in form, they are also privative in meaning; that is, they tell us of qualities which God does not possess. Eunomius' reply is to accuse Basil of using these words' privative form to pervert their meaning—God cannot be anything on the basis of a negation!

[40] Gregory has omitted something at this point, *GN* II (*J* i.399.16-18).

400.22-6	How can God be above his works on the basis of what he does not possess (310b.18-20)?[41]
401.7-10	God surpasses mortals as being immortal, corruptible things as incorruptible, begotten things as unbegotten (310b.48-51),
401.25-7[w]	Yet it is not because he *lacks* mortality or corruption that he is immortal and incorruptible (311a.23-6).

viii. *A reply to Basil,* Eun. *i.14 (544A-B)*[42]

| 403.10-12[x] | Truth bears witness to no union of natures with God (311b.33-4), |
| 403.16-18 | Nor has she inscribed any invention discovered by ourselves in Holy Scripture (311b.41-3). |

ix. *A reply to Basil,* Eun. *i.15 (545B-548B)*[43]

| 406.28-407.4[y] | Basil has unknowingly said that God is derived from nothing, for if he is, as Basil asserts, 'from none', and 'none' is equivalent to 'nothing', then God is from nothing (313a.29-38).[44] |
| 408.31-409.1 | |

[w] 401.25-7: cf. 402.8-9, 19-20   [x] 403.10-12: cf. 403.31-404.1
[y] 406.31-407.4 = 407.21-5; 406.31 = 408.18-19; 407.1-2 = 408.27-8; 407.3-4 = 404.23-4, cf. 406.14-16

---

[41] This seems to be a direct reply to Basil, *Eun.* i.10 (*PG* 29.536c), where Basil, having contended that 'unbegotten' is negative in meaning, says that God's very being cannot be numbered among the things which he is not!

[42] It is clear from his comments at *GN* II (*J* i.403.9-10) that Gregory passed over a good deal at this point. The following two fragments seem best understood as Eunomius' retort to Basil's scriptural argument in *Eun.* i.14 that, in contrast to creatures who know him 'by invention', the Father's essence is known to none but the Son and the Holy Spirit because they participate in it. Eunomius can reply that scripture bears no witness to a union of natures with God and that it contains nothing based on human invention.

[43] According to *GN* II (*J* i.404.22-3), this argument marked the end of the book. Eunomius began by quoting Basil, *Eun.* i.15 (so *GN* II (*J* i.404.24-7; 405.21-406.5)), which uses the 'reverse' genealogy of Luke 3: 23-38 to show that 'begotten' and 'unbegotten' are purely relational terms and do not refer to the essence.

[44] *J* i.406.31, 407.2 quotes Basil, *Eun.* i.15 (*PG* 29.548A3).

BOOK III[1]

i. ἐν προοιμίοις[2]

J ii:
4.20-5[a]
= 44.6-13

In accordance with the order of the (divine) natures and revelation, we assert that the Son, being begotten, may be called 'offspring of begetting', since his begotten essence and the word 'Son' make this appropriate (135b.19-25).

6.6-13[b]

The same argument applies in the case of the designations 'thing made' and 'creature'; our authority to use them derives from the relationships of the natures and the usage of the saints (136a.26-34).[3]

ii. *A reply to Basil*, Eun. *ii.2 (573c-576c)*[4]

10.25-11.8

The scriptural basis for speaking of the Son as 'thing made' and 'offspring' is Prov. 8: 22 and 1 Cor. 1: 24 (137b.27-38).[5]

35.2-5

Though 'son of the living God', the Lord is not

---

[a]4.20 = 5.2, 10-11; 4.20-1 = 5.14-15; 4.21-5 = 27.23-6, 44.21-6; 4.22-5 = 50.7-11; 4.22-3: cf. 56.19-20; 4.23 = 27.28; 4.23-4 = 34.12-15, 44.26-7
[b]6.7-8 = 6.13-14, cf. 22, 24; 6.9-10 = 7.21; 6.12-13: cf. 7.7-9, 11, 8.1, 26.27-8, 27.17

---

[1] Cf. *GN* iii.i (*J* ii.3.9, 4.19).

[2] Cf. ibid. (*J* ii.4.18). Jaeger (*J* ii.4.22 n.) connects the following fragments with Basil's refutation of Eun., *Apol.* 12.6-10 in *Eun.* ii.6 (*PG* 29.584A ff.). In view of Gregory's comments, however, it seems better to see the specific refutation of this passage as coming later and the present fragments as part of a preface to the argument as a whole.

[3] At *GN* iii.i (*J* ii.6.1) this fragment is described as being μικρὸν ὑποβάς and thus is presumably still part of the preface and not, as suggested by Jaeger (*J* ii.6.12), a reply to Basil's attack on *Apol.* 17.6-8 in *Eun.* ii.24 (*PG* 29.628c ff.).

[4] In the face of Eunomius' claim in *Apol.* 12.1-4 that his description of the Son as 'offspring' and 'thing made' was based on 'the words of the saints', Basil challenges him to name the actual passages.

[5] Gregory gives none of Eunomius' language here, but it is clear from the passage cited and the extensive refutation which follows that Eunomius responded to Basil's demand for the scriptural justification of his position by citing Prov. 8: 22 and 1 Cor. 1: 24.

	ashamed to call himself 'Son of Man' (145b. 16-20).[6]
46.21-47.16	Titles applied to the Only-begotten by scripture are to be taken in a sense befitting the divine; the same principle applies to the word 'Son' (149b.19-53).[7]

iii. *A reply to Basil,* Eun. *ii.6-7 (581B-585C)*[8]

52.4-15[c]	Who is so foolish as not to know that earthly bodies communicate their essences with passion by material means (152a.11-24)?[9]
61.8-14[d]	The Son's essence was not begotten of the Father by extension or division, but solely by the will of him who begot him (155b.8-14).[10]
66.18-25	The 'First-born of all creation' must be of the same essence as the creation itself; if that creation is of one essence with the Father, then so is the 'First-born'; if the creation is not, then neither is he (157a.44-52).[11]
73.15-17	Human beings do not 'create', they only give form to pre-existing material (159b.38-40).

[c]52.14-15: cf. 71.25   [d]61.8-14: cf. 61.25-62.4

---

[6] *J* ii.35.2-5: cf. Matt. 16: 13-17.

[7] = Rettberg, *Frag.* 2 (pp. 128-9). This fragment is clearly a reply to Basil, *Eun.* ii.2 (*PG* 29.576C), part of whose language it reproduces. *J* ii.46.22: Acts 4: 11; Matt. 3: 10 ~ Lk. 3: 9. *J* ii.46.23: 1 Cor. 3: 11; Jn. 6: 35 ff.; Jn. 15: 1; Jn. 10: 7, 9; Jn. 14: 6. *J* ii.46.23/4: Jn. 10: 11, 14. *J* ii.46.24: Jer. 2: 13, 17: 13, cf. Jn. 4: 14; Gen. 2: 9, 3: 22, 24, cf. Rev. 22: 2; Jn. 11: 25; Jn. 13: 13; Jn. 8: 12. *J* ii.47.10/11: Jn. 1: 18.

[8] Despite the suggestion of Jaeger (*J* ii.52.4-15 n.) that the following fragments refute Basil, *Eun.* ii.21-2 (*PG* 29.620A-B), it seems clear from both their content and their context that they are in fact refutations of Basil, *Eun.* ii.6 ff. (*PG* 29.581B-C ff.), Basil's contention that 'begetting' need not imply a material substratum. The following fragments seem to be Eunomius' defence of the 'natural order' of the divine natures as the basis for interpreting the word 'son' as applied to the Only-begotten.   [9] = Rettberg, *Frag.* 3 (pp. 129-30).

[10] = Rettberg, *Frag.* 4 (p. 130). There is a verbal echo of Basil, *Eun.* ii.6 (*PG* 29.581B14-C2). According to *GN* iii.ii (*J* ii.56.6-12) Eunomius here refuted Basil's prohibition of ὀνοματοποιΐα, i.e. the transformation of the scriptural words γέννησις, γεννάω into γέννημα, referring to Basil, *Eun.* ii.7 (*PG* 29.584C-585B), not (*pace* Jaeger ad loc.) directly to *Eun.* ii.22 (*PG* 29.620C-D).

[11] *J* ii.66.20, 24: Col. 1: 15.

J ii: Both agent and patient in human generation
74.2-5   and creation share the same nature (159b.
                           57-160a.2).

76.8-12ᵉ = 79.21-6 = 82.10-14 ⎫ It is the only essence established
86.28-87.3ᶠ = 91.4-7   ⎬ by the direct action of the Father
92.24-5   ⎭ which must be called 'offspring'
                           and 'thing made' and 'creature', for its begetting
                           was unmediated and it preserves its relation-
                           ship to its Begetter, Maker, and Creator
                           without separation; it is not to be compared to
                           any of the things made through it (160b.34-43,
                           164a.55-b.2, 166b.14-17).¹²

93.22-5   For the Begotten Essence, being *Only*-begotten,
                           leaves no place for any property shared with
                           another, nor is the Maker's (direct) action seen
                           to be shared (167a.2-6).¹³

96.24-97.5ᵍ   Having found nothing other than the Son's
                           essence to which begetting can be referred, we
                           believe that the names refer to the essence
                           (unless 'son' and 'begotten' are used in vain),
                           and are confirmed in separating the essences
                           (168a.15-24).¹⁴

105.5-14   Basil dishonours the begetting of the Son by
                           comparing it with human begetting (171a.
                           17-28).¹⁵

ᵉ76.9-12 = 83.13-15; 76.10-12 = 86.18-20   ᶠ86.28-87.3: cf. 76.13-15;
NB, 88.21-5 = 76.10-12 + 86.28-87.3; 87.1-3 = 91.25-7; 87.2-3 = 87.7-9
ᵍ96.25-6 = 101.9-10, 18, 101.28-102.1, cf. 102.17; 97.5 = 97.8-9, 10, 98.13-14

---

¹² *J* ii.88.21-5 = 76.10-12 + 86.28-87.3, showing that these fragments form
part of a continuous whole; *J* ii.76.13-15 is almost certainly a paraphrase of *J*
ii.86.28-87.3, not an independent fragment. According to *GN* ɪɪɪ.ii (*J* ii.92.8-12),
Eunomius' teaching at this point is based on that of Theognostus, head of the
catechetical school at Alexandria, *c*.265-82.

¹³ *J* ii.93.24: cf. Jn. 1: 18. As is evident from *GN* ɪɪɪ.ii (*J* ii.93.19-21), this
fragment is the immediate sequel to the preceding.

¹⁴ = Rettberg, *Frag.* 5 (p. 130). *J* ii.97.3-5: cf. Basil, *Eun.* ii.4 (*PG* 29.577c2-3).

¹⁵ Gregory here gives only a résumé of Eunomius' attack, though he seems to
preserve some of his language; at this point Eunomius apparently quoted Basil,
Eun. ii.24 (*PG* 29.625c).

iv. *A reply to Basil,* Eun. *ii.3* (576D–577A)[16]

112.10–116.28[h]   Basil preaches two Christs, the one divine and the other human, by perverting scripture to his own ends; then follows a *reductio ad absurdum* of Basil's interpretation of Acts 2: 36 and Phil. 2: 7, and an explanation of the real meaning of these passages (174a.21–175b.18).[17]

v. *A reply to Basil,* Eun. *ii.4* (577C)[18]

166.11–16[i]   Granted that the essences are distinct, then so also are the designations which signify them; things which have one and the same name are themselves one (193a.35–41).

---

[h]112.12 = 125.21; 112.14–15 = 128.6; 113.16, 17–18, 20, 28–114.1 = 117.22–4; 113.16–18, 115.14: cf. 124.26–7; 113.18–23: cf. 124.14–18; 113.18–19 = 125.7–8; 113.23–4 = 148.4–6; 113.26–8 = 149.8–10; 113.28–114.1 = 164.22–3; 114.3–11 = 149.10–18, 151.11–17; 114.3–9 = 150.11–16; 114.7–9 = 151.1–6; 114.9–11: cf. 143.28–9; 115.6–9 = 156.17–20, cf. 154.19–20; 115.9–17 = 141.26–142.6; 116.10–13 = 129.14–17   [i]166.11–16: cf. 80.8–10

---

[16] In discussing the meaning of Acts 2: 36, Basil denied that the Apostle intended to refer to the essence of the Only-begotten; in doing so he made a sharp distinction between the pre-existent Christ and the one 'who emptied himself' and became 'obedient unto death' (Phil. 2: 7). In what follows Eunomius accuses him of preaching two Christs.

[17] = Rettberg, *Frag.* 6 (pp. 133–7). *J* ii.112.10: Acts 2: 36; *J* ii.112.17: Jn. 1: 1; *J* ii.112.17–18: Acts 2: 36; *J* ii.112.18–20: cf. Phil. 2: 7–8; *J* ii.112.20–113.9: Basil, *Eun.* ii.3 (*PG* 29.576D–577A); *J* ii.114.3–4: Jn. 1: 1; *J* ii.114.15–16: Jn. 1: 1, 14; *J* ii.114.22–5: Phil. 2: 6–7; *J* ii.114.27: Jn. 1: 18; *J* ii.115.5–6: Jn. 1: 1; *J* ii.115.6: Jn. 1: 18; *J* ii.115.7: Jn. 1: 1; *J* ii.115.15: Jn. 1: 1; *J* ii.115.22–3: Acts 2: 36; *J* ii.116.4–5: 1 Cor. 8: 6; *J* ii.116.12–13: Jn. 1: 14; *J* ii.116.15–18: cf. Phil. 2: 6–8; *J* ii.116.19–20: 1 Cor. 2: 8; *J* ii.116.22–3: 2 Cor. 3: 17. It is not clear from Gregory's comments at *GN* III.iii (*J* ii.107.1–3) whether or not this passage was quoted in sequence. It seems probable, however, that throughout this section Eunomius did not refute Basil in order, but presented his own argument while citing passages from Basil at need.

[18] According to *GN* III.v (*J* ii.166.11), the first in this series of fragments came shortly after that in *J* ii.112.10–116.28. It is a defence of Eunomius' assertion in *Apol.* 12.3–4 (cf. 18.13–14) that the difference in the names of the divine persons shows a difference in their essences. Basil had attacked this in *Eun.* ii.4 (*PG* 29.577C) by pointing to the fact that some names refer to individuals sharing a common essence. Gregory mentions at *GN* III.v (*J* ii.166.24–168.4) that Eunomius had quoted this passage as a whole before attacking it; since he himself proposed to pass over much of it, the following fragments give only isolated portions of the argument.

J ii:	Praise of the significant concepts which reveal
168.11-12	the objects underlying them (193b.55-7).[19]
169.10-13	Who is so foolish, when speaking of human beings, as to call one thing 'a human being' and another 'a horse' by way of comparison (194a.30-5)?[20]
171.21-4 = 172.2-3	The immutability of the natural relationship between names and their object (195a.12-14).[21]
172.18-21	Not one right-thinking person has called begotten things 'unbegotten', or the God who is over all 'begotten' (195a.47-50).[22]
174.13-175.2[j]	If (as Basil contends) the names of individuals reveal genuine differences between them, the same must be said in the case of words which refer to essences; in enumerating the different names of the intelligible beings, the Apostle displays the distinction in their essences (196a.25-45).[23]
177.26-178.1	Basil's presumption in using material examples for the contemplation of intelligible realities (197a.41-7).[24]
182.25-183.2	Every individual united to the idea of an essence

[j] 174.14 = 182.19, 185.3

---

[19] According to *GN* III.v (*J.* ii.168.15-18) Eunomius here used language derived from Isocrates and Philo Judaeus.

[20] A reference apparently to Basil, *Eun.* ii.9 (*PG* 29.588c) where Basil mentions 'human being', 'horse', and 'cow' as examples of words referring directly to the things named.

[21] According to *GN* III.v (*J* ii.171.21-2), there was a small amount of material intervening between this and the preceding fragment.

[22] *J* ii.172.20-1: Rom. 9: 5.

[23] *J* ii.174.28-175.2: cf. Col. 1: 16 (so *GN* III.v (*J* ii.183.19-26)). The general reference of this passage is to Basil's argument in *Eun.* ii.4 (*PG* 29.577c) that some names (such as 'Peter' and 'Paul') refer not to essences but to individuals.

[24] It seems that more of Eunomius' language has been preserved here than has been italicized by Jaeger. It is possible that *GN* III.v (*J* ii.178.13-15) represents another fragment, but it is more probably a hypothetical argument put in Eunomius' mouth by Gregory.

exists corporeally and is joined to corruption (199a.23-6).[25]

vi. *A reply to Basil*, Eun. *ii.11-13 (592A-596D)*[26]

194.11-22[k]	We made two statements about the Son (in *Apol.* 12.10-12): (1) the Son's essence was not before it was begotten; (2) it was begotten before all other things (203b.5-19).[27]
205.17-20	Basil will be taken in his own snare (207b. 26-9);[28]
206.4-12[l]	What will he do if someone says, 'If to create is good and befits God, why did God not possess this good from the beginning and create eternally?' (207b.45-56)[29]
207.24-5, 28-208.2	If the Creator begins (to be such) from the time of the creation, then the Creator of time must begin to be (such) from the same kind of 'beginning' (208a.53-b.5).[30]

[k]194.11-14 = 200.26-201.1; 194.12-13: cf. 203.4-5, 10   [l]206.4-12: cf. 207.19-21; 206.4 = 206.14

---

[25] According to *GN* III.v (*J* ii.182.19-25) Gregory has omitted a good deal here. The point of the argument seems to be that individual exemplars of a common essence can only exist in a bodily way, i.e. where there is matter to differentiate them; purely immaterial beings (such as Father, Son, and Holy Spirit) must possess individual essences.

[26] Cf. *GN* III.vi (*J* ii.185.10-15); *J* ii.185.11 echoes Basil, *Eun.* II.11 (*PG* 29.592A). In these chapters Basil attacked Eunomius' contention that the Son was begotten before all other things 'when as yet he was not'. In the following fragments Eunomius clarifies his position and replies to Basil's arguments.

[27] = Rettberg, *Frag.* 7 (pp. 137-8).

[28] *J* ii.205.17-20 + 206.4-12 = Rettberg, *Frag.* 11 (pp. 140-1). *J* ii.205.20 (lit. 'caught with his own feathers'): cf. Aeschylus, *Frag.* 139 (Nauck p. 45). Gregory seems to have passed over some abuse of Basil here, cf. *GN* III.vi (*J* ii.205.8-12).

[29] This is a direct parody of Basil's argument in *Eun.* ii.12 (*PG* 29.593A) that if the act of begetting was 'good and befit God', God must have possessed that good and fitting thing from the very beginning.

[30] The proper extent of the fragment seems to include 207.28-208.2; Jaeger did not italicize the apodosis when resumed after an interjection. Eunomius is replying to Basil's contention in *Eun.* ii.13 (*PG* 29.596A-B) that to speak of the Son's essence as 'not being before its begetting' introduces time as a new principle between the Unbegotten and his Offspring. Eunomius replies that his phrase need no more imply such a new principle than the creation of time by God at any point would do.

J ii: 216.3-12[m]   God, as the highest good and in need of nothing, begets and creates in accordance with his own will; if, in accordance with this will, 'everything is good', then he defines not only the creature itself as good, but also the time when it should be created (211a.39-b.6).[31]

217.17-19   Before all other things that are begotten, God has dominion of his own power (212a.6-9).[32]

220.5-8[n]   When God willed to do so, it was good and proper that he should have begotten the Son, leaving no room for any enquiry as to why he did not do so earlier (213a.5-9).[33]

vii. *A reply to Basil*, Eun. *ii.15* (600C-604A)[34]

200.13-18   Basil shows his own ignorance by saying that the investigation of the terms used by the Spirit is impossible for human beings (213a.15-22).[35]

224.4-14[o]   No act of begetting goes on indefinitely, but comes to some end; if the Son was begotten, his begetting must have come to an end; if it came to an end, it must have begun; this is confirmed both by nature itself and the divine laws (214b.7-18).[36]

227.22-228.4   God shows in scripture that he rested from his works in order to show that he had also begun

---

[m] 216.3: cf. 217.17; 216.3-6: cf. 215.6-8; 216.4-5 = 216.15-18; 216.10-11 = 216.20-1   [n] 220.5-8: cf. 220.27-8   [o] 224.4-5 = 224.24-5; 224.4-6 = 226.7-9; 224.10-11: cf. 227.6; 224.12-14 = 227.8-10; 224.14 = 227.20

---

[31] = Rettberg, *Frag.* 8 (p. 139). *J* ii.216.9-10: cf. Gen. 1: 31.

[32] According to *GN* III.vii (*J* ii.217.19-23, 27-218.3), this statement is taken from Philo Judaeus; cf. Philo, *Leg. alleg.* iii.175 (Cohn and Wendland i.151.27-30).

[33] = Rettberg, *Frag.* 9 (p. 140).

[34] Basil continues his attack on Eunomius' teaching that the Son was begotten 'when as yet he was not' by examining the opening lines of the gospels, in particular Jn. 1: 1. Eunomius replies with a scriptural argument of his own.

[35] *J* ii.220.13-15: cf. Basil, *Eun.* ii.15 (*PG* 29.601A). The 'terms' (λόγοι) to be investigated are those of scripture.

[36] = Rettberg, *Frag.* 10 (p. 140); *J* ii.224.4-14: cf. Basil, *Eun.* ii.15 (*PG* 29.601C). According to *GN* III.vii (*J* ii.227.3-5), this argument is borrowed from the *Phaedrus* of Plato (cf. *Phaedrus* 245C).

them (215b.48-55).[37]

235.25-6   Cf. *Apol.* 13.7.[38]

viii. *A reply to Basil,* Eun. *ii.16 (604A-605B)*[39]

236.14-19   The Father is absolute virtue, life, and light;
                   there is no need to suppose (with Basil) that he
                   was in darkness when as yet the Son was not
                   (218b.55-219a.3).[40]

238.7-15P   It is one whose mind has been darkened by ill
                   will who ascribes the same darkness to others
                   (220a.16-22).

240.7-14   Or does scripture call the Lord 'door' and 'way'
                   in vain, if no one passes through him to the
                   contemplation of the Father? How can he be
                   'light' if he does not enlighten human beings to
                   know the transcendent Light (220b.36-46)?[41]

243.23-8q   The mind of believers leaps over every sensible
                   and intelligible essence and does not even stop
                   at the begetting of the Son but shoots beyond
                   it, eager to encounter the First in its yearning
                   for everlasting life (222a.21-7).[42]

246.27-8   Basil's doctrine is likened to that of Sabellius
                   and Montanus.

247.20-248.2   Just as begottenness is joined to the Son's
                   essence, so unbegottenness is joined to the

P238.8, 9-10 = 240.2-4   q243.25 = 244.3/4

---

[37] *J* ii.227.22-228.4: cf. Gen. 2: 1-3, Exod. 20: 11.

[38] The text given, however, is that found in Basil, *Eun.* ii.14 (*PG* 29.597B), not a direct quote of the *Apology* itself; if Gregory's allusion to this passage reflects anything in the present work, then Eunomius was quoting Basil's version of his earlier statement, not himself directly.

[39] In asserting that God cannot be known apart from the Son, Basil accused Eunomius of 'trying to see without light' in claiming to know the Unbegotten God at a stage 'when as yet the Son was not'. Eunomius in turn accused Basil of blasphemy in trying to claim that there was ever a time when the Father was in darkness.

[40] Cf. Basil, *Eun.* ii.16 (*PG* 29.604A-B).

[41] Cf. Basil, *Eun.* ii.16 (*PG* 29.604C); *J* ii.240.7: Jn. 10: 9; *J* ii.240.10: Jn. 14: 6; *J* ii.240.12: Jn. 1: 9. This and the following fragment are a response to Basil's contention ad loc. that apart from the enlightenment of the Word the mind can know nothing of God and must halt its ascent at the begetting of the Son.

[42] = Rettberg, *Frag.* 12 (p. 142).

J ii: Father's (223b.8-23).[43]
248.23-7[r]   Since God exists apart from begetting and is
                            prior to the Begotten One, he whose existence
                            derives from begetting was not before he was
                            begotten (223b.50-4).

ix. *A reply to Basil*, Eun. *ii.18 (608D-612A)*[44]

251.18-23[s]   He who is in the bosom of the I AM does not
                            possess existence simply or in the proper sense,
                            even if Basil, neglecting the distinction, uses
                            'I AM' interchangeably of both (225a.3-9).[45]

254.27-255.3[t]   For he who possesses existence and who lives
                            through the Father does not appropriate to
                            himself the status of the I AM for the essence
                            which rules even him draws the meaning of
                            'I AM' to itself (226a.24-7).[46]

264.4-12[u]   The Only-begotten himself has given the
                            Father the title which is properly his by calling
                            him alone 'good' (230a.8-17).[47]

273.24-274.2[v]   By calling the Word 'angel', scripture shows
                            through whom the I AM's message was pro-
                            claimed; by calling him 'God', it shows his
                            superiority to all the things made through him

---

[r]248.25-7 = 250.1-2   [s]251.18-19: cf. 252.5-6   [t]254.27-255.3 =
261.6, 10, 14, 21-2, 25, 28, 272.1; 255.2-3 = 262.1-3, 22-3, 272.5-6; 255.3
= 262.13, 263.1   [u]264.4-6 = 272.12-14; 264.6-12 = 272.17-23; 264.7/8 =
272.27   [v]274.1-2 = 275.10-11

---

[43] This seems to be the import of the argument; it is not clear whether this is an
actual fragment or a restatement of Eunomius' position by Gregory. It is not
italicized by Jaeger.

[44] In denying Eunomius' contention in *Apol.* 15.3-7 that his teaching about the
Son was that 'used in times past by the saints' (i.e. the authors of sacred scripture),
Basil argued that in speaking the phrase 'I AM THAT I AM' in Exod. 3: 14, the
Word showed that he shared the Father's eternity and godhead. The following is
Eunomius' refutation. Much of the argument turns on a play between the verb εἰμί
('to be') and the name ὁ Ὤν ('I AM') which is difficult to render in English.

[45] *J* ii.251.9-10: Jn. 1: 18, Exod. 3: 14; *J* ii.251.20: Jn. 1: 1; *J* ii.251.22: Exod.
3: 14. *J* ii.252.5-6 preserves a phrase, οὐδὲ ἁπλοῦς ὤν, which has apparently dropped
out at line *J* ii.251.18-19.

[46] *J* ii.255.1-2: Jn. 6: 57; *J* ii.255.3: Exod. 3: 14.

[47] *J* ii.264.6-7: cf. Mk. 10: 18, Lk. 18: 18 (cf. *J* ii.267.17-18).

(233b.57-234a.6).[48]

| 276.4-7 = 276.22-4 | He who sent Moses was the I AM; He through whom he was sent was the angel of the I AM, the God of all other things (234b.34-7). |
| 277.26-278.2 | Scripture puts the word 'angel' first and thus introduces the dialogue of the I AM (235a. 45-9).[49] |

x. A reply to Basil, Eun. ii.19 (612A-613C)[50]

281.19-24	We not only acknowledge that the Son is, but that he is Lord, Creator, and God of every sensible and intelligible essence (237a.15-19).[51]
282.4-10ʷ	He has been entrusted by the Father with the creation and providential care of all things (237a.32-9).
283.19-21	Did not earth and angel come into being when as yet they were not (237b.45-6)?[52]
283.29-284.2	It would be a lengthy task to go over the origins and essences of the intelligible beings; they do not share the nature of non-being, but differ according to the creative action which produced them (238a.1-6).
284.12-19	Basil is compared to Valentinus, Cerinthus, Basilides and other heretics and is denied the name 'Christian' (238a.22-31).[53]

ʷ 282.5 = 282.22; 282.8-9 = 282.27-9

---

[48] J ii.273.24: Exod. 3: 2; J ii.273.26: Exod. 3: 4 ff.; J ii.274.2: Rom. 9: 5.

[49] J ii.277.27: cf. Exod. 3: 2.

[50] The following fragments are a reply to Basil's contention in this chapter (cf. 612A-B) that Eunomius' position implied that the Son was actually non-existent!

[51] = Rettberg, Frag. 13 (p. 142).

[52] According to GN III.ix (J ii.283.11-15) this and the following fragments are given only 'by way of summary'. The point of the argument is presumably that other beings besides the Son, both intelligible and sensible, were created by God 'when as yet they were not', and do not therefore share the nature of non-being.

[53] Though not italicized by Jaeger, this passage surely represents Eunomius' language; it echoes Basil's similar charge in Eun. ii.19 (PG 29.612B-C). According to GN III.ix (J ii.284.6-9), a good deal has been omitted here.

xi. *A reply to Basil,* Eun. *ii.22 (620A–621B)*[54]

J ii: 284.20–5   Believing the saints, we affirm that the mystery
of godliness is not established by the sacredness
of the Names or the distinctiveness of customs,
but by accuracy of doctrine (238a.33–7).[55]

287.15–17   The Father is not only the Father of the Only-
begotten, but also his God (239a.33–5).[56]

291.25–292.7   Therefore (if Christ said, 'My God and your
God'), either the disciples are of one essence
with the Father, or the Son is not of the same
nature as the Father but serves his 'God' in the
same sense as the disciples do (241a.12–22).

xii. *A reply to Basil,* Eun. *ii.25–9 (629A–641A)*[57]

296.7–9   Cf. *Apol.* 19.12–14.

297.2–13   The different senses of the word 'light' in
scripture, in which we learn to distinguish the
begotten from the 'unapproachable light'
(242b.49–243a.8).[58]

299.21–3   Eunomius will present his proof from the facts
themselves and from holy scripture (244a.2–4).

299.26–300.4   The prologue of St John's gospel shows that the

---

[54] The 'Names' of the first fragment in this section are shown by *GN* III.ix (*J*
ii.285.26–7) to be those of the baptismal formula; the reference therefore is to Basil,
Eun. ii.22 (*PG* 29.620D), where Basil condemns those who depart from the Names
'in which they were sealed'. Eunomius' reply seems to be that veneration for the
Names simply as sounds without a proper understanding of them is pointless.

[55] = Rettberg, *Frag.* 15 (p. 144). *J* ii.284.22: cf. Matt. 28: 19; *J* ii.284.24:
1 Tim. 3: 16.

[56] *J* ii.287.17: Jn. 20: 17 (according to *J* ii.289.5–13, this passage was then quoted
in full); Jaeger is almost certainly wrong in italicizing εἰς δημιουργὸν καὶ κτίστην,
which seems to be an interpretation by Gregory.

[57] In *Apol.* 19 Eunomius had tried to answer the arguments of those who asserted
that because scripture used words such as 'light' and 'life' of both Father and Son
they must be of the same essence; he had said that 'light' must in each case be understood in a sense proper to the entity to which it was applied. Basil, in the chapters
cited, denied this and tried to show that an identity of essence was indeed implied.
The following are surviving portions of Eunomius' refutation.

[58] *J* ii.297.2–13 + 299.21–300.4 + 301.6–12 = Rettberg, *Frag.* 14 (pp. 143–4).
J ii.297.3: Jn. 1: 9; *J* ii.297.3–4: Gen. 1: 3; *J* ii.297.6–7: Matt. 5: 14; *J* ii.297.8:
1 Tim. 6: 16; *J* ii.297.9: Rom. 9: 5.

'light' mentioned there was 'made flesh' (244a. 7-15).[59]

301.6-12
= 119.11-15
If Basil can show that it was 'the unapproachable light' which was made flesh and was crucified, etc., then he can say that 'light' = 'light' (244b.7-13).[60]

303.7-10
It was the light 'made flesh' which was active for salvation; the 'unapproachable light' was not active in the bestowal of this grace (245a.33-5).

307.17-23
Basil's God is composite in that, while 'light' is property common to both persons, one 'light' is separated from the other by individual characteristics (247a.1-8).[61]

309.18-21
But if the Begotten is contrasted with the Unbegotten, the begotten Light will be equally inferior to the Unbegotten Light: the one will be light, the other darkness (247b.33-7).[62]

310.25-6
Basil has undertaken to write without any skill in logic (248b.8-12).[63]

[59] *J* ii.299.26-7: Jn. 1: 1; *J* ii.299.27-8: Jn. 1: 4; *J* ii.300.1: Jn. 1: 14.

[60] *J* ii.301.7/8: Rom. 9: 5; *J* ii.301.8: 1 Tim. 6: 16.

[61] According to *GN* iii.x (*J* ii.309.7-8), something has been omitted following this fragment.

[62] Though he does not list *J* ii.309.18-21 as a separate fragment, Rettberg (p. 144) cites it in connection with his fragment 14. It seems to follow on those which precede it as part of Eunomius' continuing effort to show the logical absurdity of Basil's argument.

[63] According to *GN* iii.x (*J* ii.310.28-311.6), Gregory has omitted the end of the book.

EUNOMII EXPOSITIO FIDEI
THE CONFESSION OF FAITH

INTRODUCTION

I DATE AND OCCASION

The *Expositio Fidei* is the last of Eunomius' surviving complete works. It was produced in connection with events following on the second ecumenical council held at Constantinople in 381. When the Emperor Theodosius the Great attempted to put the council's first canon into effect—a canon reaffirming the Nicene faith and anathematizing all others[1]—there were severe civil disturbances.[2] Theodosius tried to achieve an accommodation, if not a reconciliation, with the dissenting groups by calling a 'conference of all the heresies' to meet at Constantinople. This conference finally met in June of 383.[3] The initial plan was that there should be a free discussion of the issues,[4] but the Emperor was dissuaded from this by the efforts of Nectarius, Archbishop of Constantinople, and it was proposed that the discussion should be based instead on the writings of those Fathers who had lived before the divisions had arisen in the Church.[5] When the heretics could reach no agreement about this procedure, the Emperor suggested that each group present a written account of its teachings.[6] In thus preventing any free discussion, Nectarius achieved what was doubtless his aim—he effectively frustrated any weakening of Nicene orthodoxy as well as any positive result which might have been hoped for from the conference. In the end the Emperor accepted only the confession presented by the Novatians (it affirmed the *homoousion*) and rejected all the others.[7] He then issued an omnibus edict against heretics (25 July 383),[8] followed by another later in the same year

---

[1] J. D. Mansi, *Sacrorum Conciliorum Nova et Amplissima Collectio* iii (Florentiae: expensis Antonii Zatta Veneti, 1759), 557-560A; cf. *Cod. Theod.* xvi.5.8, dated 19 July 381, shortly after the end of the Council's first session (Mommsen i, pars posterior, p. 858), and cf. *Gothofredus* vi, p. 123a.

[2] Soc., *HE* v.10 (*PG* 67.584A-B), Soz., *HE* vii.12 (*GCS* 314.17-19).

[3] Soc., *HE* v.10 (*PG* 67.584B-c), Soz., *HE* vii.12 (*GCS* 314.19-26).

[4] Soc., *HE* v.10 (*PG* 67.584c), Soz., *HE* vii.12 (*GCS* 314.23-315.3).

[5] Soc., *HE* v.10 (*PG* 67.585A-588A), Soz., *HE* vii.12 (*GCS* 315.3-24).

[6] Soc., *HE* v.10 (*PG* 67.588A), Soz., *HE* vii.12 (*GCS* 315.24-9).

[7] Soc., *HE* v.10 (*PG* 67.589A-593A), Soz., *HE* vii.12 (*GCS* 316.3-6).

[8] *Cod. Theod.* xvi.5.11 (Mommsen i, pars posterior, p. 859).

(3 December 383),[9] and others of gradually increasing severity in
the years following. Any accommodation which might have existed
earlier between Eunomius and Demophilus, the former Arian
Archbishop of Constantinople, had by now obviously (and, be it
said, understandably)[10] broken up, for we find each representing
his respective party at the conference.[11] Eunomius joined with the
others in presenting his profession of faith.[12] That the profession
then presented and that found in our manuscripts are identical is
shown by Gregory of Nyssa's quotations and the mention of 'the
imperial decrees' in the confession itself.[13] We may therefore be
reasonably confident of the identity as well as of the authenticity of
the work now under consideration. As to its later history, we know
little. Although it was certainly an 'occasional work' in one sense, it
is clear that it was soon put to use in a broader context. Gregory of
Nyssa elected to write a refutation of it largely because it was being
used in Eunomian missionary activity and might lead many of the
'simpler sort' astray.[14] Thus this work has come down to us not only
because of its original apologetic purpose, but because as a more or
less complete summary of the Eunomian position it was admirably
suited for missionary purposes.

II. STRUCTURE AND CONTENTS

When we begin to look at the actual text of this document, we find
that it divides easily into a creed of four main sections together with
an introduction and a conclusion:

---

[9] Ibid., xvi.5.12 (Mommsen i, pars posterior, pp. 859-60).

[10] Demophilus would hardly have wished to be associated with a body already
increasingly singled out for punitive action by the government. As *Gothofredus* (vi,
p. 123a) remarks concerning *Cod. Theod.* xvi.5.8, this period sees the beginning of
really separate Eunomian activity.

[11] Soc., *HE* v.10 (*PG* 67.588B), Soz., *HE* vii.12 (*GCS* 316.1-2).

[12] N. Q. King, *The Emperor Theodosius and the Establishment of Christianity*
(London: SCM Press, 1961), p. 54, n. 1 seems clearly wrong in referring the Empress
Flacilla's successful attempt to prevent the Emperor from seeing Eunomius to this
period (Soz., *HE* vii.6 (*GCS* 307.19-23)). Apart from the fact that such an action
would have made any conference pointless, Sozomen is clearly referring to an earlier
period.

[13] Eun., *Exp. Fid.* 1.5-6 (cf. Valesius, *PG* 67.592D n.).

[14] Grg. Nyss., *Conf.* (*J* ii.320.5-10).

A more detailed examination makes it evident that Eunomius had few expectations of actually conciliating the Emperor. His pointed (and courageous) allusion to Matt. 10: 32-3[15] and emphatic assertion that he had neither added nor omitted anything[16] bear this out. This document, then, is on the whole an uncompromising presentation of Eunomius' teaching. It is not, however, a deliberately provocative one. If Eunomius could not hope to escape condemnation altogether, he could still hope to mitigate the severity of the sentence. The basic orientation of the work is scriptural—each of the three paragraphs devoted to the divine persons is in effect an exposition of the titles given them by holy scripture.[17] Indeed, the expositions of these titles are themselves almost thickets of scriptural quotations and allusions. In many ways, however, this work is chiefly notable for what it does *not* say. Apart from a few provocative phrases such as εἰς ὑπόστασιν τρισσὴν σχιζόμενον[18] (if this is the correct reading), there is a distinct muting of the characteristic Eunomian catch-phrases. We find no mention of γέννημα or ἀνόμοιος at all, and even ἀγέννητος[19] is played down in favour of the less suspect ὁ παντοκράτωρ.[20] Likewise, when speaking of the divine persons, such words as ποίημα[21] and ἔργον[22] are used very cautiously indeed. In a more positive vein, we may note that in spite of the work's generally scriptural orientation there is no attempt to try to conform to the formula ὅμοιος κατὰ τὰς γραφάς which had been popular at an earlier period. In describing the Son as ὅμοιον . . . μόνον κατ' ἐξαίρετον ὁμοιότητα καὶ τὴν ἰδιάζουσαν ἔννοιαν,[23] Eunomius indeed went as far as he well could

---

[15] Eun., *Exp. Fid.* 1.2-4   [16] Ibid., 6.2-5.
[17] Thus, the Father: Jn. 17: 3 (2.1); the Son: 2 Cor. 1: 19, Jn. 1: 49, etc., Col. 1: 15 (3.1-2); the Spirit: Jn. 14: 17, 15: 26 (4.1-2).
[18] Eun., *Exp. Fid.* 2.6-7.   [19] Ibid., 3.2, 29, 30bis.
[20] Ibid., 2.10; 3.13, 30, 32.   [21] Ibid., 4.7, 10.   [22] Ibid., 4.8.
[23] Ibid., 3.27-8.

under his own presuppositions, but as the qualifications in the lines which follow show,[24] his basic position remained unchanged. While it is obvious, then, that Eunomius tried to use scriptural and conciliatory language wherever possible, it is equally obvious that he nowhere retreated from the full rigour of his acknowledged position.

III. THE MANUSCRIPTS

Before we go on to a presentation of the manuscripts on which the present edition is based, it would be well to take into consideration the reasons which have permitted the survival of this last of Eunomius' extant complete works. As we have already remarked several times, there was no incentive for Orthodox scribes to copy heretical literature unless they had some clearly defined purpose in so doing. In the case of the *Liber Apologeticus* this purpose was to provide an illustration for the arguments of St Basil in his refutation of it. Similar motives have governed the preservation of the *Expositio Fidei*. This work has survived only because at a very early period in the history of its transmission it was included in manuscripts of its refutation by Gregory of Nyssa, his *Refutatio Confessionis Eunomii* (previously known as Book II of the *Contra Eunomium*).[25] Indeed, in three of the six known manuscripts of this work (LPZ) Eunomius' treatise is still bound up with the *Contra Eunomium* of Gregory.[26] Since these three manuscripts have already been described in detail in Jaeger's excellent critical edition of this work, we will confine ourselves to comments directly relevant to the text immediately before us.

a. *Manuscripts LN*[27]

L   *Codex Laurentianus Mediceus plut. VI, 17, fos. 4ᵛ-5ᵛ, ut videtur, saeculi xi medii.*

The *Expositio Fidei* of Eunomius occupies the second place in this manuscript (described by Jaeger, vol. ii, pp. xiv-xv), immediately following the chapter headings of (vulgate) Books II-XII of

---

[24] Ibid., 3.28-33.

[25] *J* ii.312-410 (= *Conf.*); cf. his comments, ibid., ii, pp. xvif.

[26] Of the remaining three, two (NJ) are apographs of known copies, leaving F as the sole independent witness.   [27] See p. 16 n. 89 above.

Gregory's *Contra Eunomium*, and preceding those of Book I. Apart from the name of the author, there is nothing to indicate the heretical nature of the work, but in the margin of fo. 5ʳ the word ση(μείωσ)αι draws attention to a phrase in *Exp. Fid.* 4.2-3 var. referring to the Holy Spirit: γενόμενον ὑπὸ τοῦ μονογενοῦς. The same marginal note appears at the top of fo. 5ᵛ opposite the words πεμπόμενος ὑπ᾽ αὐτοῦ καὶ παρ᾽ αὐτοῦ λαμβάνων, again referring to the Spirit (*Exp. Fid.* 4.12-13).

N   *Codex Parisinus suppl. graecus 270, fos. 466ʳ-467ᵛ, saeculi xvii.*

Among the numerous, if miscellaneous, treatises contained in this codex are found not only the *Expositio Fidei*, but also the *Liber Apologeticus* of Eunomius (see the article cited above, p. 24, section c). The several parts of the manuscript, however, appear to be quite separate, and are in different hands. The manuscript is written on paper in a single column of 34 to 35 lines, each folio measuring 28.3 × 18.5 cm. The somewhat rough hand is that of Émery Bigot(ius) of Rouen (1626-89). This manuscript is a direct copy of L, as a Latin note at the top of fo. 466ʳ informs us: *ex mˢᵗᵒ cod. Bibliot. Florentiae / iacobus Gretserus in proligomenis ait hanc expositionem Eunomii haeretici in bibliot. bavarica et in codice Livineii post Nysseni in Eunomianis libros. ex cod. mˢᵗᵒ Flor. transcribuntur.* The value of this manuscript, then, lies not in what it can tell us of the text of Eunomius, but in the fact that it was used as the basis of the first printed edition and explains many of the vagaries of the vulgate text. It formerly belonged to the Abbey of Saint-Germain-des-Prés and entered the Bibliothèque Nationale during the French Revolution.

b. *Manuscripts PZ*

P   *Codex Patmensis (Γ) 46 monasterii S. Ioannis, fos. 238ᵛ-241ʳ, saeculi x vel xi.*

While the *Contra Eunomium* is only one of several treatises by Gregory found in this manuscript, within it the *Expositio Fidei* of Eunomius immediately follows the *Refutatio Confessionis Eunomii*, commonly called Book II (the manuscript is described in Jaeger, vol. ii, pp. xxx-xxxi). The scribe has called attention to the heretical nature of the work being copied by a series of marks in the margin, though he neglected to do so on fo. 241ʳ which closes the

work. Other quotations of Eunomius in the text of Gregory himself
are similarly treated.

Z   *Codex Vaticanus graecus 1773, fos. 149ʳ-151ᵛ, saeculi xvi.*

This manuscript, described in Jaeger, vol. ii, pp. xxxi-xxxii, is a
sixteenth-century copy of the preceding (P). Although the contents
of the codex as a whole are not completely identical with those of its
exemplar, the *Expositio Fidei* occupies the same relative position
within the *Contra Eunomium* of Eunomius, i.e. immediately
following the vulgate Book II (= the *Refutatio Confessionis
Eunomii*). As in P, the *Expositio Fidei* is distinguished by a series of
marks in the margin.

c. *Manuscript F*

F   *Codex Parisinus suppl. graecus 174, fos. 146ʳ-151ᵛ, saeculi
     xvi, fortasse ineuntis.*[28]

This manuscript is composed of two otherwise unrelated sections of
different ages. The first, fos. 1ʳ-141ʳ, contains Book I of the *Contra
Eunomium* of Gregory of Nyssa (fos. 1ʳ-140ᵛ) and an extract from
a work of St Maximus together with a comment on it in an Italian
hand of the seventeenth century; the manuscript itself is also
seventeenth century.[29] The second section (following the blank fos.
141ᵛ-145ᵛ) consists of fos. 146ʳ-151ᵛ and contains the copy of the
Expositio Fidei now under discussion; it dates from the sixteenth
century, perhaps the earlier part. Apparently the two manuscripts
were already joined together prior to their entry into the Bibliothèque Nationale. Since the two sections of the work were originally
unrelated, this manuscript is unique in containing the *Expositio
Fidei* independently of the *Contra Eunomium* of Gregory. The
manuscript is written on paper in a single column of 25 to 26 lines,
each folio measuring 29.5 × 22 cm. The paper is Italian of the
sixteenth century and possesses a watermark in the form of an
anchor in a circle surmounted by a star (cf. Briquet nos. 477-532).
The hand is a rapid, somewhat angular minuscule, slightly leaning
to the right. There are no marginal notes or comments connected

---

[28] I am indebted for much of my information about this manuscript to the
kindness of Dr Charles Astruc of the Bibliothèque Nationale (personal letter dated
29 May 1979).   [29] It is mentioned, but not described in *J* ii, p. lvi.

with Eunomius' text.[30] At fo. 148ʳ, line 7, the text of the *Liber Apologeticus* suddenly breaks off at the words τῷ πνεύματι τοῦ διδόντος τὴν χάριν (*Exp. Fid.* 4.15-16 var.); then, without any external indication of a break in continuity, the same line continues (through fo. 151ᵛ) with an excerpt from the thirty-ninth and fortieth chapters of the *Oratio Catechetica Magna* of Gregory of Nyssa (*PG* 45.100A2-105B3). It is to be noted that this excerpt, which begins suddenly in mid-sentence with εἰς τὸ κτίστον καὶ τὸ ἄκτιστον, ends equally suddenly with the words μετὰ ταῦτα δέ, κατὰ τὴν αἰωνίαν ἀντίδοσιν, leaving the latter part of the chapter incomplete. This is immediately followed by eight crosses in the form of a line and cross, strongly suggesting that this marked the end of the volume. It seems, then, that in this manuscript we have an excerpt of six folios from the end of a once larger sixteenth-century codex, now attached to an entirely separate volume of the seventeenth century. Although the indications of an originally Italian provenance are quite strong, there is nothing in the volume as now constituted to indicate its previous owners. It is said by Omont to have belonged formerly to the Convent of the Feuillants at Paris, whence it passed into the Bibliothèque Nationale during the French Revolution.[31]

d. *Manuscript J*

J   *Codex Cantabrigiensis Collegii Sanctissimae et Individuae Trinitatis O.2.3 (1107), fos. 1ʳ-6ʳ, saeculi xviii ineuntis (verisimile c.1710).*

In addition to the *Expositio Fidei*, this manuscript also contains the *Liber Apologeticus* (see the article cited above, p. 24, section c), but whereas the latter is interleaved, the verso sides of the folios in the *Expositio Fidei* have been left blank, presumably to allow for a translation. The hand is the same throughout, but is not identical with any of the five or six hands visible in the *Liber Apologeticus*. The text is a straight copy of the *editio princeps* published by Valesius in 1668 (see below, section iv).

---

[30] On fo. 151ʳ there is a subject heading in connection with the excerpt from the *Oratio Catechetica Magna* of Gregory of Nyssa.

[31] H. Omont, *Inventaire sommaire des manuscrits de la Bibliothèque Nationale* iii (Paris: Ernest Leroux, 1888), p. 228, and ibid., Iᵉʳᵉ partie, Introduction, p. xvi.

Of the six manuscripts described in the preceding pages, only three, L. P, and F, are independent witnesses to the text. They will be the main basis of the present edition (questions of space unfortunately make it impossible to include the others in the apparatus). Of the three, two, L and P, are still joined to manuscripts of Gregory of Nyssa. The third, F, was also once part of a larger manuscript, perhaps even one containing Gregory's refutation. It is clear, then, that the relationship of these manuscripts to one another cannot be determined apart from their context in the larger work. With this in mind, let us look briefly at the evidence presented by the manuscripts. That all three derive ultimately from a common ancestor is sufficiently shown by the fact that all three agree in a number of incontrovertibly erroneous readings. To cite only two of the most obvious, we may mention *Exp. Fid.* 4.2-3, where all three manuscripts have the certainly wrong ὑπὸ τοῦ μονογενοῦς for Gregory's correct ὑπὸ τοῦ μόνου θεοῦ διὰ τοῦ μονογενοῦς. Again, at *Exp. Fid.* 3.2, all three read the undoubtedly incorrect χριστὸν ἀληθινὸν θεόν for the υἱὸν ἀληθινόν reported by Gregory. This last reading is particularly interesting, for it shows at least two stages of transmission prior to the diversification of the manuscripts. The error is most probably explained by assuming that one scribe misread the *nominum sacrum* Y̅N̅ as X̅N̅. A later copyist tried to make better sense of this by supplying the word θεόν to produce the reading now found in the manuscripts. If it seems clear, however, that all three derive ultimately from a common exemplar, it is equally clear no one is particularly close to any other, although L and P seem closer to one another than either is to F. We may note in this regard that whereas L and P agree against F eighteen times, F and P agree against L only seven and F and L against P only ten.[32] For a more detailed understanding of these relationships, we must look at the complex history of the text of Gregory as studied by Jaeger.[33]

In the printed editions prior to Jaeger's, the *Contra Eunomium* was presented as containing twelve books (I-XII) with an additional, longer book added to the whole as a kind of appendix (XII[b] or XIII). After prolonged study, Jaeger was able to show that

---

[32] Some of F's unique correct readings, however, represent fairly obvious scribal corrections and perhaps the influence of *g* (cf., e.g., *Exp. Fid.* 2.5, 7).

[33] The following is entirely based on Jaeger's presentation of the MS tradition.

the book labelled XII[b] or XIII had originally been Book II, while the book bearing that title in the printed editions was in fact a separate work, the *Refutatio Confessionis Eunomii* (*Conf.*), Gregory's attack on the *Expositio Fidei*. Books III–XII, on the other hand, were shown to be the ten λόγοι of Gregory's original Book III.[34] In order to avoid confusion in what follows we will reserve 'Book II' for the original second book of Gregory (= vulgate Book XII[b] or XIII), that now printed as such in Jaeger's edition; the *Refutatio Confessionis Eunomii* (= vulgate Book II) will be referred to as *Conf.*, while the vulgate Books III–XII will be designated Book III.i–x, again as in Jaeger. The origin of all this confusion is to be sought in the fact that originally all three books of the *Contra Eunomium* and the *Conf.* circulated separately. At a very early period two separate recensions grew up combining these works, designated by Jaeger Π (fourth to sixth century) and Φ (fifth to sixth century) respectively.[35] Both contained the same general order of books in the *Contra Eunomium*: Book I, *Conf.*, Book III.i–x; Book II was missing altogether. Ignoring their other differences, we may note that one of the features distinguishing Φ from Π was the presence in Φ of the *Expositio Fidei* of Eunomius immediately preceding the chapter headings of Book I. One of the two surviving representatives of this tradition is our own manuscript L. In the tenth century, in the aftermath of the renaissance of letters sparked by Photius, Book II, omitted in the earlier recensions, came to light. This discovery resulted in a new recension of the *Contra Eunomium* (designated Σ by Jaeger) which contained the following books: Book I, *Conf.*, Book III.i, Book II. While one exemplar (C) still possesses these books and these books only, most other copies of this recension represent a stage at which the remaining books of the *Contra Eunomium* had been added to the end of the whole treatise to produce the following order: Book I, *Conf.*, Book III.i, Book II, Book III.ii–x. Although the various copies of this recension all seem to go back to exemplars originating in the same workshop, manuscripts of differing traditions were used to provide the text for the various parts. Thus while the text of Book III.ii–x goes back to recension Φ in all the manuscripts, that of Book I, the *Conf.*, Book III.i, and Book II goes back to recension Π

---

[34] See the comparative table in *J* ii, pp. lviii–lix.
[35] For Π, see *J* ii, pp. xxxvii ff.; for Φ, *J* ii, pp. xiii ff.

in some cases, to recension Φ in others. Our own manuscript P, which contains the *Expositio Fidei* immediately following the *Conf.*, is one of those going back to the Φ recension. This confirms the evidence provided by our own manuscripts, which shows that while all three certainly go back to a common original they come from separate branches of the tradition. This is clearly evident in the case of L and P, and it is obvious too that the original source of F is a manuscript of the Φ tradition (perhaps one closer to L than to P). The manuscripts of the *Contra Eunomium* went through many further vicissitudes before the appearance of a printed edition, but the *Expositio Fidei* of Eunomius did not take part in them and does not appear in any of their surviving copies.

e. *Quotations from Gregory*

We have already noted several times that Eunomius' *Expositio Fidei* was refuted by Gregory in a separate work entitled by Jaeger the *Refutatio Confessionis Eunomii*. Since in the course of this work Gregory quotes very nearly 60 per cent of the whole treatise, these quotations are an important source for the text, and as such are listed in a separate register after the text and translation. The portions quoted are also italicized in the text. Apart from their textual importance, however, they also constitute one of our few opportunities to check Gregory's accuracy, an accuracy all the more important to determine since in the case of one of Eunomius' most important works, the *Apologia Apologiae*, we are wholly dependent on what he gives us. In the past the interpretation of the evidence has been severely hampered by the numerous serious discrepancies which exist between the printed text and Gregory's quotations. Indeed, Albertz found them so great that he actually thought they represented two separate editions![36] Examination of the manuscripts, however, reveals that while there are indeed two editions, one of them is the editor's (see below section iv)! There is no need to resort to the hypothesis of two ancient recensions.

In our treatment of Gregory's citations of the *Apologia Apologiae* we dealt first with his actual quotations and then passed on to his choice of material and omissions. We shall do the same here. We have already noted (p. 138) that in at least two of the cases where Gregory differs from the manuscripts his is surely the correct

---

[36] Albertz, pp. 42-3.

reading. The same phenomenon is observable in another instance where Gregory has preserved a line which has dropped out of the manuscript tradition. At *Exp. Fid.* 3.2-3, presumably due to the carelessness of a scribe, the phrase ἀληθῶς γεννηθέντα πρὸ αἰώνων has been omitted. Since this line is needed to complete the parallelism with the lines which immediately precede and follow and makes sense of the following clause, οὐκ ἄνευ τῆς πρὸ τοῦ εἶναι γεννήσεως ὀνομαζόμενον υἱόν, there is no question but that it is the correct reading. Since all of these examples are from theologically sensitive parts of the work, it is to Gregory's credit that there is no evidence of tampering for polemical purposes. Perhaps the only possible exception is at *Exp. Fid.* 2.6-7, where all of the manuscripts of Eunomius and most of the manuscripts of Gregory read εἰς ὑποστάσεις τρεῖς σχηματιζόμενον. We have followed Jaeger, however, in accepting the reading of his manuscript A as genuine, εἰς ὑπόστασιν τρισσὴν σχιζόμενον.[37] If this is indeed Gregory's original reading, there seems every reason to believe that it was also Eunomius'. While ὑποστάσεις τρεῖς is hardly an impossibility for its time, it is far more likely to be a banalization of ὑπόστασιν τρισσήν than the reverse. Certainly σχιζόμενον brings into sharp focus Eunomius' contention that the Orthodox position was fundamentally Sabellian. Whatever the true reading in this somewhat doubtful case, however, it is certainly true that neither in this nor in any other example is there any evidence of a deliberate change in the text on Gregory's part for theological or polemical reasons.

If we may be assured, then, that Gregory does not deliberately misrepresent what he does quote, there are greater problems with what he does *not*. Although as already noted Gregory quotes over half of the whole treatise, we still find that there are substantial omissions. In fact, these omissions are so substantial that Albertz regarded them as evidence for the existence of two ancient recensions.[38] Gregory omits both the Introduction (1.1-7) and the Conclusion (6.1-5) as well as Eunomius' concluding paragraph on the Future Judgement (5.1-12). Since none of these paragraphs

---

[37] Grg. Nyss., *Conf.* (*J* ii.325.9-10).

[38] Albertz, pp. 47-9; despite his recognition that many of the lacunae in Gregory must derive from the 'fragmentarischen Überlieferung' of the text (p. 47), he seems consistently to assume that what is not actually quoted did not, therefore, exist.

contain matter under dispute, however, there is nothing in them inconsistent with Gregory's stated policy of giving only a partial quotation of his opponent's statements, ἀναγκαίως κατὰ μέρος προτιθέντες τὴν περιφερομένην παρ' αὐτῶν ἔκθεσιν.[39] There is no need to suppose any lost ancient recension.

Of the paragraphs he does give us, Gregory quotes those dealing with the Father (2.1-19) and the Holy Spirit (4.1-24) virtually entire. The same is not true, however, of the second and longest paragraph, that dealing with the Son (3.1-46). Ignoring a number of minor omissions, we may note that two substantial *lacunae* are to be found at 3.16-22 and 3.41-6, while 3.29-31 is cited only very fragmentarily, and 3.39-41 is considerably abbreviated (for convenience we will treat 3.39-40 and 41-6 as a single omission). When we look at Gregory's reasons for omitting these passages, we find that for both 3.16-22 and 3.39-46 they are very similar. One of his problems in dealing with Eunomius' work was that there were many passages to which even the most determined critic would have difficulty taking exception (though this certainly did not prevent him from trying).[40] Such passages were, as Gregory puts it, like 'bread mixed with sand', sound doctrine with heresy,[41] and he gives us a specific statement as to how he proposes to deal with them:

Τὰ δὲ ἐφεξῆς τούτοις ἀσυναρτήτως προσκείμενα ὑπερβῆναί φημι δεῖν καλῶς ἔχειν, οὐχ ὡς ἀλήπτως ἔχοντα, ἀλλ' ὡς δυνάμενα καὶ παρὰ τῶν εὐσεβούντων λέγεσθαι, εἴπερ διαζευχθείη τῆς κακοτρόπου ἐμφάσεως. εἰ γάρ τι καὶ πρόσκειται παρ' αὐτοῦ τῶν εἰς εὐσέβειαν συντεινόντων, ἀντὶ δελεάσματος τὸ τοιοῦτον τοῖς ἀκεραιοτέροις προτείνεται, ἵνα συγκαταποθῇ τούτοις καὶ τὸ τῆς ἀσεβείας ἄγκιστρον.[42]

That which is incoherently set out in the following I think it best to pass over, not as being immune to criticism, but as being the kinds of things which even religious persons might say if only they were detached from their malicious context. Indeed, if there *is* anything put forth by him which might tend to true religion, it is only as bait laid out for the simple, so that they may swallow the hook of impiety along with it.

This is his justification for the omission of 3.16-22, but he gives

[39] Grg. Nyss., *Conf.* (*J* ii.320.8-9); in Albertz's defence, however, it must be said that the phrase κατὰ μέρος did not occur in the MSS on which the Migne edition was based (*PG* 45.476A).

[40] Note, e.g., his scurrilous misapprehension of the phrase ὑπηχῶν εὐχομένοις (4.17) in Grg. Nyss., *Conf.* (*J* ii.405.11-18).

[41] Grg. Nyss., *Conf.* (*J* ii.360.22-6). [42] Ibid. (*J* ii.369.12-18).

very similar reasons for his decision not to cover 3.39-46 in detail either: the uncritical will see only the teachings of Holy Scripture while the discerning will be able to recognize that none of Eunomius' work is free from heretical villainy.[43] Thus, the main reason why these large sections were eliminated was that, apart from the name of their author, there was nothing in them to which exception could be taken. While such a policy is perhaps understandable in an author who could expect his readers to have ready access to the work being refuted, for us who do not it must remain as a warning that the picture Gregory presents to us is not free from distortion.

IV EDITIONS AND TRANSLATIONS

v^v   Henricus Valesius, *Socratis Scholastici et Hermiae Sozomeni Historia Ecclesiastica* (Parisiis: excudebat Antonius Vitre, Regis & Cleri Gallicani Typographus, 1668), notae pp. 61-4.

The first appearance of this work in print was in the notes to the edition of Socrates' *Ecclesiastical History* by Henri Valois or Valesius (1603-76). Valesius makes the following comment about the source of his text: *Hanc fidei expositionem . . . manuscriptam penes me habeo, beneficio viri clarissimi ac doctissimi Emerici Bigotii. In codice quidem Bavarico,[44] et in exemplari Livineii,[45] subjecta erat libris Gregorii Nysseni* Contra Eunomium, *ut testatur Gretserus.[46] Verum in codice Florentino, ex quo Bigotius eam descripsit, praefixa erat iisdem libris* (p. 61A-B). The copy of L made by Bigotius is our own manuscript N, described on p. 135 above; it is, on the whole, a faithful copy of its exemplar. The same cannot be said, however, of the text prepared by Valesius; it differs so markedly from both the manuscripts and the quotations made by Gregory that it provoked Albertz to invent two hypothetical ancient editions of the work.[47] Some of the changes (some correct) are the

---

[43] Ibid. (*J* ii.384.8-19).

[44] This is apparently erroneous. I am informed by Dr K. Dachs, Director of the Department of Manuscripts of the Bayerische Staatsbibliothek München (in a letter dated 25 Feb. 1974) that the manuscript in question (*Cod. Bavaricus graecus 92*) does not in fact contain a copy of the *Expositio Fidei*.

[45] Apparently our own manuscript Z; cf. the comments of Jaeger, *J* ii, p. lxiv.

[46] In the introduction to the 1618 supplement to the 1615 edition of Gregory's *Contra Eunomium* (cf. Jaeger, loc. cit.).   [47] Albertz, pp. 42-3.

144   EXPOSITIO FIDEI

work of the editor;[48] others are simply errors, whether on the part of Valesius or of the printers cannot be said.[49] Perhaps the most serious is the omission of οὐκ (!) at *Exp. Fid.* 3.41, an error which significantly alters the meaning of the passage. In addition to the Greek text, Valesius also published a Latin translation in a parallel column. Both text and translation have remained the basis of the vulgate text to this day and have been many times reprinted.[50] The most accessible form of this text is that found (with minor variations) in:

v^m   J.-P. Migne, ed., *Socratis Scholastici, Hermiae Sozomeni Historia Ecclesiastica* . . . (Parisiis: apud J.-P. Migne editorem, 1864 (Patrologia Graeca LXVII)), cols. 587C-592D.

Column numbers in Migne's edition are given in the margin of the text printed below.

v^r   Christ. Henr. Georg. Rettberg, *Marcelliana. Accedit Eunomii ΕΚΘΕΣΙΣ ΠΙΣΤΕΩΣ Emendatior* (Gottingae: sumptibus Vandenhoek et Ruprecht, 1794), pp. 148-70.[51]

This second, revised edition, although based on the text of Valesius, has nonetheless been thoroughly revised on the basis of the quotations given by Gregory of Nyssa. The result has been a vastly improved text and translation accompanied by copious

---

[48] Thus καὶ ὅτι for ὅτι καὶ at 2.1; οὐκ ἄνευ γεννήσεως πρὸ τοῦ εἶναι at 3.2-3, an attempt to correct the obviously wrong οὐκ ἄνευ πρὸ τοῦ εἶναι γεννήσεως; ὁδῶν ἔργων for ἔργων ὁδῶν at 3.4-5 (the manuscripts are shown to have lost a καὶ at this point by Eunomius' treatment of similar texts elsewhere, e.g. Ephes. 2: 17 at 3.42, where there is a reversal of order separated by a καὶ); περιορωμένου for the difficult προορωμένου at 5.8 (very near to the correct παρεωραμένου). It is only fair to mention changes in which Valesius was correct (apart from mere changes in spelling): ἀρχὴν for ἀρχὴ at 3.4; ἄλλῳ for ἄλλο at 3.10; τοῦ for τὸ at 5.3-4; ὧν for ὡς at 6.2.

[49] Thus, the omission of τοῦ κυρίου at 2.2; of one καὶ at 2.7 and another at 2.10/11 (perhaps correctly); the omission of ὕλης at 2.18; Πατρὸς for πνεύματος at 3.15; οὐδὲν for οὐδὲ ἕν at 3.19; ἐπικεύσαντα for ἐπικλύσαντα at 3.34; ἐπὶ for ἐπ' at 3.39; the omission of οὐκ at 3.41 (editorial?); γενομένων for γινομένων at 5.6.

[50] Those known to me include: J. A. Fabricius, *Bibliothecae Graecae* viii (Hamburg, 1717), pp. 253-60; J. Basagne, *Thesaurus Monumentorum Ecclesiasticorum* i (Antwerp, 1725), pp. 177 ff.; N. Coletus, *Sacrosancta Concilia* . . . Stephani Baluzii & Joannis Harduini additamentis ii (Venice, 1728), 1203B-1208C; J. D. Mansi, *Sacrorum Conciliorum Nova et Amplissima Collectio* iii (Florence, 1759), 645B-650C.

[51] Reprinted in J. D. Goldhorn, ed., *Sancti Basilii . . . et Sancti Gregorii theologi vulgo Nazianzeni . . . opera dogmatica selecta* (Leipzig, 1854), pp. 616-29.

notes, many of which are still useful. This is certainly the best edition prior to that of Van Parys.

a M. Albertz, *Untersuchungen über die Schriften des Eunomius* (Wittenberg: Herrosé und Ziemsen, 1908), pp. 43-6.

Unlike the editions mentioned above, that of Albertz is not based on the text of Valesius. Misled by the many discrepancies between the quotations of Gregory and the vulgate text, Albertz supposed that each must be based on a different ancient recension; he therefore attempted in this edition to reconstruct that used by Gregory. The text thus includes only those portions of the work actually quoted by Gregory (2.1-4.24 with *lacunae*), but, while based on a misapprehension, it still provides a useful guide to the text as Gregory presents it.

p Michael Van Parys, Εὐνομίου Κυζικοῦ ἔκθεσις πίστεως, in Βιβλιοθήκη Ἑλλήνων Πατέρων καὶ Ἐκκλησιαστικῶν Συγγραφέων (Ἀθῆναι, ἔκδοσις τῆς Ἀποστολοκῆς Διακονίας τῆς Ἐκκλησίας τῆς Ἑλλάδος, 1968), vol. 38, pp. 115-18.

The text of Van Parys is the first attempt since Rettberg to produce a corrected text of the *Expositio Fidei*, and the first to attempt to do so by a re-examination of the manuscript tradition. Unfortunately, he wrongly assumed that the text of Valesius was an accurate copy of L, and used in addition only manuscript Z and the quotations of Gregory. None the less, he was able materially to improve the text at a number of points, and his certainly represents the best available text prior to the present critical edition. The text was originally prepared as part of a doctoral thesis for the University of Paris entitled *Grégoire de Nysse. Réfutation de la Profession de foi d'Eunome* (1968), and is found on pp. 110-36 of that thesis together with a French translation. It is to be regretted that the format of the series in which his edition appeared did not allow Van Parys to present either his translation or an *apparatus criticus*, since this would have greatly increased the utility of his already helpful edition.

CONSPECTUS SIGLORUM

L   Codex Laurentianus Mediceus plut. vi, 17, fos. 4^v-5^v, ut videtur, saeculi xi medii.

N   Codex Parisinus suppl. graecus 270, fos. 466^r-467^v, saeculi xvii.

P   Codex Patmensis (Γ) 46 monasterii S. Ioannis, fos. 238^v-241^r, saeculi x vel xi.

Z   Codex Vaticanus graecus 1773, fos. 149^r-151^v, saeculi xvi.

F   Codex Parisinus suppl. graecus 174, fos. 146^r-151^v, saeculi xvi, fortasse ineuntis.

J   Codex Cantabrigiensis Collegii Sanctissimae et Individuae Trinitatis O.2.3 (1107), fos. 1^r-6^r, saeculi xviii ineuntis (verisimile *c*.1710).

codd.   Codices omnes.

g   Excerpta quae in Gregorii Nysseni *Refutationis Confessionis Eunomii* libro inveniuntur (*Conf.*).

a   Textus iuxta Martini Albertz editionem excerptorum Gregorii.

v^v Textus vulgatus iuxta editionem Henrici Valesii (1668).

v^r Textus vulgatus iuxta editionem C. H. G. Rettberg (1794).

v^m Textus vulgatus iuxta editionem J.-P. Migne (1864).

p   Textus iuxta Michaelis Van Parys editionem (1968).

STEMMA

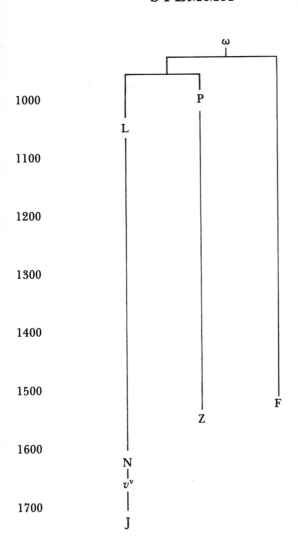

ΕΥΝΟΜΙΟΥ ΕΚΘΕΣΙΣ
THE CONFESSION OF EUNOMIUS

ΕΥΝΟΜΙΟΥ ΕΚΘΕΣΙΣ

1. Τοῦ θεοῦ καὶ σωτῆρος ἡμῶν Ἰησοῦ Χριστοῦ κατὰ δικαίαν κρίσιν φήσαντος ὁμολογεῖν ἔμπροσθεν τοῦ θεοῦ καὶ πατρὸς τοὺς ὁμολογοῦντας αὐτὸν ἔμπροσθεν τῶν ἀνθρώπων, καὶ ἀπαρνεῖσθαι τοὺς ἀρνουμένους αὐτόν,[a] καὶ τῆς ἀποστολικῆς διδασκαλίας προτρεπούσης ἡμᾶς ἑτοίμους εἶναι
5 πρὸς ἀπολογίαν παντὶ τῷ ἐπερωτῶντι λόγον,[b] καὶ τῶν βασιλικῶν προσταγμάτων ταύτην ἐπιζητούντων τὴν ὁμολογίαν, προθύμως ὁμολογοῦμεν ἃ φρονοῦμεν,

2. Ὅτι καὶ πιστεύομεν εἰς τὸν ἕνα καὶ μόνον ἀληθινὸν θεὸν[a] κατὰ τὴν αὐτοῦ τοῦ κυρίου διδασκαλίαν, οὐκ ἐψευσμένῃ φωνῇ τιμῶντες αὐτόν (ἔστι γὰρ ἀψευδής),[b] ἀλλ᾽ ὄντως ὄντα φύσει τε καὶ δόξῃ θεὸν ἕνα, ἀνάρχως, ἀϊδίως, ἀτελευτήτως μόνον, οὐ τὴν οὐσίαν καθ᾽ ἥν ἐστιν εἰς χω-
5 ριζόμενον ἢ μεριζόμενον εἰς πλείους, ἢ ἄλλοτε ἄλλον γινόμενον, ἢ τοῦ εἶναι ὅ ἐστι[c] μεθιστάμενον, οὐδὲ ἐκ μιᾶς οὐσίας εἰς ὑπόστασιν τρισσὴν σχιζόμενον (πάντη γὰρ καὶ καθάπαξ ἐστὶν εἷς, κατὰ τὰ αὐτά τε καὶ ὡσαύτως διαμένων μόνος), οὐ κοινωνὸν ἔχων τῆς θεότητος, οὐ μερίτην τῆς δόξης, οὐ σύγκληρον τῆς ἐξουσίας, οὐ σύνθρονον τῆς βασι-
10 λείας (εἷς γάρ ἐστι καὶ μόνος θεὸς[d] ὁ παντοκράτωρ), θεὸς θεῶν,[e] βασιλεὺς τῶν βασιλευόντων καὶ κύριος τῶν κυριευόντων,[f] ὕψιστος ἐπὶ πᾶσαν τὴν γῆν,[g] ὕψιστος ἐν οὐρανοῖς, ὕψιστος ἐν ὑψίστοις, ἐπουράνιος, ἀληθινὸς ἐν τῷ εἶναι ὅ ἐστιν ἀεὶ[h] καὶ διαμένων ἀληθινὸς

---

1. [a] Matt. 10: 32-3   [b] 1 Pet. 3: 15   2. [a] Jn. 17: 3   [b] Titus 1: 2
[c] Cf. Exod. 3: 14   [d] Jn. 17: 3   [e] Ps. 49(50): 1   [f] 1 Tim. 6: 15
[g] Pss. 82(83): 19, 96(97): 9   [h] Cf. Exod. 3: 14

Title: εὐνομίου ἔκθεσις L: ἔκθεσις εὐνομίου P: ἡ τοῦ δόγματος εὐνομίου, ἔκθεσις F
2. 1 καὶ[1] LF: om. P   2 αὐτόν g: codd. om   4 ἀϊδίως LPg: δίως F   5 ἢ[1] LPg: καὶ F   ἄλλον LPg: ἄλλο Fg var.   6 ἐστι LPg: ἔστιν F   οὐδὲ g: οὔτε codd.
6-7 ὑπόστασιν τρισσὴν g ad 325.9-10: ὑποστάσεις τρεῖς codd.g ad 326.6, 19   7 σχιζό-
μενον g: σχιματιζόμενον L: σχηματιζόμενον PFg var.   κατὰ Fg: καὶ κατὰ LP
8 διαμένων LFg: μένων P   9 μερίτην g: μεριστὴν codd.   10 ἐστι LPg: ἐστιν F   ὁ παντοκράτωρ g ad 327.27: παντοκράτωρ codd.g ad 331.22
11 βασιλεὺς g: καὶ βασιλεὺς codd.   καὶ codd.g var.: om. g   12/13 ἐπουράνιος g: ἐπουρανίοις F: τοῖς ἐπουρανίοις LP   13 ἐν τῷ εἶναι ὅ ἐστιν ἀεὶ codd.: ἐν τῷ εἶναι ἀεὶ ὅ ἐστι g   διαμένων g: διαμένειν F: διαμένει LP

THE CONFESSION OF FAITH

1. Our God and Saviour Jesus Christ has said by a just decree that he will acknowledge before his God and Father everyone who acknowledges him before men;[a] apostolic teaching likewise urges us always to be prepared to make a defence to anyone who asks us for an account of our faith;[b] since, therefore, imperial decrees have asked us for just such a confession, we readily acknowledge that which we also profess:

2. We believe in 'the one and only true God'[a] in accordance with the Lord's own teaching, not honouring him by means of a lying name (for he cannot lie),[b] but reverencing him as he really is: both by nature and in glory 'one God', beginninglessly, everlastingly, unendingly 'only'. As regards the essence in respect of which he is one, he is not divided or separated into many, nor has he at any time become something else, or changed from being what he is,[c] nor yet out of single essence has he been split up into a threefold substance (for he is absolutely and altogether 'one', remaining uniformly and invariably 'only'); he has none to partake of his Godhead, none to divide his glory, none to inherit his authority with him, none to share the throne of his kingdom (for the Almighty is the 'one and only God'),[d] 'God of gods',[e] 'King of kings and Lord of lords',[f] 'Most High over all the earth',[g] Most High in the heavens, Most High in the highest, heavenly, 'true' in that he is what he is forever[h] and remains true in his works, true in his

ἐν ἔργοις, ἀληθινὸς ἐν λόγοις, ἀρχῆς ἁπάσης, ὑποταγῆς, ἐξουσίας,
M 588 βασιλείας ἀνώτερος, τροπῆς καὶ μεταβολῆς ἐλεύθερος | ὡς ἀκήρατος, οὐκ
ἐν τῷ γεννᾶν τὴν ἰδίαν οὐσίαν μερίζων, καὶ ὁ αὐτὸς γεννῶν καὶ γεννώ-
μενος, ἢ ὁ αὐτὸς πατὴρ γινόμενος καὶ υἱός (ἔστι γὰρ ἄφθαρτος), οὐκ
ἐν τῷ ποιεῖν ὕλης ἢ μερῶν ἢ φυσικῶν ὀργάνων προσδεόμενος (ἔστι γὰρ
πάντων ἀπροσδεής).

3. Πιστεύομεν καὶ εἰς τὸν τοῦ θεοῦ υἱόν,[a] τὸν μονογενῆ θεόν,[b] τὸν
πρωτότοκον πάσης κτίσεως,[c] υἱὸν ἀληθινόν, οὐκ ἀγέννητον, ἀληθῶς γεννηθέντα πρὸ αἰώνων, οὐκ ἄνευ τῆς πρὸ τοῦ εἶναι γεννήσεως ὀνομαζόμενον
υἱόν, πρὸ πάσης κτίσεως γενόμενον, οὐκ ἄκτιστον, ἀρχὴν ἔργων ‹καὶ›
5 ὁδῶν τοῦ θεοῦ[d] καὶ ἐν ἀρχῇ ὄντα,[e] οὐκ ἄναρχον, σοφίαν ζῶσαν, ἀλήθειαν
ἐνεργοῦσαν, δύναμιν ὑφεστῶσαν, ζωὴν γεννητήν (ὡς υἱὸν θεοῦ ζωογονοῦντα
τοὺς ζῶντας καὶ ζωοποιοῦντα τοὺς νεκρούς),[f] φῶς ἀληθινὸν φωτίζον πάντα
ἄνθρωπον ἐρχόμενον εἰς τὸν κόσμον,[g] ἀγαθὸν καὶ χορηγὸν ἀγαθῶν (ὡς
ἀγαθότητι καὶ δυνάμει γεννηθέντα τοῦ πατρός), οὐχὶ τῷ γεννήσαντι
10 συμμερισάμενον τὴν ἀξίαν, οὐκ ἄλλῳ τινὶ τὴν πατρικὴν οὐσίαν, οὐ τὴν
βασιλείαν, ἀλλὰ γενόμενον ἐκ γεννήσεως ἔνδοξον καὶ τῆς δόξης κύριον[h]
καὶ λαβόντα παρὰ τοῦ πατρὸς τὴν δόξαν[i] (οὐ τῆς ἐκείνου μεταλαβόντα
δόξης, ἀμετάδοτος γὰρ ἡ δόξα τοῦ παντοκράτορος, καθὼς εἶπε, Τὴν δόξαν
μου ἑτέρῳ οὐ δώσω),[j] δεδοξασμένον παρὰ τοῦ πατρὸς πρὸ τῶν αἰώνων,[k]
15 δοξαζόμενον ὑπὸ τοῦ πνεύματος δι' αἰῶνος καὶ πάσης λογικῆς καὶ γεννητῆς οὐσίας, δορυφορούμενον ὑπὸ πάσης ἐπουρανίου στρατιᾶς (κύριος
γάρ ἐστι καὶ βασιλεὺς τῆς δόξης,[l] ὡς υἱὸς θεοῦ καὶ θεός), δημιουργὸς

3. [a]2 Cor. 1: 19, Jn. 1: 49, etc.   [b]Jn. 1: 18   [c]Col. 1: 15   [d]Prov.
8: 22   [e]Jn. 1: 1   [f]Cf. Jn. 5: 19-29   [g]Jn. 1: 9   [h]1 Cor. 2: 8
[i]2 Pet. 1: 17, cf. Jn. 17: 3   [j]Isa. 42: 8, 48: 11   [k]Cf. Jn. 17: 5
[l]1 Cor. 2: 8, Ps. 23(24): 7-10

14 ἀρχῆς Pg: ἀρχὴ LF   17 ἔστι γὰρ LPg: ἔστιν F, γὰρ om.   18 ἔστι LPg:
ἔστιν F   19 πάντων codd.: παντὸς g   3. 1-2 τὸν πρωτότοκον codd.g ad
348.5: τὸν om. g ad 342.18   2 υἱὸν ἀληθινὸν: χριστὸν ἀληθινὸν θεὸν codd.
2-3 ἀληθῶς . . . αἰώνων g: om. codd.   3 τῆς PFg: om. L   4 ἀρχὴν Fg:
ἀρχὴ LP   ‹καὶ›sic conieci (cf. Rettberg): codd. om.   5 ἐν ἀρχῇ ὄντα g:
ἐν ἀρχῇ ὄντα λόγον codd.   6 ζωογονοῦντα codd.: ζωοποιοῦντα g   7 φωτίζον
PFg var.: φωτίζων L: φῶς φωτίζον g   8 καὶ LFg: om. P   9 γεννήσαντι PFg:
μερίσαντι L   10 ἄλλῳ PFg: ἄλλο L   12 τὴν codd.: om. g   13 παντοκράτορος codd.g ad 361.19 f., 27, 363.19, 364.10: παντοκράτορος θεοῦ g ad 363.7
14 δεδοξασμένον . . . αἰώνων LFg: om. P   παρά g: ὑπὸ LF   15 δοξαζόμενον
g: δεδοξασμένον codd.   γεννητῆς PFg: γενητῆς Lg var.   16 δορυφορούμενον
LF: δορυφορούμενος P   17 ἐστι LP: ἐστιν F

words. He is superior to all rule, subjection, power, or kingship; he is free from change or alteration since he is uncompounded. In begetting he does not divide his own essence, nor are begetter and begotten the same, nor does the same Father become also 'Son' (he is incorruptible); in creating he has no need of matter, parts, or physical instruments (he is without need of anything).

3. We also believe in 'the Son of God',[a] 'the Only-begotten God',[b] 'the First-born of all creation':[c] a genuine 'son', so not unbegotten; genuinely 'begotten' before the ages, so not without an act of begetting prior to his own existence to be called 'Son'; 'born' before 'all creation', so not uncreated;[1] 'beginning of the works and ways of God',[d] and existing 'in the beginning',[e] so not without beginning; living Wisdom, operative Truth, subsistent Power, begotten Life (it is as Son of God that he is the life-source of living creatures and the giver of life to the dead),[f] 'true light that enlightens every man coming into the world';[g] he is good and the supplier of good things (he was begotten of the Father in goodness and in power), but he does not partake of the status of the one who begot him or share with any other the Father's essence or his kingdom; rather, becoming glorious and 'the Lord of glory'[h] as a result of his begetting and 'receiving glory from the Father'[i] (he does not participate *in* his glory for the glory of the Almighty is incommunicable, as he himself says, 'My glory I will not give to another'),[j] he has been glorified 'from the Father' before the ages,[k] and is glorified throughout eternity by the Spirit and by every rational and begotten essence; he is attended by the whole heavenly army (he is both 'Lord' and 'King' of glory,[l] being both Son of God

[1] As with the explanation of Prov. 8: 22 which follows, each of the preceding three clauses draws out the implications of the biblical titles with which this paragraph commences.

ἀθανάτων καὶ θνητῶν, δημιουργὸς τῶν πνευμάτων καὶ πάσης σαρκός (πάντα γὰρ δι' αὐτοῦ ἐγένετο, καὶ χωρὶς αὐτοῦ ἐγένετο οὐδὲ ἕν),[m] βασιλεὺς
20 καὶ κύριος πάσης ζωῆς καὶ πνοῆς τῶν δι' αὐτοῦ γενομένων (πάντα γὰρ αὐτῷ παρεδόθη παρὰ τοῦ πατρός,[n] κατὰ τὴν ἁγίαν αὐτοῦ φωνήν, καὶ πάντα δέδωκεν ὁ πατὴρ ἐν τῇ χειρὶ αὐτοῦ),[o] ὑπήκοος πρὸς τὴν τῶν ὄντων δημιουργίαν καὶ γένεσιν, ὑπήκοος πρὸς πᾶσαν διοίκησιν, οὐκ ἐκ τῆς ὑπακοῆς προσλαβὼν τὸ εἶναι υἱὸς ἢ θεός, ἀλλ' ἐκ τοῦ υἱὸς εἶναι καὶ γεννηθῆναι μονογενὴς
25 θεὸς[p] γενόμενος ὑπήκοος ἐν ἔργοις, ὑπήκοος ἐν λόγοις, μεσίτης ἐν δόγμασι, μεσίτης ἐν νόμοις, τοῦτον ἴσμεν υἱὸν τοῦ θεοῦ καὶ μονογενῆ θεόν,[q] τοῦτον ὅμοιον τῷ γεννήσαντι μόνον κατ' ἐξαίρετον ὁμοιότητα κατὰ τὴν ἰδιάζουσαν ἔννοιαν, οὐχ ὡς πατρὶ πατέρα (οὐ γὰρ εἰσὶ δύο
M 589 πατέρες), | οὐδὲ ὡς υἱῷ υἱόν (οὐκ ὄντων δύο υἱῶν), οὐδὲ ὡς ἀγεννήτῳ
30 ἀγέννητον (μόνος γάρ ἐστιν ἀγέννητος ὁ παντοκράτωρ καὶ μόνος ὁ μονογενὴς γεννητός), ἀλλ' ὡς υἱὸν πατρί, ὡς εἰκόνα καὶ ὡς σφραγῖδα πάσης τῆς τοῦ παντοκράτορος ἐνεργείας καὶ δυνάμεως,[r] σφραγῖδα τῶν τοῦ πατρὸς ἔργων καὶ λόγων καὶ βουλευμάτων, τοῦτον ὁμολογοῦμεν ἕνα, τὸν ἐν ὕδασιν ἐπικλύσαντα τὴν γῆν, τὸν πυρὶ καταφλέξαντα Σοδομίτας, τὸν ἐπι-
35 θέντα δίκην Αἰγυπτίοις,[s] τὸν θέμενον τοὺς νόμους κατ' ἐπιταγὴν τοῦ αἰωνίου θεοῦ,[t] τὸν ἐπὶ τῶν προφητῶν ὁμιλήσαντα τοῖς παλαιοῖς,[u] τὸν καλέσαντα τοὺς ἀπειθοῦντας,[v] τὸν λαβόντα πᾶσαν τοῦ κρίνειν τὴν ἐξουσίαν (ὁ γὰρ πατὴρ κρίνει οὐδένα, τὴν κρίσιν γὰρ πᾶσαν δέδωκεν τῷ υἱῷ),[w] τὸν ἐπ' ἐσχάτων τῶν ἡμερῶν γενόμενον ἐν σαρκί,[x] γενόμενον ἐκ γυναι-
40 κός,[y] γενόμενον ἄνθρωπον ἐπ' ἐλευθερίᾳ καὶ σωτηρίᾳ τοῦ γένους ἡμῶν,

---

[m]Jn. 1: 3   [n]Matt. 11: 27   [o]Jn. 3: 35, cf. Jn. 13: 3   [p]Jn. 1: 18
[q]Cf. the creed of the fourth Council of Sirmium, AD 359 (Hahn 163)   [r]Cf. Col.
1: 15, Jn. 6: 27   [s]Gen. 7: 10-24, 19: 24-5; Exod. 14: 26-31; cf. 3 Macc. 2: 4-8
[t]Exod. 3: 1 ff., 20: 1 ff., etc.; Rom. 16: 26 (cf. g 383.20-384.5)   [u]Cf. Heb. 1: 1
[v]Cf. 1 Pet. 3: 20   [w]Jn. 5: 22 (cf. g 384.14-16)   [x]Cf. Heb. 1: 2   [y]Gal. 4: 4

---

19 ἐγένετο, καὶ LP: ἐγένητο, καὶ F   25 ὑπήκοος ἐν ἔργοις, ὑ. ἐν λόγοις codd.g ad
370.23-4: ὑπήκοος ἐν λόγοις, ὑ. ἐν ἔργοις g ad 369.24-5, 371.6-7, 372.19-20
26 νόμοις codd.: νόμῳ g   τοῦ LF: om. P sed corr.   27 μόνον . . . ὁμοιότητα
codd.g ad 377.2-3: κατ' ἐξαίρετον ὁμοιότητα μόνον g ad 375.1-2   28 κατὰ g: καὶ
codd.   29-30 οὐδὲ ὡς υἱῷ ὑ. . . . . οὐδὲ ἀγεννήτῳ ἀ. codd.: ut videtur οὔτε ὡς
ἀγεννήτῳ ἀ. . . . οὔτε ὡς υἱῷ ὑ. g (cf. 377.9-13): ὡς ἀγεννήτῳ ἀγέννητον Pg: ὡς γέννητον
ἀγεννήτῳ LF   30-1 μόνος ὁ μονογενὴς γεννητός P (cf. g): μόνος υἱὸς ὁ μονογενὴς LF
(υἱὸς bis F)   31 ὡς[s] codd.: om. g   36 τῶν LF: om. P   38 τὴν κρίσιν γὰρ πᾶσαν
P: τὴν γὰρ κρίσιν πᾶσαν L: τὴν κρίσιν πᾶσαν F   δέδωκεν LP: δέδωκε F   39 ἐν σαρκί
codd.: ἄνθρωπον g

and God); he is maker of both immortals and mortals, maker of
spiritual beings and of all flesh (for 'all things were made through
him and without him was not one thing made'),[m] King and Lord of
the whole life and breath of the things made through him (for in
accordance with his own holy voice, 'all things have been delivered
to him by his Father',[n] and 'the Father has given all things into his
hand'),[o] obedient with regard to the ordering and creation of all
existing things, obedient with regard to all governance, not made
'Son' or 'God' because of his obedience, but, because he is 'Son' and
was begotten 'Only-begotten God',[p] obedient in his works, obedient
in his words, mediator in doctrine, mediator in law; he it is whom
we acknowledge as Son of God and Only-begotten God.[q] Only he
resembles his begetter with a most exact likeness in accordance with
the meaning which is proper to himself: not as Father to Father
(there are not two Fathers), nor yet as Son to Son (there are not two
Sons), neither as Unbegotten to Unbegotten (only the Almighty is
unbegotten and only the Only-begotten is begotten), but as the
image and as the seal of the whole activity and power of the
Almighty,[r] the seal of the Father's deeds, words, and counsels. Him
we acknowledge as 'one': the one who overwhelmed the earth
beneath the waters, who consumed the people of Sodom by fire,
who laid just retribution upon the Egyptians,[s] who gave the Law in
accordance with the command of the eternal God,[t] who in the time
of the prophets spoke to the people of old,[u] who called back those
who were disobedient,[v] who received the whole power of judgement
('the Father judges no one, but has given all judgement to the
Son'),[w] who in these last days was born in the flesh,[x] 'born of
a woman',[y] born a man for the freedom and salvation of our race,

οὐκ ἀναλαβόντα τὸν ἐκ ψυχῆς καὶ σώματος ἄνθρωπον, τὸν διὰ γλώσσης καὶ
στόματος εὐαγγελισάμενον τὴν εἰρήνην τοῖς ἐγγὺς καὶ τοῖς μακράν,ᶻ τὸν
γενόμενον ὑπήκοον μέχρι σταυροῦ καὶ θανάτου,ᵃᵃ καὶ μὴ ἰδόντα διαφθοράν,ᵇᵇ
ἀλλ' ἀναστάντα τῇ τρίτῃ τῶν ἡμερῶν, καὶ μετὰ τὴν ἀνάστασιν ἀνακεφα-
45 λαιωσάμενον τοῖς ἑαυτοῦ τὸ μυστήριον,ᶜᶜ καὶ καθήμενον ἐν δεξιᾷ τοῦ
πατρός, τὸν ἐρχόμενον κρῖναι ζῶντας καὶ νεκρούς.

4. Καὶ μετὰ τοῦτον πιστεύομεν εἰς τὸν παράκλητον, τὸ πνεῦμα τῆς
ἀληθείας, τὸν καθηγητὴν τῆς εὐσεβείας,ᵃ γενόμενον ὑπὸ τοῦ μόνου θεοῦᵇ
διὰ τοῦ μονογενοῦς καὶ τούτῳ καθάπαξ ὑποτεταγμένον, οὔτε κατὰ τὸν
πατέρα, οὔτε τῷ πατρὶ συναριθμούμενον (εἷς γάρ ἐστι καὶ μόνοςᶜ πατὴρ
5 ὁ ἐπὶ πάντων θεός),ᵈ οὔτε τῷ υἱῷ συνεξισούμενον (μονογενὴς γάρ ἐστιν
ὁ υἱός, οὐδένα ἔχων ἀδελφὸν ὁμογενῆ), οὔτε μὴν ἄλλῳ τινὶ συντασσόμενον (ἁπάντων γὰρ ἀναβέβηκε τῶν διὰ τοῦ υἱοῦ γενομένων ποιημάτων
γενέσει καὶ φύσει καὶ δόξῃ καὶ γνώσει, ὡς πρῶτον ἔργον καὶ κράτιστον
τοῦ μονογενοῦς, μέγιστόν τε καὶ κάλλιστον), εἷς δὲ καὶ οὗτος ὢν καὶ
10 πρῶτος καὶ μόνος,ᵉ καὶ πάντων προύχων τῶν τοῦ υἱοῦ ποιημάτων κατὰ
τὴν οὐσίαν καὶ τὴν φυσικὴν ἀξίαν, πᾶσαν ἐνέργειαν καὶ διδασκαλίαν
ἐξανύει κατὰ τὸ δοκοῦν τῷ υἱῷ, πεμπόμενος ὑπ' αὐτοῦᶠ καὶ παρ'
αὐτοῦ λαμβάνων καὶ ἀναγγέλλων τοῖς παιδευομένοις καὶ τῆς ἀληθείας
καθηγούμενος,ᵍ ἁγιάζων τοὺς ἁγίους, μυσταγωγῶν τοὺς προσιόντας τῷ
15 μυστηρίῳ, διανέμων πᾶσαν δωρεὰν τῷ νεύματι τοῦ διδόντος τὴν χάριν,ʰ συνεργῶν τοῖς πιστοῖς πρὸς κατανόησιν καὶ θεωρίαν τῶν δια-

---

ᶻEphes. 2: 17   ᵃᵃPhil. 2: 8   ᵇᵇActs 2: 27, 13: 37, cf. Ps. 15(16): 10
ᶜᶜCf. Matt. 28: 18-20   **4.** ᵃJn. 14: 17, 15: 26, cf. 16: 13   ᵇJn. 5: 44,
1 Tim. 1: 17   ᶜCf. Jn. 17: 3   ᵈRom. 9: 5   ᵉCf. 1 Cor. 12: 9, 11, 13
ᶠJn. 15: 26   ᵍCf. Jn. 16: 13-15   ʰAt this point the text of Eunomius'
confession terminates in codex F

41 ἐκ LPg: τῆς F   44 τῇ τρίτῃ (τρίτ F) τῶν ἡμερῶν LF: τριήμερον P
4. 2 γενόμενον codd.: γενόμενος g   2-3 ὑπὸ τοῦ μόνου θεοῦ διὰ τοῦ μονογενοῦς g:
ὑπὸ τοῦ μονογενοῦς codd.   3 τούτῳ PF: τοῦ L: hic habet L adnotationem
ση(μείωσ)αι in marg.   4 συναριθμούμενον codd.: συναριθμούμενος g
5 συνεξισούμενον codd.g ad 398.19-20: συνεξισούμενος g ad 397.24   6 ὁ υἱός g:
om. codd.   ἀδελφὸν codd.g ad 399.8: om. g ad 397.25   6/7 συντασσόμενον
LPg: συναττόμενον F   9 δὲ codd.: γὰρ g   10 τῶν LPg: om. F
11 φυσικὴν LPg: δυσικὴν F   12 ἐξανύει codd.: ἐξανύειν g ad 402.10, 403.1: ἐξάνυσον
g ad 402.6   ὑπ' codd.g ad 402.7: παρ' g ad 403.7   14 καθηγούμενος codd.:
ἡγούμενος g   15 τῷ ... χάριν LF: om. P et fortasse g (cf. 404.20)   νεύματι
sic recte coniecit Rettberg et Van Parys: πνεύματι LF   16 πρὸς LPg ad 405.9:
εἰς g ad 404.23

yet not taking upon him 'the man' made up of body and soul. With tongue and voice 'he preached peace to those who were near and to those who were far off';[z] he 'became obedient unto the cross and unto death',[aa] and yet 'did not see corruption',[bb] but rose again the third day and after his resurrection summed up the mystery for those who were his own;[cc] he is seated at the right hand of the Father; he will come again to judge the living and the dead.

4. After him we believe in 'the Counsellor, the Spirit of truth', the teacher of godliness:[a] he was brought forth by the Only God[b] through the Only-begotten and was made subject to him once and for all; he is not on the same level as the Father nor is he numbered along with the Father (for 'the God who is over all'[d] is 'one and only'[c] Father), nor is he made the equal of the Son (the Son is 'only-begotten' and has no brother begotten like himself), nor yet is he placed in the same category as any other being (he transcends all the creatures made through the Son in origin and nature and glory and knowledge, being the first and most mighty work of the Only-begotten, the greatest and most beautiful; rather, since he too is 'one' and 'first' and 'only'[e] and surpasses all the works of the Son in essence and in dignity of nature, he brings every activity and teaching to completion in accordance with the Son's will, being sent from him[f] and receiving from him and declaring it to those who are being instructed and guiding them into truth:[g] he sanctifies the saints, initiates those approaching the Mystery, distributes every gift at the command of the Giver of grace, assists those who believe in the apprehension and contemplation of what has been

τεταγμένων, ὑπηχῶν εὐχομένοις,[i] ὁδηγῶν πρὸς τὸ συμφέρον,[j] κρατύνων
πρὸς εὐσέβειαν, φωτίζων τὰς ψυχὰς τῷ φωτὶ τῆς γνώσεως, καθαίρων τοὺς
λογισμούς, δαίμονας ἀπείργων[k] καὶ νοσοῦντας θεραπεύων, ἀρρωστοῦντας
20 ἰώμενος, πλανωμένους ἐπιστρέφων, θλιβομένους παρακαλῶν, ὀκλάζοντας
ἀνορθῶν, πονοῦντας ἀνακτώμενος, ἀγωνιζομένοις ὑποφωνῶν, δειλανδροῦν-
τας θαρσύνων, ἀπάντων κηδόμενος, καὶ πᾶσαν φροντίδα καὶ πρόνοιαν
εἰσφερόμενος εἰς προσαγωγὴν τῶν εὐνουστέρων καὶ φυλακὴν τῶν πιστο-
τέρων.

5. Πιστεύομεν ἐπὶ τούτοις καὶ εἰς τὴν γενησομένην ἀνάστασιν διὰ
M 590 τοῦ σωτῆρος αὐτῶν τῶν δια | λυθέντων σωμάτων μετὰ τῶν οἰκείων καὶ μερῶν
καὶ μορίων, οὐδενὸς ἐλλείποντος οὔτε ἐνηλλαγμένου τῶν τοῦ ἑκάστου τὸ
σῶμα συμπληρούντων κατὰ τὸν παρόντα βίον, ἔτι μὴν καὶ τὴν ἐπὶ τούτοις
5 κρίσιν τῶν κακῶς δοξαζομένων ἢ βεβιωμένων, καὶ πάντων ὁμοῦ τῶν κατὰ
τὴν παροῦσαν ζωὴν γινομένων ἔργων καὶ λόγων καὶ ἐνεργείων, πράξεων,
ἐνθυμημάτων, νοημάτων, μηδενὸς τὸ παράπαν λανθάνοντος τῶν μεγίστων ἢ
τῶν ἐλαχίστων, μηδενὸς παρεωραμένου τῶν ἐνθέσμως ἢ παρανόμως εἰρ-
γασμένων ἢ πεπραγμένων, τῆς συμμέτρου καὶ δικαίας ἐπιμετρουμένης
10 δίκης, καὶ τοὺς μὲν εἰς τέλος ἀσεβήσαντας ἢ ἁμαρτήσαντας πρὸς τὴν
ἀτελεύτητον κόλασιν παραπεμπούσης, τοὺς δὲ ὁσίως καὶ δικαίως βιώσαν-
τας πρὸς τὴν αἰωνίαν ζωὴν ἀναφερούσης.

6. Ταῦτα καὶ φρονοῦμεν· παρὰ τῶν ἁγίων μαθόντες, καὶ φρονοῦντες
πιστεύομεν, οὐδὲν ὑπ' αἰσχύνης ἢ δέους παρέντες ὧν ἐμάθομεν, οὔτε
μὴν ὑπ' αἰσχύνης ἢ φιλονεικίας προστιθέντες πλεῖον ἢ διαστρέφοντες,
οὐδὲ συνειδότες οὐδὲ ἀπηχὲς ἢ δύσφημον, ὁποῖα πλάττουσι καθ' ἡμῶν
5 οἱ συκοφαντοῦντες ἢ διαβάλλοντες, ὧν τὸ κρίμα ἔνδικόν ἐστιν.[a]

---

[i]Cf. Rom. 8: 26   [j]Cf. Ps. 142(143): 10, 1 Cor. 12: 7   [k]Cf. Matt. 12: 28
6. [a]Rom. 3: 8

---

17 ὑπηχῶν Pg: ὑφηχῶν L   19 καὶ L: om. P(g?)   ἀρρωστοῦντας Pg: τοὺς
νοσοῦντας L   20 πλανωμένους ἐπιστρέφων LP: om. g ad 406.21, sed cf. 407.4-5
21 ἀγωνιζομένοις LP: τοῖς ἀγωνιζομένοις g   22 θαρσύνων LPg var.: θρασύνων g
κηδόμενος Pg: κηδεμόνα L   καὶ[1] g: om. LP   23 εἰσφερόμενος Pg: εἰσφερό-
μενον L   5. 1 καὶ P: om. L   2 καὶ L: om. P   3-4 τῶν τοῦ ἑκάστου τὸ
σῶμα P: τῶν τὸ ἑκάστου σῶμα L   5 κακῶς P: ἐπὶ κακῶς L   8 παρεωραμένου
P: προορωμένου L   ἢ παρανόμως bis L   10 ἢ ἁμαρτήσαντας L: ἢ ἀσεβήσαντας P   12 αἰωνίαν L: αἰώνιον P   6. 2 ὧν P: ὡς L

commanded, inspires those who pray,[h] leads us to that which is advantageous,[i] strengthens us in godliness, enlightens souls with the light of knowledge, cleanses our thoughts, binds demons[j] and heals the sick, cures the diseased, raises the fallen, refreshes the weary, encourages the struggling, cheers the fainthearted; he is the guardian of all and exercises every care and providence for the advancement of the better-disposed and the protection of the more faithful.

5. After these things, we also believe in the resurrection to be brought about through the Saviour of our actual dissolved bodies together with their own proper parts and members, nothing being lacking or altered of that which went to make up the body of each in this present lifetime. Moreover, we also believe in the judgement after these things of that which has been thought or done wickedly, as well as of all the actions, words, and activities, deeds, conceptions, or thoughts which have been done in this present life; not one thing overlooked, lawful or unlawful, which had been done or accomplished. The proper and appropriate retribution will be meted out to each: those who have lived godlessly and remained in sin to the very end will be sent to everlasting punishment; those who have lived devout and righteous lives will be borne up to life everlasting.

6. These things, then, we profess, having learned them from the saints, and, professing them, believe. We have neither passed over anything we have learned out of shame or fear nor have we added anything extra or distorted anything out of shame or love of rivalry; nor, indeed, have we even been conscious of any discordant or derogatory thing of the kind trumped up against us by detractors or slanderers — 'their condemnation is just'.[a]

APPENDIX

CITATIONS OF THE *EXPOSITIO FIDEI* BY GREGORY OF NYSSA

EF	Conf.	EF	Conf.
2.1-4	320.11-16 (320.25-6; 321.4-5; 322.21-2; 323.8-9, 23; 324.10-11)	25-6	373.20-1
		26-7	Cf. 374.25-7
		27-9	377.2-5 (374.28-375.2; 377.1; cf. 379.7-8, 9; 377.18)
4-8	325.6-12 (325.24-5; 325.20-2; 326.14-18; 326.5-9; 327.3-5)	29	377.11-12, 21
8-11	327.23-8 (328.25; 329.22-3, 24 f.; 330.14-15; 331.1-2, 5; 329.14, 21 f.; 331.22-3; 332.19)	29-30	377.9-10, 27 (cf. 378.3-4)
		30-1	Cf. 378.1, 11-12, 18-19
		31	379.16
11-12	332.20	31-2	381.18-20 (379.23-4, cf. 26; 380.21-2; 381.6-7; 378.26; 379.1)
12-14	332.25-8 (333.4-5; 333.3; cf. 371.6-7)		
14-15	333.13-14	32-3	381.24-5, cf. 382.19-21, 23, 24-5
15-17	334.7-11; 335.3-6; 337.23-6 (335.10; 336.2-3; 334.17-19, 21-3; 337.4-7)	33-5	Cf. 383.6-9
		35-6	383.20-1, cf. 323.19-22
		36	Cf. 363.1-2
17-19	340.12-14	38	Cf. 384.14-16
3.1-4	342.17-22 (348.4-7; 352.19-21; 353.11; 343.12-14; 355.6-7; 356.15; 342.27; 348.10; 356.18)	39	384.29-30
		41	384.30-385.2
		44	Cf. 387.8-14
		4.1-2	389.7-8 (390.13-14; 391.21-2)
4-5	Cf. 358.7-360.4	2	392.13-14
5	360.5	2-3	392.23-4; 395.6-7
5-6	360.26-361.4	3	396.3-4; 397.2
6-8	361.6-10	3-6	397.21-5 (398.19-20; 399.7-8)
9-14	361.14-21 (367.25-7; 361.25-8; 363.4-7; 363.19; 364.9-10; 365.1, 21)	6-9	400.22-401.1 (401.6)
		9-14	402.2-9 (403.20-1; 404.2-3; 402.9-10; 403.7-9)
14	368.11-12		
15-16	368.26-8	14	404.7-8
22-5	369.20-5 (cf. 370.22-4; 371.6-7; 372.19-20)	14-15	404.12-13
		15	404.20

EF	Conf.	EF	Conf.
16–17	404.22–4; 405.9–10	19–21	406.20–3 (407.4–5, 9–10, 14–15, 19–20)
17	405.11–12; 405.19		
17–18	405.22–3	21	408.3–4
18	406.4–5	21–2	409.7
18–19	Cf. 406.9–10	22–3	409.21–3
19	406.13	23–4	410.2–3

THE FRAGMENTS OF EUNOMIUS

INTRODUCTION

FRAGMENT i

In addition to the larger works of Eunomius which, whether complete or fragmentary, have come down to us, a number of fragments have also been preserved. The first of these is contained in the pseudo-Athanasian *Dialogus de Sancta Trinitate* ii.6 (*PG* 28.1165A-B),[1] and has come down to us in connection with what is described as a 'letter' of Eunomius' teacher Aetius (it is part of his *Syntagmation*).[2] In the section of the *Dialogus* which introduces it, it is described as follows:

Ἀνόμοιος. Λάβε, ἀνάγνωθι τὴν ἐπιστολὴν Ἀετίου, καὶ εἰπὲ πρὸς αὐτήν. Ὀρθόδοξος. Αὐτὸς ἀνάγνωθι. Ἀνόμ. Εἰσὶ μετ' αὐτῆς καὶ σχόλια Εὐνομίου. Ὀρθ. Καὶ αὐτὰ ἀνάγνωθι.[3]

Anomoean. Here! Read this letter of Aetius and see if you can answer that! *Orthodox.* Read it yourself. *Anom.* There are some *Scholia* of Eunomius with it. *Orth.* Read those too.

The actual *Scholia* are introduced by the following title:

Σχόλια Εὐνομίου. καὶ πρὸς αὐτὰ Ὀρθοδόξου.[4]

The *Scholia* of Eunomius and (the reply) of the Orthodox to them.

It is abundantly clear, then, that the *scholia* in question are notes, marginal or otherwise, added to the letter (*Syntagmation*) of Aetius. What is not so clear is how far they extend. In the case of the quotation from Aetius made in the same dialogue, the passages taken from his work extend far beyond that specifically identified as such,[5] but it is only because we possess the treatise as a whole that we are able to identify them. The same may be true here. Although short of actually finding the complete document there is no way to

---

[1] On the vexed question of the real author of these dialogues see A. Heron, 'The Two Pseudo-Athanasian Dialogues Against the Anomoeans', *JTS* 24 (1973), 101-22.

[2] (Ps.-)Ath., *Dial.* ii.10-29 (*PG* 28.1173A-1201B).   [3] Ibid., ii.5 (*PG* 28.1164D).

[4] Ibid., ii.6 (*PG* 28.1165A). I have omitted the reference to the Orthodox response in the text printed below.

[5] The quotation specifically identified as Aetius' is found at *Dial.* ii.10 (*PG* 28.1173A-B), but the quotations from it actually continue throughout *Dial.* ii.11-29 (*PG* 28.1173B-1201B).

be certain, it seems reasonable to suppose that there were other *scholia* besides that specifically identified as such in the text. In that case, it is not impossible that in addition to the passage actually entitled *scholia*, the other questions and statements ascribed to the Anomoean in the following passages are also from the same source. Unfortunately, in the absence of the document itself there is no way to ascertain the truth, and we have therefore printed in what follows below (p. 176) only that passage actually headed *scholia* in the text.[6] We can be almost certain, however, that whatever the status of the other passages in the *Dialogus*, the one under discussion was not Eunomius' only comment on Aetius' work. We can therefore legitimately ask to which passage it was originally attached. Since it clearly cannot apply to the opening section of Aetius' 'letter' quoted under that heading in the *Dialogus*,[7] it must be intended to go with one of the chapters in the main body of the work. That on which it seems to provide the most apposite comment is the central section of Aetius' chapter 18 (quoted in the *Dialogus* at ii.20 (*PG* 28.1188C)), which seems to imply the same distinction between God's will and his essence which is the subject of the *scholia*. In any case, the opening words of our fragment seem to flow quite naturally from the last part of Aetius' statement on this subject, and, while recognizing the conjectural nature of this suggestion, we have therefore printed out the passage just prior to the *scholia* themselves.

When we turn to the question of this fragment's authenticity, there seems little reason to doubt it. It is quoted together with a passage from the *Syntagmation* of Aetius which is certainly genuine, and moreover seems to provide a relevant comment on at least one of the chapters of that work. We find, too, that the ideas which it expresses are found elsewhere in Eunomius,[8] and that such additions as it makes (notably the idea of the multiplicity of God's acts of will) appear to be logical consequences of his teaching.[9] The only hesitation we might feel is due to the tendency of obscure authors to be displaced by better known ones in the course of trans-

[6] It must be said, however, that there is no obvious way to connect these passages with Aetius' *Syntagmation*. The passages are *Dial.* ii.7 (*PG* 28.1165C, 1168A bis), 8 (1168B), 9 (1168D), 10 (1172C).

[7] (Ps.-)Ath., *Dial.* ii.10 (*PG* 28.1173A-B).

[8] Eun., *Apol.* 23.4-24.4, cf. *Apol. Apol.* iii (*J* ii.224.4-14).

[9] Cf., e.g., Eun., *Apol. Apol.* i (*J* i.72.12-73.3).

mission. It is not impossible that these *scholia* might have been composed by one of Eunomius' humbler followers and subsequently ascribed to the heresiarch himself. However, since the name of the author occurs not only in the title, but also in the body of the dialogue, and since the thought expressed in the fragment is coherent with the rest of Eunomius' teaching, this possibility seems to us hypothetical at best.

The text presented below is that of Migne with some slight revision, mostly in terms of punctuation. The only substantive change is the addition of οὔσης at i.5 as required by the sense and witnessed by Codex Parisinus graecus 1258, fo. 325ᵛ and the Latin translation printed in Migne.[10]

FRAGMENT ii

Our next fragment has come down to us in Socrates, *HE* iv.7 (*PG* 67.473B-C), and in terms of content is perhaps among the most interesting. Yet it is precisely because of this content that its authenticity has been called into question, for in it Eunomius makes the claim to know God's essence as God knows it himself. Whatever difficulties this may raise, however, it is important to realize in evaluating their significance that Socrates himself clearly believed that he was presenting a genuine fragment of Eunomius. This is shown by the words with which he introduces the passage (ii.1-3), for it is precisely because he wishes to show that his earlier statements were not his own inventions that he now quotes Eunomius verbatim (κατὰ λέξιν). This must be kept in mind as we look at the objections which have been raised against this fragment's authenticity.

It has been suggested[11] that this fragment is in fact simply an expansion of a similar statement ascribed to Eunomius' teacher Aetius by Epiphanius. A comparison of the two texts, however, reveals substantial differences between them. The statement ascribed by Epiphanius to Aetius is as follows:

ἐφαντασιάσθη γὰρ οὗτος ὕστερον εἰπεῖν, αὐτός τε καὶ οἱ ὑπ᾽ αὐτοῦ μεμαθητευ-
μένοι, ὅτι 'οὕτως, φησί, τὸν θεὸν ἐπίσταμαι τηλαυγέστατα καὶ τοσοῦτον αὐτὸν
ἐπίσταμαι καὶ οἶδα, ὥστε μὴ εἰδέναι ἐμαυτὸν μᾶλλον ὡς θεὸν ἐπίσταμαι.'[12]

---

10 Variants given by Migne are printed in the apparatus in the form he gives them.
11 Albertz, p. 54. 12 Epiph., *Haer.* 76.4.2 (*GCS* iii.344.18-21).

For afterwards this fellow (the man himself, that is, and those who had been instructed by him) deluded himself to speak thus: 'I know God', he says, 'with perfect clarity, and I know and understand him to such an extent that I do not understand myself better than I know God.'

It is obvious in reading this passage that it is part of the same general community of ideas as that found in our own fragment. Indeed, we can see certain verbal resemblances between the two: ἐπίσταται in Eunomius parallels ἐπίσταμαι in Aetius, εἰδείημεν and οἶδεν parallel οἶδα and εἰδέναι, and μᾶλλον is used in both. The fact is, however, that despite these verbal reminiscences the differences are even more striking. Even ignoring the fact that the verbs are used in different persons, there is the striking absence in the passage quoted by Socrates of Epiphanius' τηλαυγέστατα, and the addition of such words as γινωσκομένη and ἀπαραλλάκτως is worth noting as well. All of this goes to show that there cannot be any direct literary link between the two, and this is confirmed by the fact that the only work of Epiphanius with which Socrates shows any familiarity is the *Ancoratus*.[13] Moreover, there is yet another reason for suggesting that the passage quoted by Socrates cannot be a development, even indirect, of that found in Epiphanius, a reason which is one of our chief grounds for taking Socrates' claim to be quoting Eunomius directly seriously. That is, that Socrates does not portray Eunomius as claiming a perfect knowledge of God in himself, but rather a knowledge of God's οὐσία or essence. It is precisely because he does *not* mention the essence that one suspects Epiphanius of giving, not a direct quotation, but rather what he understood Aetius to be saying. This suspicion is strengthened by his mention in the sentence immediately following of the things he had 'heard' about Aetius.[14] Moreover, there is another difference between the ideas expressed in the two passages. Eunomius, according to Socrates, asserted that he knew God's essence as well as God knew it himself, whereas according to Epiphanius, Aetius said that his knowledge of God was equivalent to his own knowledge of himself. This difference makes it even more difficult to believe that Socrates' passage depends even indirectly on that of Epiphanius. This impression is strengthened when we discover that there is an independent witness to this tradition given by Theodoret of Cyrus:

[13] Soc., *HE* v.24 (*PG* 67.649B).
[14] Epiph., *Haer.* 76.4.2(*GCS* iii.344.22-3).

Ἐτόλμησε γὰρ εἰπεῖν, ὡς οὐδὲν τῶν θείων ἠγνόησεν, ἀλλὰ καὶ αὐτὴν ἀκριβῶς ἐπίσταται τοῦ θεοῦ τὴν οὐσίαν, καὶ τὴν αὐτὴν ἔχει περὶ τοῦ θεοῦ γνῶσιν, ἣν αὐτὸς ἔχει περὶ ἑαυτοῦ ὁ θεός. Εἰς ταύτην ὑπ᾽ αὐτοῦ τὴν μανίαν ἐκβακχευθέντες οἱ τῆς ἐκείνου λώβης μετεσχηκότες, τολμῶσιν ἄντικρυς λέγειν, οὕτως εἰδέναι τὸν θεόν, ὡς αὐτὸς ἑαυτόν.[15]

For he dared to assert such things as not one of the saints ever perceived: that he knows the very essence of God perfectly, and that he has the same knowledge about God as God has about himself! As for those who shared his disfigurement, in their Bacchic frenzy they rushed under his leadership into the same madness, and dared to say outright that they know God as he knows himself!

As in the case of Epiphanius, there are indications that this is not a quotation from a written document, but a statement of Eunomius' position as understood by Theodoret himself.[16] We note, for instance, that in the second part of the statement which he ascribes to Eunomius, and in that which he attributes to his followers, he describes them as claiming to know God himself rather than the essence of God. There are, however, striking similarities between this passage and that given by Socrates. We note that both use ἐπίσταμαι in the third person, both speak of the οὐσία of God, and both assert that Eunomius' knowledge about God is the same as that which *God* has about himself (i.e., they do not portray Eunomius as claiming that his knowledge of God is as great as his *own* self-knowledge, as in the passage from Epiphanius). Thus, Theodoret's statement clearly represents a form, even if a variant one, of the tradition preserved by Socrates. Indeed, this accusation seems to have been one of the stock weapons in the Orthodox arsenal.

If there is no justification, then, for seeing the passage quoted by Socrates as a simple development of that given by Epiphanius, we may well ask what reasons there are for questioning its authenticity. We have already noted that Socrates' whole reason for reproducing the passage at all was that he did believe it to be genuine, for he used it as proof of the veracity of his own statements. It seems, then, that the chief reason for hesitating before pronouncing it genuine is

[15] Thdt., *Haer.* iv.3 (*PG* 83.421A); cf. also Chrys., *Incomp.* ii.158-9 (*SC* 28bis, 154), (ps.-)Ath., *Dial.* i.1 (*PG* 28.1117A, 1117C/D), Cyril Alex., *Thes.* 31 (*PG* 75.441B-C, 445D, 449A-B).
[16] Cf. Theodoret's mention of oral knowledge in the passage preceding this one, *Haer.* iv.3 (*PG* 83.420D-421A).

its content. If we can find a place for this doctrine within Eunomius' system, we will presumably be justified in accepting the fragment as genuine; if not, we will not. Unfortunately, a discussion of this issue would take us beyond the limits of this Introduction, and we must content ourselves at this time with the simple statement that in our view Eunomius did indeed make a statement of this kind and that the form of it preserved in Socrates is perhaps as close as any to what he may really have said.

The text presented below is identical with that of Migne; in the absence of a critical text we have collated the manuscripts of Socrates at this point, but have found no significant variants.[17]

FRAGMENT iii

This third fragment is taken from a *florilegium* of texts dealing chiefly with the interpretation of Matt. 26: 39 ('nevertheless, not as I will, but as thou wilt') and bearing chiefly on the Monophysite and Monothelite controversies. It is to be found in Codex Vaticanus graecus 1409, fos. 178ᵛ-183ʳ included among the works of Anastasius of Sinai (the fragment of Eunomius occurs on fo. 179ʳ).[18] Like most of the other texts in the *florilegium*, including two from Aetius,[19] it deals with Christ's will in relation to that of the Father. The fragment itself is preceded by the title (iii.1-2):

Εὐνομίου πρωτοστάτου τῆς 'Αρείου θυμελικῆς ὀρχήστρας, ἐκ τῆς περὶ υἱοῦ τρίτου λόγου, κεφ. ιθ'.

From the nineteenth chapter of the third book *Concerning the Son* of Eunomius, the leader of Arius' theatrical dancing-floor.

---

[17] I am grateful to the Revd George Dennis, SJ, of the Catholic University of America for allowing me to use his microfilm copies of these MSS: Codex Patmensis 688, fo. 69ʳ (13th c.), Codex Alexandrinensis 60 (86), fo. 329ᵛ (13th c.), Codex Laurentianus Mediceus plut. 70.7, fos. 296ᵛ-297ʳ (10th c.), Codex Laurentianus Mediceus plut. 69.5, fo. 108ʳ (11th c.), Codex Marcianus gr. 2.339 (916), fos. 237ʳ-237ᵛ (14th c.), Codex Marcianus gr. 2.337 (691), fos. 274ᵛ-275ʳ (15th c.).

[18] This collection has been reprinted in Migne at *PG* 89.1180c-1189d; for convenience when referring to the collection as a whole we will refer to Migne. On collections of this kind see Theodor Schermann, 'Die Geschichte der dogmatischen Florilegien', *TU* 28 (1904/5), 43-6, and also F. Diekamp, *Doctrina Patrum de Incarnatione Verbi* (Münster: Aschendorffsche Verlagsbuchhandlung, 1907), p. lxv.

[19] Anast. S., *Monoph.* (*PG* 89.1181a-b). They are discussed by G. Bardy, 'L'Héritage littéraire d'Aétius', *RHE* 24 (1928), 826-7, and by V. Grumel, 'Les textes monothélites d'Aétius', *EO* 28 (1929), 164-6.

Since all but a few of the works quoted in this *florilegium* are now either wholly or partly lost, it is difficult to ascertain with what accuracy their titles are given. Many of these designations are only generally descriptive, and, indeed, the passages quoted from Aetius are themselves said to come from a work Περὶ υἱοῦ.[20] Because, then, so many of the headings of these fragments seem to be general descriptions rather than titles strictly so-called, we might be in doubt as to whether the title quoted above refers to an otherwise unknown work of Eunomius or to a known work under a different name,[21] were it not for additional information given us by Nicetas Acominatos, quoting Philostorgius:

Ὁ μὲν οὖν Ἀπολινάριος καὶ ὁ Βασίλειος κατὰ τῆς ἀπολογίας ἧς Εὐνόμιος ἐξήνεγκεν ἐγραψάτην. τοῦ δὲ Γρηγορίου . . . διαγνόντος ὁπόσον αὐτῷ πρὸς ἐκεῖνον ἦν τὸ τῆς δυνάμεως μέσον καὶ τὴν ἡσυχίαν ἀσπασμένον, μόνον δέ τινα τῶν Εὐνομίου κεφαλαίων ἐν τῷ Περὶ υἱοῦ λόγῳ ἀνατρέψαντος ὡς ἐν εἴδει τῆς πρὸς Ἀνομοίους ἀντιρρήσεως . . .[22]

So then, Apollinarius and Basil wrote against the *Apology* which Eunomius had brought out, and Gregory . . . discerning the extent of the gap between his own and his opponent's powers, and desiring nothing but peace, having only refuted some of Eunomius' chapters in the book *Concerning the Son* as in the shape of a reply to the Anomoeans . . .

Although this passage is not entirely unambiguous (it is possible to understand it as referring to a book by Gregory of Nazianzus *Concerning the Son*),[23] when taken together with the title of the fragment found in Anastasius of Sinai it none the less seems to confirm the existence of a separate work by Eunomius going under the title Περὶ υἱοῦ, *Concerning the Son*. We note that in both passages the title is identical and the work is spoken of as being divided into κεφάλαια. Albertz, in his somewhat hesitant discussion of this fragment, says that it must have belonged to 'ein sonst unbekanntes umfangreiches Werk des Eunomius',[24] no doubt basing this description on the mention of a 'third book' in the title

[20] Anast. S., *Monoph.* (*PG* 89.1181A-B); the headings of the other works in the collection are similarly obscure.
[21] As noted by Albertz, p. 54.   [22] Philost., *HE* viii.12a (*GCS* 114.16-22).
[23] As was apparently done by J. Bidez, the editor of the *GCS* Philostorgius, since he cited ad loc. the third and fourth theological orations, *De Filio*, of Gregory of Nazianzus; if this is the case, however, the reference must be to the fourth, which does refer to *capitula* of a sort, Grg. Naz., *Or.* 30.12 (Mason 125.7-128.7).
[24] Albertz, p. 54.

given by Anastasius. However, despite the conventional translation of λόγος by 'book' in the above, there is no real reason to assume a large work is intended. This supposition is strengthened by the mention of the κεφάλαια into which the work is divided, since this suggests a treatise divided into relatively small sections in the manner of the *Syntagmation* of Eunomius' teacher, Aetius. Thus it seems likely that in the treatise *Concerning the Son* ascribed to Eunomius we are in fact dealing with a short dogmatic work divided into at least three sections and composed of short 'chapters'. We may also note another possibility. The *Syntagmation* of Aetius mentioned above has come down to us as a separate work quoted entire by Epiphanius,[25] but it is also described in the pseudo-Athanasian *Dialogus de Sancta Trinitate* as being from a letter of Aetius.[26] Since this is undoubtedly its proper literary form,[27] it is not at all impossible that the treatise *Concerning the Son* of Eunomius, which is similar to the work of Aetius in other respects, was similar in this as well, and that in this fragment we are in fact dealing with one of the lost letters of Eunomius. Naturally, until such time as further fragments are found, this and other speculations can only remain interesting conjectures.

When we turn to the problem of authenticity, however, we are faced with an entirely different set of problems. In the past the chief reason for viewing this fragment with suspicion has been that its title refers to an otherwise unknown work.[28] However, the fact that the existence of this work can apparently be verified from a passage in Philostorgius suggests that this consideration may be given less weight than heretofore. Moreover, while the teaching found in the fragment is nowhere discussed as such in Eunomius' other extant writings, it is not inconsistent with his position. We may note, for instance, the characteristic Eunomian distinction between κτιστός and ἄκτιστος, and that the difference of wills flows naturally from the difference between ἀγέννητος and γέννημα. The only reason, indeed, we might have for hesitating is that the collection from which this fragment comes was made for a specific polemical purpose, to serve in the Monothelite and Monophysite

[25] Epiph., *Haer.* 76.11.1–12.37 (*GCS* iii.351.21–360.4).

[26] (Ps.-)Ath., *Dial.* ii.5, 10 (*PG* 38.1164s, 1173A/B).

[27] Cf. L. R. Wickham, 'The Syntagmation of Aetius the Anomoean', *JTS* 19 (1968), 533–4; hereafter referred to as 'Syntagmation'.   [28] Cf. Albertz, p. 54.

controversies, and that several of the other fragments contained in it are suspect or show signs of tampering.[29] Since there is nothing in this particular fragment which shows such signs, it is difficult to know how to evaluate it, and indeed quite eminent scholars have been divided.[30] We can only say that in our view the negative evidence is insufficient to establish its inauthenticity, and that until such time as more turns up the best policy is to treat it as probably authentic.

FRAGMENT iv

This fourth fragment stands in a somewhat different category from the others. It has come down to us in the *Ecclesiastical History* of the sixth-century Nestorian author, Barhadbešabba 'Arbaia (*PO* 23.281.2-4). As we have tried to show elsewhere,[31] there are two sources for this writer's information about Eunomius, the *Ecclesiastical History* of Socrates, and the lost *Contra Eunomium* of Theodore of Mopsuestia. The present fragment is inserted into a section of the work which is otherwise a verbatim translation of Fragment ii quoted by Socrates. It comes between the introductory clause and the fragment itself, so that it immediately follows the words '. . . for he asserts the following in these very words' (ii.2-3). It seems, then, that Barhadbešabba intended these words of Socrates to apply to his own fragment as well, and that he believed that this too was a genuine quotation from Eunomius. The question is, was he justified in believing this?

Probably he was. At any rate, there is nothing in the fragment inconsistent with Eunomius' thought, and much that is closely parallel. The crucial phrase in this respect is the second one, to the effect that the Father had 'poured the whole power of God into the Son'. In what context are we to see it? A passage in Eunomius' *Expositio Fidei* suggests part of the answer, for the Son is there

---

[29] Cf. Grumel, op. cit., and M. Spanneut, *Recherches sur les écrits d'Eustathe d'Antioche* (Lille: Facultés Catholiques, 1948), pp. 41 f., 82, 126.

[30] Though neither scholar has made a specific study of the matter, J. Paramelle is of the opinion that these fragments of 'Anastasius' are probably false, whereas the late Marcel Richard felt that they were probably authentic (personal letter of J. Paramelle, dated 13 Feb. 1978).

[31] R. P. Vaggione, 'Some Neglected Fragments of Theodore of Mopsuestia's *Contra Eunomium*', *JTS* 31 (1980), 403-70.

described as being '. . . ὡς εἰκόνα καὶ ὡς σφραγῖδα πάσης τῆς τοῦ παντοκράτορος ἐνεργείας καὶ δυνάμεως . . .'[32] An even closer parallel is to be found in the *Liber Apologeticus*, for in that work Eunomius asks 'τίς γὰρ αὐτόν τε τὸν μονογενῆ γινώσκων . . . οὐκ ἂν ὁμολογήσειεν ⟨ἐν⟩ αὐτῷ θεωρεῖσθαι πᾶσαν τὴν τοῦ πατρὸς δύναμιν;'[33] These passages undoubtedly give us the kind of context in which a statement such as that found in our fragment is to be understood. It seems, then, that while there is no known example of precisely this way of putting it in the surviving works of Eunomius, and no entirely certain use of 1 Cor. 1: 24,[34] there is nothing in this passage which is inconsistent with its being by Eunomius. We may note, too, that the presence of a specific citation of Holy Scripture helps to assure us that this is a genuine quotation and not simply a generalized statement of the Eunomian position.

The question which this naturally raises is, where did Barḥadbešabba get such a quotation? Obviously no certain answer is possible, but we can weigh the probabilities. He may have taken it from some completely known work and simply inserted it as one of the 'single phrases' he mentions in his preface as sometimes adding to the text.[35] But since it is very doubtful that he would have leafed through some full-scale refutation of Eunomius' teaching looking for an appropriate quotation, and very unlikely that he possessed any actual work of Eunomius,[36] the kind of *florilegium* in which Fragment iii is found might be a better possibility. On the other hand, the most likely possibility is also the most convenient, the *Contra Eunomium* of Theodore of Mopsuestia which, as we hope we have shown, was one of the sources used in this section of his work. In that case, this fragment would be Theodore's version of something in the *Apologia Apologiae*. Unfortunately, in the absence of Theodore's work itself, there is no way to be sure.

---

[32] Eun., *Exp. Fid.* 3.31-2, cf. *Apol.* 26.9-10.   [33] Eun., *Apol.* 24.13-15.

[34] Cf., however, *Apol.* 19.3-4; there is also some evidence that Eunomius used this passage in the third book of his *Apologia Apologiae*, cf. *J* ii.10.25-11.8 and the Summary, p. 116 above.

[35] Barḥad., *HE.*, Introduction (*PO* 9.496.7-10).

[36] Though this is not quite impossible. Eunomius' *Apology* has come down to us in manuscripts of Basil's refutation of it, and since we have reason to believe that Barḥadbešabba possessed that work (cf. *HE* 14 (*PO* 23.282.11-13)), it is not impossible (if unlikely) that he also had Eunomius'. In the present instance, of course, the *Apology* is not the source of our fragment.

The text of Barhadbešabba's history is based on a unique manuscript (British Museum MS Or. 6714), and unfortunately the text as it stands in the manuscript at this point is very obscure. F. Nau (*PO* 23.281, trans. 3-4) has translated the opening line (*F* 4.1-2) as follows: 'Le Père (a rapport) au Fils seulement et celui-ci au Saint-Esprit.' It is difficult to know what that might mean even in translation! Another possibility might be: 'The Father (is the Father) with respect to the Son only, and he to the Holy Spirit.' This makes some sense of the first clause (by reading a lot into it) but still leaves the second obscure. A further point to be considered is the reason behind Barhadbešabba's interpolation at this point. Socrates used his quotation as an illustration of the enormity of Eunomius' heresy. If Barhadbešabba has amplified this, it is probably because nowhere else does he more than hint at what Eunomius' heresy was, and he now needed something which would indicate the heretic's general position. In that case, one would expect the inserted phrase to reflect the main point of the heresy, not one of its more obscure *dicta*. The probable solution, then, is to be sought in a corruption of the text. We have assumed that the verb ܒܪܐ 'to create' dropped out from before ܠܒܪܐ 'the Son' so as to give the reading found in the manuscript. This emendation has the advantage of making good sense, fulfilling the expectations mentioned above, and explaining the error; it seems to us very probably correct.

EUNOMII FRAGMENTA

FRAGMENTUM i

Scholia Eunomii super Aetii Syntagmatio

[Cf. Aetii *Syntag.* ιη´: Εἰ ἡ ἀγέννητος οὐσία κρείττων ἐστί γενέσεως, οἴκοθεν ἔχουσα τὸ κρεῖττον, αὐτὸ οὐσία ἐστὶν ἀγέννητος. οὐ γὰρ βουλόμενος ὅτι βούλεται γενέσεώς ἐστι κρείττων, ἀλλ᾽ ὅτι πέφυκεν.][a]

Σχόλια Εὐνομίου[b]

῞Οτι ἡ θέλησις καὶ ἡ βούλησις οὐ ταὐτὸν τῇ οὐσίᾳ τοῦ θεοῦ· ἡ μὲν γὰρ θέλησις καὶ ἄρχεται καὶ παύεται, ἡ δὲ οὐσία οὔτε ἄρχεται οὔτε παύεται, τὸ δὲ ἀρχόμενον καὶ παυόμενον τῷ μήτε ἀρχομένῳ μήτε παυομένῳ τὸ αὐτὸ εἶναι οὐ δύναται. καὶ ἄλλως, εἰ ταὐτὸν ἦν τῇ οὐσίᾳ τοῦ
5 θεοῦ ἡ βούλησις, ἐχρῆν μιᾶς οὔσης τῆς οὐσίας, μίαν εἶναι καὶ τὴν θέλησιν· εὑρίσκονται δὲ κατὰ τὴν διδασκαλίαν τῶν θείων γραφῶν οὐ μία θέλησις, ἀλλὰ πολλαὶ θελήσεις, τῆς γραφῆς λεγούσης, Πάντα ὅσα ἠθέλησεν ἐποίησε·[c] πολλὰ οὖν ἠθέλησε καὶ οὐχ ἕν. ἐναργέστερον δὲ ἰδεῖν ἐπὶ τῆς κοσμοποιΐας, ἠθέλησε γὰρ εἶναι τὸν κόσμον, καὶ ὑπέστη κατὰ
10 τὴν αὐτοῦ θέλησιν, καὶ διαμένει τὸ γενόμενον,[d] ἄλλο δέ ἐστιν ἡ διαμονὴ παρὰ τὴν θέλησιν τῆς δημιουργίας. ἐπηγγείλατο δὲ καὶ μετασχηματίσαι τὸν κόσμον·[e] θελήσας ἄρα μετασχηματίζει. οὐ μόνον δὲ πολλαί, ἀλλὰ καὶ διάφοροι αἱ θελήσεις· ἠθέλησε γὰρ καὶ οὐρανόν,[f] ἠθέλησε καὶ ἥλιον,[g] ἠθέλησε καὶ γῆν·[h] τῶν δὲ θελημάτων διαφόρων ὄντων, ἀνάγκη
15 διαφέρειν καὶ τὰς περὶ αὐτῶν θελήσεις· καὶ ἐπὶ τῶν νοητῶν δὲ ὡσαύτως.

---

[a] Aetius, *Syntagmation*: L. R. Wickham, 'The Syntagmation of Aetius the Anomoean', *JTS* 19 (1968), 542 = Epiph., *Haer.* 76.12.18 (*GCS* iii.355.19-21), (ps.-)Ath., *Dial.* ii.20 (*PG* 28.1188c)   [b] (Ps.-)Ath., *Dial.* ii.6 (*PG* 28.1165A-B)   [c] Ps. 113: 11 (115: 3)   [d] Gen. 1: 1-2, cf. Ps. 148: 5-6   [e] Gen. 1: 9 ff.   [f] Gen. 1: 6-8   [g] Gen. 1: 16   [h] Gen. 1: 9-10

Σχόλια Εὐνομίου sic scripsi: Σχόλια Εὐνομίου καὶ πρὸς αὐτὰ Ὀρθοδόξου Migne
5 οὔσης τῆς codex Parisinus gr. 1258, fo. 325ᵛ necnon et translatio Latina Mignei: om. Migne   10 ἐστιν *v*: σοι MS Palat.: τι Paris., Felck

THE FRAGMENTS OF EUNOMIUS

FRAGMENT i

The Scholia of Eunomius on the Syntagmation of Aetius

[Cf. Aetius, *Syntag*. 18: 'If the unbegotten essence is superior to generation, possessing this superiority as an inherent quality, it is unbegotten in respect of its very essence. For it is not such by way of purpose, because it purposes to be superior to generation, but because it is so by nature.']ᵃ

*The Scholia of Eunomius*ᵇ

. . . because the will and the purpose of God are not identical with his essence: the act of willing has both a beginning and an ending, while the divine essence neither begins nor ends, and it is impossible that that which begins and ends should be identical with that which has neither beginning nor ending. Besides, if the purpose of God were identical with his essence, then, since there is only one essence, there would have to be only one act of willing. But we find in fact that according to the divine Scriptures there is not just one act of willing but many such acts, for Scripture says, 'Whatever things he willed to make, he made.'ᶜ He willed many things, therefore, and not just one. We can see this even more clearly with regard to the creation of the world: God willed the world to be and it came into existence in accordance with his will and that which was brought into existence endured;ᵈ yet the permanence of the creation is something different from the act of willing which created it. God also gave a command to change the shape of the world,ᵉ hence it was after willing it that he changed it. But the acts of willing are not only numerous, they are also distinct: God willed 'heavens',ᶠ he willed 'sun',ᵍ he willed 'earth'.ʰ If the things which he willed are distinct, the acts of willing concerning them must also be distinguished, and the same principle will apply in the case of the intelligible beings.[1]

---

[1] Consistently with Eunomian usage elsewhere (e.g., *Apol.* 25.10-12) the 'intelligible beings' refer (though not exclusively) to the Son and Holy Spirit.

FRAGMENTUM ii

Fragmentum a Socrate Scholastico transmissum [a]

Ἵνα δὲ μὴ δόξωμεν λοιδορίας χάριν ταῦτα λέγειν, αὐτῆς ἐπάκουε τῆς
Εὐνομίου φωνῆς, οἷα σοφιζόμενος περὶ θεοῦ λέγειν τολμᾷ, φησὶ γὰρ κατὰ
λέξιν τάδε· Ὁ θεὸς περὶ τῆς ἑαυτοῦ οὐσίας οὐδὲν πλέον ἡμῶν ἐπίσταται,
οὐδέ ἐστιν αὕτη μᾶλλον μὲν ἐκείνῳ, ἧττον δὲ ἡμῖν γινωσκομένη, ἀλλ᾽
5 ὅπερ ἂν εἰδείημεν ἡμεῖς περὶ αὐτῆς, τοῦτο πάντως κἀκεῖνος οἶδεν, ὃ δ᾽
αὖ πάλιν ἐκεῖνος, τοῦτο εὑρήσεις ἀπαραλλάκτως ἐν ἡμῖν. ταῦτα μὲν καὶ
ἄλλα πολλὰ τοιαῦτα Εὐνόμιος σοφίσματα ποιῶν οὐκ ᾐσθάνετο.

FRAGMENTUM iii

Fragmentum operis Eunomii 'De Filio' [a]

Εὐνομίου πρωτοστάτου τῆς Ἀρείου θυμελικῆς ὀρχήστρας, ἐκ τῆς περὶ
υἱοῦ τρίτου λόγου, κεφ. ιθ'.

Καταβέβηκα γάρ, φησί, ἐκ τοῦ οὐρανοῦ οὐχ ἵνα ποιῶ τὸ θέλημα τὸ
ἐμόν, ἀλλὰ τὸ θέλημα τοῦ πατρός. [b] ὅρα τὸν κατελθόντα ἄνωθεν λόγον
5 ἀκυροῦντα τὸ ἴδιον θέλημα ὡς μὴ συμφωνοῦν τῷ ἀκτίστῳ θελήματι τοῦ
πατρός, διὰ τὸ κτιστὴν ἔχειν τὸν λόγον καθάπερ τὴν φύσιν, οὕτω καὶ
τὸ θέλημα.

FRAGMENTUM iv

Fragmentum a Barḥadbešabba ʿArbaia transmissum [a]

ܟܘܗܢ . ܢܘܒܠܕ ܐܪܬܝܠ ܐܪܒܕ . ܝ̈ ܪܝܐ
ܐܪܒܕ . ܗܝܐ̈ܠܐ ܘܠܝܠ ܠܝ ܗܠܒܐ . ܐܪܒ̈ܕ ܐܘܐܠ
. ܗܝܐ̈ܠܐ ܘܗܠܬܝܠܐ ܘܠܝܠ ܠܝ ܢܘܗܘ . ܗܣܘܩ

Frag. ii. [a] Socrates, *HE* iv.7 (*PG* 67.473B-C)   **Frag. iii.** [a] Anastasius of Sinai,
Contra Monophysitas Testimonia (*PG* 89.1181B-C)   [b] Jn. 6: 38   **Frag. iv.**
[a] Barḥad., *HE* 14 (*PO* 23.281.2-4)   [b] 1 Cor. 1: 24

Frag. iv. 1 ⟨ܟܝܒ⟩ sic conieci: cod. om.

FRAGMENT ii

A Fragment transmitted by Socrates Scholasticus[a]
But so that we should not seem to be saying these things purely for the sake of abuse, listen to Eunomius' own voice—the sorts of things which, in his subtlety, he presumes to say about God—for he asserts the following in these very words: 'God does not know anything more about his own essence than we do, nor is that essence better known to him and less to us; rather, whatever we ourselves know about it is exactly what he knows, and, conversely, that which he knows is what you will find without change in us.' *And indeed, in producing this and many other similar contrivances, Eunomius did not even recognize them for the absurdities they were.*

FRAGMENT iii

A Fragment of a work 'Concerning the Son'[a]
From the nineteenth chapter of the third book 'Concerning the Son' by Eunomius, the leader of Arius' theatrical dancing-floor:

For he says, 'I have come down from heaven, not to do my own will, but the will of the Father.'[b] Note that the Word who came down from above set aside his *own* will since it was not in accord with the uncreated will of the Father—for just as the Word has a created nature, so also he has a created will.

FRAGMENT iv

A Fragment transmitted by Barḥadbešabba ʿArbaia[a]
For he said: 'The Father ‹created› only the Son, and the Son the Holy Spirit—indeed, he (the Father) poured the whole power of God into the Son, for he is "the power and the wisdom of God".'[b]

APPENDIX I

THE QUOTATIONS IN THE
THESAURUS OF CYRIL OF ALEXANDRIA

The quotations contained in the *Thesaurus de Sancta et Consubstantiali Trinitate* of Cyril of Alexandria are both of unique interest and also present a number of unique problems. The source of much of the work is the third of Athanasius' discourses *Contra Arianos*, but it is also clear that Cyril made use of another treatise as well, perhaps the lost *Contra Eunomium* of Didymus the Blind.[1] In any case, as it now stands the work contains a number of excerpts described as coming ὡς ἐκ τῶν Εὐνομίου, though exactly what that means is not clear. There is thus no way to tell whether the work used by Cyril was directed against some specific Eunomian writing or against the Eunomian position in general. What is certain is that they have been reworked by Cyril prior to their insertion in his own treatise. Although it is clear, then, that these quotations may not be from any specific work and must be used with some caution, we have treated them much as we did the excerpts given by Gregory from the *Apologia Apologia*: we have given first the column number in Migne *PG* 75, together with the chapter heading, and then below it a brief résumé of the contents of the fragment. Only those passages which are specifically ascribed to Eunomius or Aetius will be included, with the exception of those in *Assertio xxxi* which clearly reflect distinctively Eunomian teaching.

Assertio v

57B-C. Ἀντίθεσις ὡς ἐκ τῶν Εὐνομίου.

If the Father exists beginninglessly and unbegottenly forever while the Son was begotten, how can the thing begotten fail to be circumscribed by a beginning?

60D. Ἐρώτησις ὡς ἐκ τῶν Εὐνομίου.

Let those who say the Son is co-eternal answer: did the Father cease begetting? He did cease. Then the Son has a beginning of his being in the Father's ceasing to beget.

---

[1] For a detailed study of this work see J. Liébaert, *Saint Cyrille d'Alexandrie et l'arianisme. Les sources de la doctrine christologique du 'Thesaurus' et des 'Dialogues sur la Trinité'* (Lille: Facultés Catholiques, 1948).

69A. *ΑΛΛΟ.* ὡς ἐξ ἀντιθέσεως τῶν Εὐνομίου.

We too confess that the Son is coeternal with the Father for the Father had the power to be able to beget him even before he did so.

69C-D. *ΑΛΛΟ.* Ὡς ἐξ ἀντιθέσεως τῶν Εὐνομίου.

If the Son is coeternal in the way you say and the Father never became active for the begetting of the Son, how could he have been begotten? If he did become active and bear him, then the thing begotten must have a beginning of existence.

Assertio vi

72D-73A. Ἀντίθεσις ὡς ἐκ τῶν Εὐνομίου.

And how can you avoid acknowledging the diminution of the Father's essence if the Son came forth from him as a part of him? If you want to retain the Father's immutability, you must acknowledge that the Son is from without and that his coexistence is in the potentiality in the will alone.

73D-76A. Ἀντίθεσις ὡς ἐκ τῶν Εὐνομίου.

If you want to say that the Son came forth from the Father's essence, you must first confess that he pre-existed within him. If the Father begat no other Son, you will have to say he was deprived of the power to beget, for the Son was no longer within him as before.

77A-B. *ΑΛΛΟ.* Ἐρώτησις ὡς ἐκ τῶν Εὐνομίου.

The Father was perfect before he begot the Son, but if in begetting he was divided into a dyad, how could he remain perfect unless there were some superabundance in his essence to fill up what was missing? If this does not befit the divine nature, then the Father did not beget the Son from himself but created him to be like himself in all things.[2]

81C-D. *ΑΛΛΟ.* Ἀντίθεσις ὡς ἐκ τῶν Εὐνομίου.

If the Father begat the Son from himself and yet is 'another' in respect of him in having his own hypostasis, all the Father has will be divided between them. Either, then, the Father no longer has perfect glory, having divided it with the Son, or if he has it, he has taken it back to himself again.

Assertio vii

96C. *ΑΛΛΟ.* Ἀντίθεσις ὡς ἐκ τῶν Εὐνομίου.

Did the Father beget the Son willingly or unwillingly? If the Son existed as another within him, he did not beget by choice, but by nature; if the Son

---

[2] The formula ὅμοιος κατὰ πάντα is found in the Fourth Creed of Sirmium (Hahn 163), but was omitted in the related Creeds of Thracian Nike (Hahn 164) and Constantinople (Hahn 167). If genuine here it must presumably refer to the will.

was not within the Father but was begotten by his will, then the will existed before him and the Son is not coeternal.

97B. *ΑΛΛΟ.* Ὡς ἐξ ἀντιθέσεως τῶν Εὐνομίου.

If it was not by choice but by nature that the Father begat the Son, then he did not himself have knowledge of him but derived it from his nature. If this is ridiculous, then it was by will, knowing that he would be, that the Father begat the Son.

100A. *ΑΛΛΟ.* Ὡς ἐξ ἀντιθέσεως τῶν Εὐνομίου.

The Father begat the Son either by his will or by nature. If it was by his nature alone, then he was begotten unwillingly; if it was by both, God is composite, being made up of both.

100B-C. *ΑΛΛΟ.* Ὡς ἐξ ἀντιθέσεως τῶν Εὐνομίου.

Answer this, you who say the Son is the reflection of the Father:[3] Light or fire in a lamp shines outward but does not itself fill everything. If the Father is the light and the Son his reflection, the Father's essence cannot fill everything, for there must be a place for the reflection. If the Father does fill everything, where is there a place for the essence of the begotten?

Assertio ix

112B-C. *ΑΛΛΟ.* Ὡς ἐξ ἀντιθέσεως τῶν Εὐνομίου.

The Father's essence does not admit of begetting while the Son was begotten; how then can the Son be *homoousios* with him?

113B. *ΑΛΛΟ.* Ἀντίθεσις ὡς ἐκ τῶν Εὐνομίου.

Anything derived from a source is secondary to the source; therefore the Son is secondary to the Father, not *homoousios*. If he is *homoousios*, the one Godhead must be cut in two; the Son cannot be *homoousios*.

113D. *ΑΛΛΟ.* Ὡς ἐξ ἀντιθέσεως τῶν Εὐνομίου.

If the Son is *homoousios* with the Father, why is he not 'good' in the same sense as he? For Christ says, 'No one is good but God alone' (Mk. 10: 18), including himself. He is good, but not in the same sense as the Father.

Assertio x

124D. Ἀντίθεσις ὡς ἐκ τῶν Εὐνομίου.

How can the Son be *homoousios* with the Father if the Father is also his God (citing Jn. 20: 17; Matt. 27: 46)? Things of the same nature cannot be gods to one another by nature.

---

[3] Perhaps an allusion to Heb. 1: 3.

125c. Ἀντίθεσις ὡς ἐκ τῶν Εὐνομίου.

How can the Son be *homoousios* with the Father if the Father is the source of his being? Everyone agrees that the Father is not from any source.

128c. *ΑΛΛΟ. Ὡς ἐξ ἀντιθέσεως τῶν Εὐνομίου.*

How can the Unbegotten be *homoousios* with the begotten? Great is the difference between them.

129a. *ΑΛΛΟ. Ἀντίθεσις ὡς ἐκ τῶν Εὐνομίου.*

A thing cannot be completed if it did not have a beginning. If the Father ceased to beget the Son, and this cessation is a completion, the Son had a beginning.

132b-c. *Πρότασις ὡς ἐκ τῶν Ἀετίου.*

How can an identity of essence between Father and Son be saved if the one is Unbegotten and the other begotten? One would have to say there was no difference at all and call the Father 'begotten' and the Son 'unbegotten'.[4]

133b. *ΑΛΛΟ. Ὡς ἐξ ἀντιθέσεως τῶν Ἀετίου.*

If God is indivisible in essence, the Son was not begotten by a division of essence but established by an act of power. How can the nature thus established be of the same essence as the one which established it?

Assertio xi

140b-c. Ἀντίθεσις ὡς ἐκ τῶν Εὐνομίου.

There can be no greater or less with respect to essence. If the Son, then, says 'the Father is greater than I' (Jn. 14: 28) he cannot be *homoousios* with him.

144d. Ἀντίθεσις ὡς ἐκ τῶν Εὐνομίου.

The Saviour said, 'The Father is greater than I' (Jn. 14: 28). If he spoke the truth the Father *is* greater, and if he is, the Son is unlike him and therefore not *homoousios*.

Assertio xix

313a-b. Ἀντίθεσις ὡς ἐκ τῶν Εὐνομίου.

If the Son is the Word and is also *homoousios* with the Father, he differs in nothing from him; let him therefore be called both Word and Father. But the sense of Scripture and the teaching of the Apostles does not allow this: it knows the Father as Father and the Son as Son, and thus as different in essence. The Son is thus not the Word of the Father in the true sense and does not come forth from him but is separate by nature.

---

[4] See Aetius *Synt.* 6 in Epiph., *Haer.* 76.12.6 (*GCS* iii.353, 16-18).

316c-d. Ἀντίθεσις ὡς ἐκ τῶν Εὐνομίου.

In the Gospels the Son speaks to the Father and is answered by him (Jn. 12: 28). How then can the Son be the Word of the Father in the true sense? Either the Word was speaking to itself or the Son is different from the immanent Word which is in the Father by nature and spoke to him at the Father's will.

317b-d. ΑΛΛΟ. Ἀντίθεσις ὡς ἐκ τῶν Εὐνομίου.

In holy Scripture the Father speaks to the Son (Gen. 1: 26; Jn. 12: 49, cf. 8: 26). Did the Father tell the Son what he knew or what he did not know? If he told him what he did not know, he learned from the Father and is different from him in nature. If he knew, why tell him? Therefore the Son did not know; he is not the immanent Word and does not know the Father's will apart from that Word.

321a-b. Ἀντίθεσις ὡς ἐκ τοῦ Εὐνομίου.

Who is so foolish as not to say that names are different from their underlying objects? The one is a visible object, while the other is not visible but audible only. Because the Son is called 'Word' he is not what some people think he is; he is called 'Word', but he is something different by nature.

321d-324a. Ἀντίθεσις ὡς ἐκ τῶν Εὐνομίου.

How can the Son be the Word and Wisdom of God if Wisdom is knowledge, while the Word is the bare utterance of the thing spoken? Knowledge does not have an independent existence nor is the Word a living being. The Son is a living being and is thus neither Knowledge nor Wisdom nor Word. Moreover, like cannot be *in* like. If he were the Word of God, how could the Father speak to him (Gen. 1: 26)?

325a. Ἀντίθεσις ὡς ἐκ τῶν Εὐνομίου.

The name 'Word' is not sufficient to manifest the essence of the Son. He is called by many other names which are bare designations without independent existence.

325c. Ἀντίθεσις ὡς ἐκ τῶν Εὐνομίου.

Scripture calls the Son 'Word' not because he has his existence from the Father by nature or is himself the Immanent Word, but because he hears the Word of the Father and declares it to us. For the same reason he is called 'Sanctification' and 'Righteousness' (1 Cor. 1: 30).

Assertio xxv

412c. Ἀντίθεσις ὡς ἐκ τῶν Εὐνομίου.

If the Son is True God, how can Scripture include him among created beings by calling him 'the First-born of all creation' (Col. 1: 15)? He must himself be of the same nature as those things of whom he is the chief.

Assertio xxvi

413C. Ἀντίθεσις ὡς ἐκ τῶν Εὐνομίου.

If the Son is equal to the Father, how could he say, 'It is not mine to grant' (Mk. 10: 40, Matt. 20: 25)? This is the language of one who lacks authority; how can he be equal to the Father who possesses all authority?

Assertio xxviii

421D-424A. Ἀντίθεσις ὡς ἐκ τῶν Εὐνομίου.

How could one who is not perfect be equal to the Father in essence? The Son is said to have 'grown in wisdom' (Lk. 2: 52), while the Father, being in need of nothing, does not grow.

Assertio xxxi

441B-C. Ἀντίθεσις ὡς ἐκ τῶν δι' ἐναντίας.

The Wisdom of God is Unbegotten and this is its own proper being. Therefore God, who knows what this is, knows himself altogether. But God knows himself to be Unbegotten. There is no difference, therefore, between him thinking this about himself and us believing that this is the way he is.

445D. Ἀντίθεσις ἐκ τῶν λεγόντων εἰδέναι τὸν Θεὸν ὡς αὐτὸς ἑαυτόν.

The word 'Unbegotten' means either something revelatory of the essence of God or signifies something accidental to him. But nothing can be accidental in the divine essence. 'Unbegotten', then, is significant of the essence. If this is so, God knows that he is Unbegotten, and if someone else knows this, he will know God wholly, as God knows himself.

449A-B. Ἀντίθεσις ἐκ τῶν αὐτῶν διὰ τῆς εἰς ἄτοπον ἀπαγωγῆς.

God knows his own nature exactly and truly. If we do not know it just as he does, we are found to think of what pertains to him falsely and distortedly. He whose knowledge is not like that of the one who truly knows will not truly understand but errs altogether.

APPENDIX II

ALLEGED UNPUBLISHED
FRAGMENTS OF EUNOMIUS

The possible existence of unpublished fragments of the lost works of Eunomius has been suggested repeatedly over the past century and a half. The issue was originally raised in the *Bibliotheca Graeca* of Fabricius/ Hareles,[1] and subsequently taken up by both M. Albertz[2] and L. Abramowski.[3] It must now be reported that none of the possibilities suggested by Fabricius/Hareles shed any new light on Eunomius' literary remains. In what follows, we shall discuss each of the suggested possibilities in turn (including some not mentioned by Fabricius/Hareles) and attempt to identify the manuscript in question and evaluate its authenticity:[4]

1. *In bibl.* Scorial. *regis Hispan.* Eunomii *et orthodoxi contra Eunomium dialogus, cuius initium ab impii Aetii epistola ducitur, secund.* Montfauc. *bibl. biblioth. MSSt. ii. p. 619 A.*

The manuscript described by Fabricius/Hareles following Montfaucon[5] is to be identified as MS Escorial Gr. 371, fos. 421^r-428^r,[6] and is a rearranged version of the second of the five pseudo-Athanasian *Dialogi de Sancta Trinitate* (*PG* 28.1157D-1201C). The 'impii Aetii epistola' is that found at *PG* 28.1173A/B, and in the manuscript begins the dialogue. In this manuscript the single *Dialogue* ii is broken up into two separate dialogues in the following order: *Dialogue* i (fo. 421^r) = *PG* 28.1173A-1201C; *Dialogue* ii (fo. 426^r) = *PG* 28.1157D-1173A.

2. Oxon. *in bibl. Bodlei. inter codd.* Cromwell. *nr. 291. fragmenta* Seueriani, Eunomii *et aliorum.*

This manuscript is to be identified as Codex Oxon. Bodleianus Cromwell 7, pp. 579-81,[7] and contains a short dialogue entitled Ἐρώτησις Εὐνομίου

---

[1] J. A. Fabricius, G. C. Hareles, *Bibliotheca Graeca*, editio nova ix (Hamburgi: apud Carolum Ernestum Bohn, 1804), p. 211, note *ss.*

[2] Albertz, p. 55.   [3] L. Abramowski, 'Eunomius', *RACh* vi, col. 938.

[4] The headings which precede nos. 1, 2, 4, 5, 6, 8 are the descriptions given by Fabricius/Hareles.

[5] B. de Montfaucon, *Bibliotheca Bibliothecarum Manuscriptorum Nova* i (Parisiis: apud Briasson, 1739), p. 617D. Hareles's reference to p. 619A is an error.

[6] Described in G. de Andrés, *Catálogo de los Codices Griegos de la Real Biblioteca de el Escorial* ii (Madrid, 1965), p. 280.

[7] Described in H. O. Coxe, *Bodleian Library Quarto Catalogues* i (Oxford: Bodleian Library, 1969), col. 126.

πρὸς τὸν μέγαν Βασίλειον. While this dialogue was apparently composed for didactic purposes, it contains no fragments of Eunomius; his participation is limited to the asking of short questions, of which the first may be taken as representative: τί ἐστι θεὸς τὸ πᾶσι περισπούδαστον; The same dialogue is also found with variations in MS Tübingen gr. Mb 2 (K 16), fo. 287ʳ, MS Tübingen gr. Mb 3 (K 15), fo. 148ᵛ,[8] and Codex Vaticanus Bibliothecae Angelicae graecus 28, fo. 60ᵛ.[9]

3. *Codex Oxon. Bodleianus Canon 41, fos. 83ʳ-84ʳ.*[10]

Although this manuscript is mentioned neither by Fabricius/Hareles nor by his modern followers, it contains a short dialogue entitled Εὐνομίου αἱρετικοῦ ἐρώτησις πρὸς τὸν ἅγιον Ἀμφιλόχιον ἀπὸ τῶν εὐαγγελικῶν ῥημάτων. In fact it contains only a single set of questions by Eunomius followed by relatively lengthy replies of 'Amphilochius'. A more detailed examination reveals that it is actually an independently circulating excerpt from the life of St Amphilochius appended to the *Menologion* of Simeon Metaphrastes (par. 5-6, *PG* 116.961B-963A). It contains no independent information about Eunomius.

4. *Inter codd. Vossian.* Eunomii catechesis religionis christianae. *secundum catal. codd. Angliae etc. pag. 60. vol. ii. nr. 2210. Contra in bibl.* Leidensi *inter codd. Vossian. pag. 395. nominatur* Eunomii τοῦ δυσσεβοῦς apologeticus, *contra quem scripsit antirrheticos sermones Magn. Basil.*

This manuscript, described in the catalogue mentioned by Fabricius/ Hareles as *Eunomii catechesis religionis christianae,*[11] is to be identified as Codex Vossianus graecus Q.13, fos. 22ʳ-38ᵛ. It is in fact a copy of the *Liber Apologeticus* and is the manuscript designated V in our own edition.[12]

5. *et p. 397 citatur* Eunomius de mercede meretricis non admittenda in templum, graece.

The title, *Eunomius de mercede meretricis non admittenda in templum,* is derived from an early catalogue of the Library of the University of Leiden.[13] The manuscript in question is undoubtedly Codex Vossianus

---

[8] Described in W. Schmid, *Verzeichnis der griechischen Handschriften der Königlichen Universitätsbibliothek zu Tübingen* (Tübingen, 1902), pp. 5 and 7.

[9] Described in P. Franchi de' Cavalieri and G. Muceio, 'Index codicum graecorum Bibliothecae Angelicae', *Studi Italiani di Filologia Classica* iv (1896), p. 57.

[10] Described in Coxe, op. cit., col. 45.

[11] Cf. *Catalogi Librorum Manuscriptorum Angliae et Hiberniae* ii (Oxoniae: E Theatro Sheldoniano, 1697), p. 60, no. 2210.

[12] See above, pp. 22-3.

[13] *Catalogus Librorum . . . Bibliothecae Publicae Universitatis Lugduno-Batavae* (Lugduni apud Batavos: Sumptibus Petri Vander Aa, 1716), p. 397.

graecus Q.30, fos. 256^r–259^r,[14] and is in fact a pseudo-Philonic work based on a passage in the *De Specialibus Legibus*.[15]

6. Vindobon. *in cod. caesar xlii. nr. 6 sunt* Mathusalae *monachi montis Sinai excerpta de S. Trinitate ex Hermete Trismegisto, Platone, Aristotele et* Eunomio. *v* Lambec. *comm vii. p. 175*.

This manuscript is to be identified as MS Vindobonensis Phil. Gr. 110, fo. 246^r.[16] It contains a fragment ascribed to 'Eunomius' which is part of a collection entitled Πλουτάρχου ἀποφθέγματα φιλοσόφων περὶ τριάδος. The fragment itself reads as follows: Εὐνομίου· τοῦ ὑπερτάτου τῶν ὅλων αἰτίου, προσεπινοεῖται οὐδέν. ἄλλο δὲ ὡς αὐτὸς ἐξ αὐτοῦ. ἄλλος οὐκ ἀλλοῖος:— As the title of the collection indicates, this fragment is part of a series of attestations to the doctrine of the Trinity by Greek philosophers. Apart from 'Eunomius', the other philosophers cited in the collection are (ps.-)Plato, (ps.-)Aristotle, and Hermes Trismegistus.[17] This, together with the announced purpose of the collection itself, goes to suggest that the 'Eunomius' in question is not the heretical Bishop of Cyzicus, but a Greek philosopher of the same name. In view of this, the most likely possibility is that this fragment derives from a Neo-Pythagorean source, and that the 'Eunomius' named as its author is in fact Εὔνομος, described in the tradition as the brother of Pythagoras.[18]

7. Gregorii Abu-l-Farag (Barhebraeus), *Liber Candelabri Sanctuarii, pars iii* (PO *27, 582, 25-7*).

Although this reference was unknown to Fabricius/Hareles, it is well worth our attention because, like entry no. 6, it contains a quotation from someone named 'Eunomius'. The quotation is one of a series listed under the heading 'Pagan Witnesses', and intended to illustrate a discussion of the procession of the Holy Spirit. Other witnesses cited include Hermes Trismegistus (*PO* 27.582, 13; 584, 4), an Oracle of Elea (*PO* 27.582, 20),

---

[14] Described in K. A. De Meyeier, *Bibliotheca Universitatis Leidensis, Codices Manuscripti* vi (Leiden, 1955), p. 108.

[15] Philo, *Spec. Leg.* i.280-4 (Cohn and Wendland v, 67, 20-69, 22; cf. the comments, ibid., p. xx).

[16] Described in H. Hunger, *Katalog der griechischen Handschriften der Österreichischen Nationalbibliothek* i (Vienna: Georg Prachner Verlag, 1961), p. 219.

[17] What are fundamentally the same fragments are found in a somewhat different form in Richard Bentley's *De Ioannes Malalae Chronographia Epistola*: (ps.-)Plato at *PG* 97.724B; (ps.-)Aristotle at *PG* 97.722D; and Hermes Trismegistus at *PG* 97.722C. That ascribed to 'Eunomius' is not included.

[18] Cf. Diogenes Laertius viii.2, and the Suda s.v. Πυθαγόρας (*Adler* iv, 262, 23, no. 3120). Cf. also entry no. 7 below, which gives another similarly ascribed fragment in a collection of pagan authors.

(ps.-)Plutarch (*PO* 27.584, 1), (ps.-)Aristotle (*PO* 27.584, 10), (ps.-)Sophocles (*PO* 27.584, 12), and (ps.-)Plato (*PO* 27.584, 15). Our own fragment reads as follows:

ܣܗܕܘܬܐ ܕܬܠܬ. ܐܘܢܘܡܝܣ ܦܝܠܘܣܘܦܐ ܐܡܪ.
ܡܒܘܥܐ ܕܐܒܐ ܠܐ ܡܬܚܒܠܢܝܬܐ ܕܐܡܝܢ ܪ̈ܕܝܗ̇.
ܕܒܨܒܝܢܗ ܐܝܬ ܠܗ ܚܝܠܐ ܫܘܐ ܒܬܘܩܦܐ. ܕܢܗܘܐ
ܡܢܗ ܗ̇ܘ ܚܝܠܬܢ ܒܟܠ ܡܠܬܐ. ܟܕ ܐܝܬܘܗܝ ܘܗܘ
ܒܟܝܢܗ ܐܚܝܕ ܟܠ܀

Witness Three: The Philosopher Eunomius said, 'The fountain of the Father is incorruptible, its flow everlasting; by his will[19] he possesses a power equal in force (to himself), so that the Almighty Word is from him by nature, since he also is Omnipotent by nature.'

The general context in which this fragment is found, as well as the designation of the 'Eunomius' in question as 'the Philosopher', is sufficient to show that the reference cannot be to our own heresiarch, and, indeed, must be to a non-Christian. It is a reasonable supposition, then, that the 'Eunomius' intended is the brother of Pythagoras, as in our item no. 6 above, and that the fragment found in Barhebraeus is yet another sample of Neo-Pythagorean literature.[20]

8. *In* Nicetae Choniatae Acominati *panoplia dogmatica, (cod. Baluz.) tom. v. est enarratio de Aetii et* Eunomii *haeresi; deinceps capita, quibus Eunomius probare nititur, filium post patrem ortum remque esse creatam: sub haec propositiones quaedam haereticae Aetii et Eunomii, earumque refutationes, teste* Montfaucon. *in palaeographia gr. pag. 329.*

This manuscript is to be identified as Codex Parisinus gr. 1234,[21] and is a copy of the *Thesaurus Orthodoxiae* of Nicetas Acominatus which has been heavily interleaved with extraneous matter. As noted by Montfaucon,[22] this manuscript does indeed contain a series of 'propositions' ascribed to Eunomius; however, they are identical with those in the printed text of the *Thesaurus* at v.41–53 (*PG* 139.1401C–1418A). These are of so general a nature that it is impossible to believe that they are direct quotations of a specific work. Rather, they are to be taken as propositions assembled by Nicetas as generally illustrative of the Eunomian position rather than actual quotations.

19 Reading the suffix as masculine.

20 On this and the preceding entry, see Hasmut Erbse, *Fragmente griechischer Theosophien* (Hamburg: Hansischer Gildenverlag, 1941), pp. 138–9, especially p. 138 n. 279.

21 Cf. H. Omont, *Inventaire sommaire des manuscrits de la Bibliothèque Nationale* (Paris: Ernest Leroux, 1898), Ière Partie, p. 273.

22 B. de Montfaucon, *Palaeographia Graeca* (Parisiis: apud Ludovicum Guerin . . . Viduam Joannis Boudot . . . et Carolum Robustel . . ., 1708), p. 329.

9.   *Codex Vaticanus graecus 495, fo. 227ʳ.*

This manuscript[23] contains a passage entitled παϱαλογισμὸς Εὐνομίου.
Unfortunately, upon examination it proves to contain no words at all
except those incidental to its purpose. It is a small diagram dealing with the
relationship between the natures of the Father and the Son according to
Eunomius. It contains no quotations whatsoever.

[23] Described in R. Devreese, *Codices Vaticani Graeci* ii (Rome, 1937), p. 319.

INDEXES

I: PASSAGES FROM SCRIPTURE AND OTHER SOURCES

NOTE. For the books of the Old Testament the numbering of the Septuagint has been followed. For works appearing in the preceding edition references are to paragraph and line number; for the *Apologia Apologiae* references are to volume, page, and line number in Jaeger's 2nd edn. of the *Contra Eunomium* of Gregory of Nyssa (*J*). The following abbreviations are used throughout for the works of Eunomius: *A* = *Liber Apologeticus*; *AA* = *Apologia Apologiae*; *EF* = *Expositio Fidei*; *F* = *Fragmenta*.

A. SCRIPTURE

Genesis

1: 1-2	*F* i.9-10
1: 3	*AA* i.284.31-2, ii.297.3-4
1: 6	*AA* i.284.32
1: 6-8	*F* i.13
1: 9	*AA* i.285.1
1: 9 ff.	*F* i.11-12
1: 9-10	*F* i.14
1: 11	*AA* i.285.2a
1: 11-12	*AA* i.282.12-14
1: 14 ff.	*A* 10.6-8
1: 16	*F* i.13-14
1: 20	*AA* i.285.2b
1: 26	*Thes.* xix (*PG* 75.317B-324A)
2: 1-3	*AA* ii.227.22-228.4
2: 9	*AA* ii.46.24
2: 19-20	*AA* i.303.1-6; 342.21-9
3: 22, 24	*AA* ii.46.24
7: 10-24	*EF* 3.33-4
19: 24-5	*EF* 3.34

Exodus

3: 1 ff.	*EF* 3.35-6
3: 2	*AA* ii.273.24; 277.27
3: 4 ff.	*AA* ii.273.26
3: 14	*A* 8.3; 17.2; 28.4; *AA* ii.251.19-20, 22; 255.3; *EF* 2.6, 13
14: 26-31	*EF* 3.34-5
20: 1 ff.	*EF* 3.35-6

3 Maccabees

2: 4-8	*EF* 3.33-5

Psalms

15(16): 10	*EF* 3.43
23(24): 7-10	*EF* 3.17
49(50): 1	*EF* 2.10
54(55): 20	*A* 10.9
82(83): 19	*EF* 2.11-12
96(97): 9	*EF* 2.11-12
113: 11 (115: 3)	*A* 23.18-19; *F* i.7-8
142(143): 10	*EF* 4.17
146(147): 4	*AA* i.350.8-9
148: 5-6	*F* i.9-10

Proverbs

8: 22	*A* 12.2-3; 17.13-14; 26.15-16; *AA* ii.10.25-11.8; *EF* 3.4-5
8: 22, 23, 25b	*A* 28.23-4

Isaiah

42: 8	*EF* 3.13-14
48: 11	*EF* 3.13-14

Jeremiah

2: 13	*AA* ii.46.24
17: 13	*AA* ii.46.24

B. OTHER SOURCES

II: PROPER NAMES

III: IMPORTANT WORDS